LETTERS

TO THE GRANDCHILDREN

Winner of the 2018 New Mexico-Arizona
Book Awards for Anthologies

LETTERS

TO THE GRANDCHILDREN

A FAMILY'S LIFE

DAN WADE

AUTHOR — COMPILER

Letters to the Grandchildren:
A Family's Life

Copyright ©2018 Dan Wade

ISBN: 978-1-940769-88-2

Publisher: Mercury HeartLink
Silver City, New Mexico

Printed in the United States of America

contact the author: *danwade955@gmail.com*

Mercury HeartLink
www.heartlink.com

TABLE OF CONTENTS

CHAPTER 1
FAMILY NOT FORGOTTEN —11

CHAPTER 2

YOU CAN NEVER HAVE TOO MUCH FUN —61

CHAPTER 3
CHARACTER(S) REVEALED —117

CHAPTER 4

PASSING DOWN —169

CHAPTER 5

A DIFFERENT TIME —199

CHAPTER 6

GOOD TIMES HUNTING —257

CHAPTER 7
WHATEVER IT TAKES —305

CHAPTER 8

LESSONS FROM LIFE —337

This book of family stories is dedicated to our Grandchildren.

May you go far and soar high,

while never forgetting where you came from.

ACKNOWLEDGEMENTS

This collection of family stories has been a joy to write and assemble. In starting this project, I had no idea that we would so quickly have one hundred stories of our family's life and history. I hope that you find them a joy to read and that they are a great resource for the Grandchildren. Sincere thanks go to my beautiful, loving wife Daina for her work on and patience with these stories she has been invaluable. Editing, suggestions, encouragement, organization, and word processing are just a few of her contributions. Without her help, this book of stories could not have happened.

I am grateful to the many members of the family who have contributed stories, sayings, comments, and many encouraging words. We were blessed to find a publisher, Stewart Warren, who has become a friend. He has directed us through the process of putting a book together and referred us to an editor/ writing coach named Charlie McKee of Editor's Proof. Charlie has gently but firmly introduced me to *The Chicago Manual of Style* and has had an incredible impact in making this a better product. In her, we also gained a new friend. A special thanks to Charlie. The illustrations were done by José Daniel Oviedo Galeano. He worked diligently to understand my descriptions. My sister Jenny Chilson did the work on the homeplace picture, making it not quite so painful to look at. Thanks, Sis.

I really had no idea of the amount of work it takes to put a book together when this all started, and, without these good people's help, it would not have happened. My dear Uncle Haskell and Aunt Willie Mae's incredible work researching our family history has been invaluable, and our entire family owes those two good people an eternal debt of gratitude.

Credit for the success of this book, if any is due, belongs to all who assisted in making the book possible. Any errors, omissions, or stories that you wish had not been told are entirely the responsibility of the author.

INTRODUCTION

A LETTER TO THE GRANDCHILDREN by Dan Wade

This book of stories, Grandchildren, is to introduce you to the people and times that came before you. Our world changes so fast. I believe it is important that you have an understanding of the world your people came from.

My grandmother Minnie Ozella Wade rode a horse sidesaddle and saw Indians when they were still living the old ways. My grandfather Jesse Felix Wade was a cotton farmer. He had inherited the forty-acre home place where he raised his family in the Big Creek community just outside of Laurel, Mississippi. Needing to farm more land, he spent several years sharecropping on different farms about fifty miles to the north. It was after one good year of farming that he proudly bought his first truck—a big, used, flatbed Chevy. He was in his forties; gear shifts and gas pedals were brand new to him. After tearing down some fence trying to drive the truck out of the sales lot, his thirteen-year-old son Noel became the official driver for the family. I don't think Grandfather ever mastered that new technology, the automobile.

His father, my great-grandfather had grown up in the same community and continued to farm there after coming home from fighting in the Civil War. My dad worked on a Depression Era works program, the WPA (Works Progress

Administration). He also worked as a carpenter during World War II at a top-secret weapons plant in Tennessee. Dad had asthma as a young man, and, by his mid-forties, it had progressed to the point that his doctor told him to move west to a drier climate or face more suffering. Dad would joke years later that he had moved west after being blessed with asthma.

As for me, after fighting a losing battle with COPD (Chronic Obstructive Pulmonary Disease), I was blessed with a lung transplant. During my recovery, I thanked the Lord for granting me some more time here on earth. I also asked for direction. *What should I do with this gift of life?*

So far, I have been given direction for three projects: the first was to be kind in all my interactions; the second was to volunteer at the police department; and the third was to get these family stories written and assembled. I continue to work at all three. Being kind is more than not being rude; it requires some effort. The police have discovered that I can file, hang pictures, and move furniture. And here are the stories.

THE BEGINNING

THE HOME PLACE BY DAN WADE

The old house has been abandoned since 1971. I think that was the year Dad and his brothers moved their ninety-one-year-old mother, Minnie Ozella, to town, so she could get a little help. You can see time has been hard on it; part of the roof has fallen, and the porch is almost gone. Standing here looking at that old wreck, I think back to another time, and this is what I see. On the front porch are the four brothers: Vardaman, Noel, Haskell, and Heber, all sitting in rocking chairs with cane bottoms, visiting quietly and enjoying each other's company. Their two sisters, Beulah and Lola, are missing. They had both died some years before while giving birth. The yard is full of kids chasing fireflies, climbing trees, and playing. While we played, we kept one ear tuned for story time to start.

Soon the ladies would finish cleaning up after supper and come outside to join the rest of us. Grandmother would always have a bowl of peas to shell. Then one brother would say to another "Do you remember that time," and off they would go; one story after another, some side-splitting funny and some not funny at all. The kids aren't playing any more. We are sitting on the edge of the porch, in the tree, or on the grass, hanging on to every word. Every now and then, on the hour and the half hour, we are interrupted by the ding-dong of the cuckoo clock.

Then when I look closer, I can see a bunch of us crowded around the table for breakfast. I see plates full of thick Brer Rabbit syrup, real cane syrup, a spoonful of homemade butter mashed into the syrup with a fork, then a big old cat-head biscuit dragged through the plate.

Then I see myself crawling under the covers in that back bedroom where Dad and I would sleep. Somehow those sheets would be freezing. I see Grandmother admiring the three-inch fish I caught using a safety pin and sewing thread in that little pond by the house.

I don't see a dilapidated old house that had been added onto over the years. An indoor bathroom was added in 1969. I don't see a house falling down that, on its best day, really wasn't much.

This is what I see: I see life, love, and laughter, a home place, a beginning, a connection. The children who grew up there have had children of their own, and they have had children. We have all scattered to different points around the world and have had many different experiences, but this we all have in common: the home that was created by Jessie Felix and Minnie Ozella Wade in 1895. Judging by the character of the children that they raised, those two created a fine home. There are many finer houses but few, very few, better homes. They were my grandparents, my children's great-grandparents, and their children's great-great-grandparents. That spans three centuries.

I don't know where any of us are going, but I know where we all came from.

That's what I see. Look close, and you can see it too. Just look a little closer.

CHAPTER 1

FAMILY NOT FORGOTTEN

OUR FIRST WINTER IN COLORADO
BY DAN WADE

In 1963, my family had been living outside of Roswell, New Mexico, for about ten years. They had moved there from Mississippi, where Mom and Dad had been born. Their parents and grandparents had been born there as well. Mississippi was home, and their roots were deep. After they got married and started a family, Dad got a job at the Masonite plant. He worked hard, saved money, and built their first house on a farm that they were able to buy on payments near the small community of Myrick. I believe their new house was one of the first in the area to be wired for electricity. In his mid-forties, Dad's breathing was getting increasingly difficult. He was diagnosed with asthma, and his doctor told him that moving to a dry climate was his only chance to get better. Dad and Mom were forced to move and take their four children. Jerry was the oldest at fifteen, then Wallace at ten; Donna was seven; and Jenny was three. They left their lifelong home, families, and friends behind, loaded the car and headed west. They sold their farm in Myrick and used the money from that sale to put money down on a new farm just outside of Roswell, New Mexico.

Before moving his family, Dad had driven west by himself to scout around for a nice place to live, raise their children, and make a good living. He drove all the way to Arizona on two-lane roads. This was long before interstate highways and bypasses, so he must have seen every signal light in three states. He checked out Phoenix and Tucson, Arizona, before turning back and choosing Roswell for their next home. It was a nice, growing town in eastern New Mexico with a major Air Force base as the largest employer. Dad got his family moved out to Roswell and started working in New Mexico, first as a carpenter, then as a superintendent for a couple of different companies. While he worked, he completed an Audel correspondence course on general construction. After a few years, Dad decided he was ready to take the test for his contractor's license. He studied hard and passed the test on his second try. On the first test, he did the math on paper and ran out of time. On the second test he used an adding machine. Soon after Dad started building on his own. He would continue to work with some of the good men he got to know in Roswell for his entire career.

My parents also farmed cotton and raised sheep in the early years after moving to New Mexico. I don't think either endeavor was very profitable, because the neighbor's dogs killed a lot of their sheep. Dad used to say that nobody ever admitted to owning a dog that he shot while it was chasing our sheep. I'm not sure, but I think the deep irrigation well went dry, and they had to quit farming cotton. I just remember a few things about that farm and the old house we lived in when I was born. One thing I do remember is Dad building a high, mesh, wire fence around our yard. At three to five years old, I was bad to go and hide in the outbuildings, and I wouldn't answer when they called, hoping I guess that someone would come looking for me. They thought the fence would keep me in the yard. Boy, were they wrong! The wire mesh made a good ladder, and it didn't slow me down at all. Next they tied bells on my shoes. I guess that helped because they could find me. Whenever I moved, the bells rang.

I was about five years old when Dad built us a new house on the far side of the farm, and they sold the old house and half the property. We didn't farm after moving into the new house, but we did have livestock—horses, a few cattle, and a bunch of chickens with a mean rooster that terrorized me. That was Mom's first nice, new, modern house with indoor facilitates. We only lived there for a few years before the Air Force base moved out of Roswell. When that happened, it was a disaster for the economy of Roswell. We needed to sell out quickly while it was still possible to sell. Roswell's population would soon drop by seventy-five percent, and property values would fall to almost nothing. It would take over thirty years for the town to recover. Somehow, Mom and Dad were able to sell the house and a couple of acres, keeping about twenty acres that would come in handy years later. Dad had just finished building a "spec" house in town that he planned to sell for a profit. When the base moved out, they were lucky enough to get it sold for cost, but there was no profit.

I think Dad saw this crash in the building business as an

opportunity to go after his longtime dream: a cattle ranch in the Rocky Mountains! Dad went ranch shopping much like he had scouted for a place to live when they left Mississippi, but this time our oldest brother Jerry went along to find a place for his family as well. They went scouting for new homes in southwest Colorado. Jerry had gone to work with Dad after coming home from college and starting his family. He had married Hulene Wilson, a pretty Oklahoma girl he had met in college. Alicia, their first born, was just a baby at that time, and Terry, his oldest son, would join us soon. After scouting Colorado with Dad, Jerry and Hulene bought a little convenience store and gas station with living quarters in the back. Southwest Colorado was a beautiful area with a nice small town, Bayfield. It was a great place for a family, but it didn't turn out to be a great place to make a living. After moving our family to Colorado, Dad discovered that there just wasn't enough work there for him to make a good living. He would spend most of the next ten years working away from home back in New Mexico. Jerry would sell his store and move his family back to New Mexico because that's where he and Dad found work after struggling to make a living in Colorado for a year or two. They would work together for many years until Dad finally retired.

Dad made a deal to purchase a little ranch in a beautiful valley called Wallace Gulch. Local legend said it had once been a stagecoach stop and a rustler's headquarters. The ranch was about four hundred acres with an old house, barn, and outbuildings. The house was at least sixty years old and hadn't been lived in for a long time. For the last ten or fifteen years, it had been leased out as a hunting camp in the fall and sat vacant the rest of the year. Hunters aren't really known for taking great care of camps, and vacant houses don't ever improve.

I've long wondered how much Dad told Mom about the situation we were moving into. I can remember Dad coming home to Roswell and telling all of us about the new home we were moving to and being shown lumps of coal. We were all amazed. How could a rock burn? We heard about winter snows, rushing rivers, towering mountains, and lush green valleys. All of us kids were excited, hearing about the mountains and the snow. We were going pioneering!

We moved into our new home in Colorado on the night of November 16, 1963. I know that because the sixteenth is my sister Donna's birthday. There were three feet of snow on the ground when we got there, and the temperature was well below zero. Wow, us kids were excited! We could see our breath inside the house. We couldn't wait for tomorrow to play in the snow. Dad got the fire going in the coal stove while we all carried in the bed covers that we needed for that first night. We thought standing around the stove was good fun.

The house was great (from an eight-year-old's point of view). It had a bay window in the twelve-foot-by-twelve-foot living room and columns between the living room and the fifteen-foot-by-fifteen-foot kitchen/dining/family room. We had ten-foot ceilings and ornate, purple, vinyl flooring throughout.

The vinyl wasn't more than forty or fifty years old, and it was only worn completely through in the traffic areas. Some of the walls had been used for dartboards, all the walls had holes where posters had been hung, and none of them had seen a paint brush for a while! Dad had set up some sawhorses with planks on top for a temporary kitchen. I think he had a propane cook stove hooked up, and we had a hose bib for running water. That's what we had. What we didn't have was: hot water, a sink, a bathroom, a real kitchen, or a place for my sisters, Wallace, and me to sleep. Mom and Dad took the one small bedroom, about eight feet by ten feet. I don't know if they had a mattress or not that first night. All four of us kids got to sleep on the living room floor. We all thought it couldn't get much better than that, and it was a great adventure. I'm sure we used every blanket my folks owned. Even with the coal stove going, it was freezing cold, and we could still see our breath.

I'm guessing Dad intended to have the house more habitable before he moved us all in. I don't know why, but somehow he had run out of time and had to move us before the house was ready. It would have made sense for us kids to change schools at Christmas break just a few weeks later. Even with his good intentions, I wonder what he and Mom talked about after they went to bed that first night. Did they discuss the "two-holer" outhouse that you needed snow boots and a shovel to get to? Or did they talk about washing dishes in a bucket with water heated on the stove? Was anything said about driving four miles through snowdrifts to town, having barely even ever seen snow? I never heard one word of complaint from Mom, but I'm not real sure that Dad didn't.

Wallace, Donna, Jenny, and I were all welcomed at our new school, and my sisters and I had a great time. We were happy at our new school, and we were having a blast at home. We made snowmen of every size. We pressed the snow into blocks and built Eskimo igloos and made snow ice cream (just add a little sugar and vanilla). We didn't have sleds yet, so we used scrap plastic and started our education in snow sledding. In front of the house was a spring-fed, sub-irrigated area that spread out and flooded an area about one hundred yards by two hundred yards and, when it froze, we had an almost perfect ice skating rink. The ice had a few ripples and some rough spots, but we loved it. There was only one obstacle to overcome for us to go ice skating: we didn't have skates! No problem. Mom always saved plastic bread sacks, and we tied them on over our socks and skated like the pros.

While my sisters and I played on the ice and in the snow, Mom, Dad, and Wallace worked to make the house more livable. Between the house and the coal cellar, there was an unfinished hallway that was pretty wide, maybe five feet, and it would eventually be our "laundry room" or the place where the hot water heater and the washing machine sat. The dryer was a clothes line outside unless it was too cold. Off the hall there was a walk-in closet on one side and an unfinished room on the other that Dad would turn into a bathroom. That was a big priority. We needed everything: all the plumbing, electricity, flooring, wallboard, and paint. Dad could do all of that work himself. I don't think there was any craft involved in building a house that he couldn't do and do well. He also had the number two priority to do, which was the kitchen cabinets, counter tops, water heater, and all the plumbing and drain lines. Of course, there was all the household organizing to do as well. Just the logistics of keeping us all fed and the household on track was plenty for Mom to do.

All of that was the easy part. Wallace had the bulk of the hard part: the septic system! His job was hand digging a thirty-foot-long, three-foot-deep ditch and then an eight-foot-by-eight-foot-by-eight-foot-deep hole for the septic tank. After that, he still had to dig another fifty-foot-long-by-three-foot-deep ditch for the drain line. The reason those ditches were three feet deep was to protect the drain lines from freezing, because the first two feet of the ground was frozen as hard as a rock. Wallace did all of that digging with a bar and a pick, one chip at a time, after he had shoveled three feet of snow off the ground. Dad had a lot of work to do inside, I was eight years old, Donna and Jenny helped where they could, and Jerry was busy with his own business. So it was up to eighteen-year-old Wallace to dig that frozen ground, and it needed to be ready for use as soon as Dad was finished inside.

Well, after some time, the plumbing got done, the cabinets got built and painted bright yellow with white trim, and the septic system got finished. We had a bathroom! Dad had sheet-rocked and painted the walls of the old storage area, tiled the floor, and installed a bathtub, toilet and sink. The path to the outhouse got snowed over from lack of use. The washing machine got hooked up, and Mom didn't have to wash clothes in a washtub anymore. The clothes were hung on a line to dry. When it was too cold to hang clothes outside, Mom would put lines up inside the house to dry them on. That first winter passed, and Donna, Jenny, and I couldn't have had more fun. It was a great adventure.,

Since I've been grown, I've thought back on that time, and I wonder how our Mom and Dad made it. It must have been overwhelming. Dad was our leader, and he had led Mom and us kids into that situation. For them, it must have been like camping in the Arctic with a construction zone inside the tent. They had made a solemn pledge when they married never to argue or have cross words in front of their kids, and they didn't, as far as I know. That first winter must have been a real test for that pledge, but they passed it. There were some loud silences but no cross words!

Over the years, Dad bought more land, and there were many more improvements to the house. Wallace moved into the bunkhouse, Dad built a nice new bedroom for himself and Mom, and Donna and Jenny got the bedroom they had moved out of. After a couple of years, they expanded the closet, and I got a nice bedroom. Eventually we even got some heat in the living room. It was an old house with add-ons, patches, and unfinished repairs. It was far from being a good house by today's standards. We didn't really notice that it wasn't really a very good house. For us it was a great home!

JERRY, WALLACE, AND THE RATTLER
by Wallace Wade

In 1953 the family moved out to Roswell from Mississippi. We were living at the "old place," and one of the fence posts on the far west side of the place had rotted out. Dad had given Jerry and me the task of replacing it. Jerry grabbed the new post, and I took the posthole digger, and we started walking the quarter mile or so to the fence line that needed the work. I was rambling on, talking nonstop about who knows what, when— without warning or a word—Jerry whipped an arm out hitting me straight across the chest with his forearm knocking me flat on my back and sending the posthole digger flying. I came up off the ground mad as all-get-out, fists balled up thinking a fight was in order, to find Jerry pounding the ground right where my next step would have been with the post. Turns out my next step would have been right on a three-foot-long rattlesnake. Jerry and I fought a lot as boys and that was the only time I was ever OK with him hitting me.

UNCLE HASKELL ON HORSEBACK
BY DAN WADE

On one of Uncle Haskell's and Aunt Willie Mae's visits to Colorado, Donna, Jenny, and I decided to take Uncle Hack horseback riding. When we asked him if he wanted to go, he thought it was a great idea. So we got saddled up and headed out. Donna was mounted on her big black horse Gander, Jenny was riding a fast little quarter horse mare called Little Red, I was riding my great horse Firecracker, and we had Uncle Haskell mounted up on Jubilee—a good gentle mare that we put all of our visitors on. For all his love of horses, he really wasn't very comfortable being on horseback, and he sure wasn't used to the mountains of Colorado. Our home place was a valley, bordered on both sides by hills. We had a trail we liked to ride; it crossed the valley and climbed up the hills to the top of the ridge. Then we would cross into some Bureau of Land Management (BLM) land for a few miles. On it were some old roads where we could really let the horses go and some old homesteads to explore. After that we would come back down off the ridge about a mile up the valley. It was a great five-mile ride, with some steep grades and long flats that we had taken many times.

We planned to take about half of that ride with Uncle Hack, but we never made it to the top of the ridge. After leaving the corrals, we all rode across the valley in good form, just walking the horses along, taking it easy. We could tell Uncle Hack was a little uneasy riding Jubilee at first, but he started getting more comfortable as we crossed the valley and started up the gentle slope around the bottom of the hill. He got uneasy again as the hill got steeper and the trail got narrower. Uncle Haskell said with concern in his voice, "Don't you think these horses need a rest?" We had just gotten started; of course, the horses weren't tired. My sisters and I just laughed and said, "Don't worry, the horses are fine," and rode on. The hill got steeper, and the trail narrowed as we got higher. After the third switchback, Uncle Hack insisted in no uncertain terms that we stop to rest the horses. So we stopped about half way up the side of the hill and rested the horses. The three of us were a little slow to catch on, but we finally came to realize that Uncle Hack was frightened by the steepness of that hill. He had never been on anything like it. Of course he was scared; it was his first time being on horseback on the side of a mountain. Anybody would be. Those hills were home to us. We were up and down them all the time, never giving it a second thought. It had never occurred to us that they might be steep mountains to a man from Mississippi. We had forgotten that it had taken time for us to get used to those hills as well. We all talked while the horses "rested" and then decided it would be better for the horses to go back down and ride in the valley. We had a great ride, and Uncle Haskell got more comfortable being in the saddle after we got down off the hill.

From then on, my sisters and I learned to think more about our visitors' experience and comfort level when planning to take them for a ride.

CAMPING THROUGH COLORADO
BY ANN MORGAN

In 1970, the year my husband James Morgan graduated from college, we decided to take our first big vacation, along with his brother Burney, his wife Katy, and their son Todd. Todd was three years old at the time. We bought a ten-foot-by-ten-foot tent and some camping gear, which we packed into a small rental trailer, and hit the road in a Pontiac LeMans pulling the trailer.

We drove from Vicksburg, Mississippi, to Walsenburg, Colorado, nonstop except for necessities. I don't remember our exact itinerary (it was only about forty-five years ago), but our first stop was at a campground near Cripple Creek, Colorado. We set up camp in the rain, got out our little camp stove, and heated a can of Dinty Moore Beef Stew for supper, huddled in the tent. We had five cots. Four of them were stacked, two on each side of the tent for the four of us—Katy and I on the top bunks—with Todd on a cot in the middle. This made wall-to-wall cots, so there was no getting up at night. That is when I learned that if you rub against the tent wall when it is wet outside, the dampness will come through. My hair would get soaked at night.

Another stop we made was at Estes Park when it was still just a small town. We camped beside a small stream where you could fish, but it cost ten cents per inch of anything you caught. We thought that was a good deal, so James and Burney went fishing. They caught a few, and we paid for the fish. It did not dawn on us until later that we would have to throw away half of the fish when they were cleaned. Oh, well, live and learn.

We drove through Rocky Mountain National Park, pulling that trailer. We traveled on some very narrow, twisting roads with sheer drops on one side—quite exciting, especially when meeting another car. That is where we found the first snow. Todd had never seen snow, so we had to stop and let him experience it. It didn't matter that it was dirty; it was snow!

Another place that we camped was near the Maroon Bells. The campground was very empty, and it was cloudy and dreary that evening. I don't think anyone else was camped there. The guys hiked up to a lake to fish (free this time!), and Katy and I climbed up in our bunks with a lantern burning. We were talking quietly when we heard footsteps in the gravel outside that sounded like they were heading toward the tent. Katy and I froze. We knew the guys were not back that soon. The steps came closer, and then a voice asked, "Anybody here?" Finally, Katy squeaked out "Yyyyyyyeeeeeessssss." The voice answered, "This is the Ranger. I was just checking to see if everything is ok." Nice of him, but he really had us terrified.

Somewhere along the line, we also drove to the top of

Pikes Peak. It was extremely cold, and the sun was really bright, but it was quite an experience. I am sure these stops are not in the correct sequence, but we also went to see Black Canyon of Gunnison National Park. We drove across the bridge over the canyon and then walked back out on the bridge. The bridge was built with big gaps—they seemed huge—between the boards. It was a little unnerving to be able to look straight down below for about a mile. We didn't stay there very long!

Our last stop was Durango, and from there we went to visit Uncle Heber and Aunt Betty Sue. I don't recall how that visit was arranged, but we were welcomed with open arms. We must have stayed two or three days. I remember several good meals. They took us out to a nearby lake and then kept Todd for a day while we went to Mesa Verde and toured in the area. Todd was a real trooper; the only time he cried on the whole trip was when he fell and hit his knee. He didn't even cry when he fell in the lake! Great trip and great visit, but it was time to go home and get back to work!

THANKSGIVING IS AN EVENT
BY APRIL WADE TURK

Thanksgiving in our family is not for the weak. We take it very seriously.

It has always been about a day of being together. The first thing is always the food. Everyone takes on a dish or dishes. It makes me smile to think about all that goes into the dinner. When I was a little kid watching, everyone cooking looked so smooth. Dinner always seemed to magically appear, and it was always yummy.

As I got older, I learned that Thanksgiving dinner is not easy. It takes a lot of work to get everything prepared, keep it warm, and get everything on the table.

The turkey is the priority. It takes the longest to cook and everything centers around it. But what about the mashed potatoes? In our family, you must have mashed potatoes. Of course, you cannot forget the bread. Also, for some it would not be a Thanksgiving meal without the sweet potato casserole. Don't forget the gravy, because you must have that as well. And always have cranberry sauce. It may still be in the kitchen in the can, but the cranberry sauce is never forgotten, even if it's also never eaten.

After the blessing, it is time to get down to business. There is always a quick family meeting, before everyone starts eating, to discuss protocol: do we pass food in a clockwise or counterclockwise direction? It is the one time a year that everyone can easily agree on a decision, and there are rarely objections. Platters of food start moving right away, and plates are quickly full. Now all the serving dishes are out of order, and you have to find room for everything on the table again.

There is usually another round—or often two—for those who want another serving. Then there is a calm. Everyone sits back to express how full they are and how they cannot imagine taking another bite.

This is when Thanksgiving is not about the turkey anymore. Now it's about dessert. Pecan pie, chocolate pie, pumpkin pie, cakes, and cookies, and you simply cannot forget the banana pudding.

Cleanup is next. Dishes are washed, tables and chairs put away, trash taken out, and leftovers placed in the fridge. Some may try to watch the football game. Others will talk and catch up. Many will do both at the same time—especially when the Cowboys are playing. Soon it will be time for the first round of games.

While I don't think anyone has ever needed serious medical attention, we take our games as seriously as our food. You can easily get a few bruises—or even clotheslined—while playing Red Rover. We just take it to another level. Dominoes! You better bring your A game and know the rules. Even my kids can count by fives, and they're quick to correct you if your math is wrong.

As it gets later in the day, part of the family starts to head home. Everyone that is left takes a break for a bit and spends time laughing about the games, telling a few stories, and having another helping of dessert or maybe a turkey sandwich.

After raiding the leftovers, discussion turns to the next round of games. Trivial Pursuit. Pictionary. Charades. They're all possibilities. It is game time, after all. This can go on for a while, sometimes into the late hours of the night.

After a full day, stomachs may hurt because of all the food—or is it all of the laughter? It's hard to tell. It's now so late that it has crossed from Thanksgiving to Black Friday. A few of the hardest-core partygoers will catch midnight madness sales on their way home. The rest crawl into bed to recover from a full day of food, family, and fun. We look forward to our next Thanksgiving and vow that we will begin endurance training, so it won't hit us as hard next year.

MOM AND DAD
by Dan Wade

In 1984 I was between paychecks when Dad's birthday, February 19, came around. Going to a store and buying a gift was not an option; neither was doing nothing. I needed to do something! My solution was to write a tribute to my Dad. So that's what I did. I wished Dad "Happy Birthday" and explained that my only gift was a letter that I had written; then I read it out loud to both Mom and Dad. This story is an expanded version—that came to include Mom—of that tribute to James Heber Wade, the youngest son of Jesse Felix and Minnie Ozella Wade, born February 19, 1911, in Soso, Mississippi.

It is said that the good Lord works in mysterious ways. If I had been able to afford a gift, I might have never told Dad how important he was in my and all of our lives. I think he probably knew it without being told, but it was still good for him and Mom to hear it said out loud, and I will be forever grateful that they heard it from me.

I was the last to leave home when I graduated from high school in 1973 and went off to pursue my own hopes and dreams. Dad and Mom decided to sell our place in Colorado where my sisters and I had grown up. Dad had recently recovered from a terrible bout with the flu, but just barely. The flu that year had killed a lot of people, and it had been a real close call for Dad. Mom wanted to get him away from the snow and cold. Also, with my leaving home, she didn't want Dad working the ranch by himself.

So, after giving it some thought, they agreed to sell the ranch and move back to Roswell. Wallace and Nancy were already living there. They had bought a laundry business and a house a year or two before. Roswell was a nice town, still recovering from the loss of the Air Force base ten years before. Mom and Dad were able to buy a good house in a nice neighborhood for about half what a nice house would cost in another town. It was the first time for Mom to have a modern house, in town, with windows that all worked, air conditioning, and heating that warmed the whole house. There was trash pickup and landscaping front and back. They were "uptown." After selling the ranch, they could finally afford to spend a little money. For their new house, Mom was able to buy brand new, shag carpeting, a big overstuffed couch, chairs with end tables and lamps to match, and a brand-new dining room set. Jerry bought Mom a brand new, big, fancy Buick Electra with a vinyl roof, cloth seats, and electric windows. He wanted to do something special for her. He took her old car in trade—just said he had a need for it. Mom loved that new car. With the exception of the dining room set, everything they bought was bright red, including the Buick! I had never known until then that Mom had a favorite color. I guess there was a lot I didn't know about Mom. I think now that maybe the chicken neck wasn't really her favorite piece of chicken.

All the time I was growing up, about the only things Mom spent money on for the house were new plastic drapes for the bay window every year or two and shelf paper for the cabinets, all from Woolworth's five and dime. One time, back in Colorado, we did get new carpet in the living room, but we didn't buy it; the carpet was left over from a house Dad built, and he installed it himself. Mom was glad to have the sculptured green carpet cover the purple flowered, forty- or fifty-year-old vinyl flooring, but it wasn't something she had picked out.

After getting settled into their new house, Dad built a big workshop on the twenty acres that they had kept when they sold out years before. At sixty-five years old, he built it by himself and then got it all set up for woodworking. He had plans to do woodworking projects like a lot of retired people do. That lasted long enough for him to build Jerry a nice big dining table with benches that his family still treasures. Using two-by-four-inch blocks, he also built my daughter April a great little play table that she loved. Dad enjoyed woodworking, and he was a true craftsman, but he wasn't really a project kind of guy. He soon got bored with "projects" and went out and found himself a ranch to lease about thirty miles from town on the Pecos River. It was there that Dad said the rattlesnakes were so big that he needed a longer shovel handle! The ranch had a good bit of irrigated alfalfa. Dad bought some cows, and the haying equipment came with the lease. There was plenty of work to do every day. He was back to farming and ranching, doing what he loved.

We didn't know what the problem was at first, but for some time Dad had been having trouble with his balance. It was just an occasional stumble at first, but what we later learned was that it was multiple sclerosis (MS). It kept progressing, and, after a couple of years, he was crawling from the tractor to the baler because he couldn't walk. That's when he knew it was time to say goodbye to farming and ranching. As Dad's MS progressed, he went from using a cane to arm crutches and then to a walker over several years. He clung tenaciously to independence. When he lost full use of his legs, he got his truck fitted with hand controls. As hard as that disease was on this proud man, he continued to work every day. After selling his cattle, haying equipment, and Mom's red-carpeted house in Roswell, Mom and Dad packed up and moved to Farmington. Jerry and I and our families were already there. Wallace and his family and Donna would soon move there, too. Jerry had started a modular home business and needed Dad's help. Dad went to work and set up and ran the wall and truss plant. There was nothing wrong with his mind. He strived to live a purpose-filled life. Dad used a walker in a way that did not invite sympathy, and sympathy sure wasn't welcomed. The way he saw it, he was blessed to be able to use it. Things could always be worse.

Mom's mother passed away; she was "Mimi" to the grandkids. Mom's father "Pawpaw" had died suddenly only a month earlier. Of course, all of us who could do so went to

Mississippi to pay our respects to our grandmother and support Mom. Losing both her parents so close together was just about more than she could take. We were all of some comfort to her, but the one she looked to the most for strength and support was our Dad—her husband, Heber. Dad was right by her side every step throughout the thousand-mile trip, the viewing at the mortuary, and the church service. The trip and the heat were brutally hard on him. By the time we got to the cemetery for the graveside service, Dad was exhausted. It was understood by all of us that, instead of going out in the heat and humidity, he would stay in the air-conditioned car and get a little rest. Mom had insisted on it. Dad had already done more than anyone expected. Using his walker to get across the soft, grassy lawn to the grave site would be more than a little difficult. It was hard for him to move around with his walker on concrete, much less moving it on a lawn.

We drove the cars into the cemetery, and the five of us brothers and sisters then walked Mom the one hundred feet or so to the grave site. There was a shade tent set up over about a dozen chairs for close family and older people. Mom took a chair, with her brother Chuck on one side and an empty chair on the other. None of us even considered sitting there; that was where Dad would have sat. Everyone was in place. The preacher was about to start the service when someone said softly, "Wait." We all looked back; Dad was coming across the soft lawn. He had somehow managed, without help, to open the door, lift his crippled legs out of the car, unfold his walker, and struggle up to his feet. He had already done more than anyone thought he could or should do, but—as he saw it—he wasn't finished. His wife Betty Sue still needed him. Here he came across the lawn, painfully slowly, dragging his feet—one step, move the walker, rest, one more step, move the walker, rest a little more, then do it again. Dad was a proud man. Even with the heat and humidity not one of us moved to help him; we all knew better. Finally, after what seemed like forever with all of us watching, he made it to the chair beside his wife Betty Sue, drenched with sweat but right where he belonged. Dad knew that, even though she'd asked him to stay in the car and rest, she still needed his support. We could all see that Mom was glad he was there and relieved that he'd made it; things were better now that her husband Heber was with her. He was fulfilling his responsibilities, doing what was needed, without complaint or excuse. Dad didn't know how to conduct himself in any other way. One of his favorite saying was, "When it's too tough for the rest of them, that's just the way I like it." Well, Dad had plenty to like!

Dad was, in the finest sense of the word, a "man." Throughout his life, he had laid a marker down for his sons—Jerry, Wallace, and me— to measure ourselves against, to judge how far we had progressed in our own quest to become men. Dad used to say that he was "Smiling Jim." I can see him now, sitting on his three-wheeled electric cart with his legs and arm crippled from MS, an egg-sized lump on his head from melanoma, a tube running into a plastic bag taped to his leg, with a big chew of beechnut in his cheek, his good felt hat sitting crooked on his head because of that lump, and the biggest smile you ever saw. Thinking of Dad with that big smile, you know what? I don't have any problems!

THE GIRLS

by Jenny Wade Chilson

Once Dan was born, our family was complete. There was Mom, Dad, Jerry, Wallace, Dan, and The Girls. That is right. The Girls. Donna and I actually had names, but for some reason, few relatives seemed to know them; we were "The Girls." Mom and Dad kind of treated us like we were one unit. We got one bed. We had matching clothes. Rather, we had the same clothes, only Donna got to wear them for a year or two before I got them. When Donna misbehaved, The Girls got punished. When Donna got mumps on a hunting trip, The Girls both had to leave. We would visit in Mississippi each year, and everyone remembered Jerry's name, Wallace's name, and little Dan's name, and, of course, they remembered The Girls.

Starting when I was about nine years old, though, someone started noticing that we were two individuals. Finally, I wasn't part of a pair! I was being noticed as an individual! Uncle Charlie started differentiating between us! We would arrive at Grandmother's house each year and go bounding up onto her porch to give our hugs to her and to her brother, Uncle Charlie. Uncle Charlie would hug Donna and say, "You're the pretty one!" Then, I would go to him for a hug, and he would say, "Your sister is the pretty one!" When our visit was done and we would be on the porch again to say our goodbyes for another year, Uncle Charlie would do the same thing. A hug to Donna would include, "You're the pretty one," and my hug goodbye would include, "Your sister's the pretty one." Ha ha. This lasted into our teens and until Uncle Charlie died. Mom and Dad were never bothered by it and never gave me any sympathy, saying that words couldn't hurt me. I don't remember anything else Uncle Charlie ever said to me, but I do remember those words! And, I am sure The Pretty One remembers, too! By the way, my name is Jenny.

NINE-YEAR-OLD DRIVES TO ALBUQUERQUE
BY DONNA WADE

Picture this: in the 1960s the road called "550" between Colorado and Albuquerque, New Mexico, was just a sheep trail—two lanes with many cattle guards and barely paved. Along this road, you would see flocks of sheep with a loyal dog standing watch and sometimes cattle resting on the warm pavement. Along comes a car, and you can hear screams from the girls—Jenny and Donna (The Pretty One), ages twelve and fourteen. "Turn! You're gonna to hit the fence!" The driver, barely able to see over the steering wheel, was nine-year-old Dan. In the back seat, reading a comic book, was big brother Jerry. Just another story of being scared, so scared.

WINTER FUN IN THE SNOW
by Donna Wade

Snow, don't want it! It's been many a year, but there was a time when I liked it. It meant that the summer work and play were over for a while. I can remember thinking, *now life will slow down,* but the chores that had to be done were actually harder when you had to walk through two or three feet of snow. Those cows and horses had to be fed and the elk chased away, but we always had time for play on weekends and holidays. We had two stock ponds, one near the house at the bottom of a rocky hill and the other about one mile to the west up the valley. We would take shovels and clear the snow off the frozen pond by the hill. Clearing snow with a shovel is very hard work, but—once that was done—we would take the toboggan, load ourselves on it, and down the hill we would go. When we hit the frozen ice, we would become airborne and end up out in the snow on the other side of the pond. Talk about fun! When the frozen ice over the pond melted a little, there were times we did not get airborne, and we ended up wet and cold.

Once a pond was cleared of the snow and had the sun on it, it would freeze and became the best ice-skating rink. We would put on our ice skates and spend hours doing our best imitation of ice skaters. We would try to go backwards, twirl, and play hockey; it was all so much fun.

One day, Jenny and I met up with a neighbor from up the valley. Her name was Jody, and the three of us thought we were ice skating pros until Jenny fell through the ice and went into the water under the frozen ice. This was truly a life and death situation. Jody and I got her out, but it was hard to do without falling in ourselves. We were so scared after it was over but did not hesitate to do what was needed at the time of the crisis. All those ranch chores and our crazy wild ways had taught us to be self-reliant, and it sure came in handy that day!

Christmas Day on the ranch was always a family fun day. About midday after we found our "Santa Gift" and after a great breakfast, we would all go out and play. I remember Dad loading up the sled and us three kids in the back of the truck and driving up the valley where the road became steep. When he got to the peak in the road, he would stop and put the sled on the snow-covered road. I would lie down on the sled, Jenny on top of me, Dan on top of her. Dad would give us a push, and off we would go flying down that road. It seemed to go on for miles—so much fun. My hips were always bruised during the winter because this is how three kids rode one sled.

THE COMBINE
BY DAN WADE

At the 2016 Wade family reunion, at a lake south of Jackson, Mississippi, I got a chance to visit separately with my cousins RV and Harlin Dean Smith. They each told me a story. There is nothing unusual about being told a story. It often happens when people visit, right? The funny thing is, it was almost the same story but at different times and places with different people.

RV and Harlin Dean both grew up farming cotton with their father, and they both continued farming after growing up. RV also had a career as a school principal. By the 1960s, they had gone from growing cotton to growing soybeans. A large combine is used to harvest soybeans. I have never been around a combine, but I have seen those large, cone-shaped hoppers on the front. I am told that it's hard to get down in the bottom of them to do some work and even harder to get back out. Of course, things would occasionally break or need adjustment down in the bottom of those hoppers. Because of the difficulty with getting in and out of the hopper, fixing a gear or replacing a part was hard for one man. Sure as the world, once you were down there with your tools and what you thought you needed, you needed something you didn't have. If you were by yourself, you might spend half a day crawling in and out. Having a helper made all the difference.

Both cousins told about a time when their combines broke down. You know, equipment never breaks at a good time, and harvesting soybeans is like any other crop. When it is ready to harvest, it is ready. You need to get busy and get it done. Every minute is important. That adds a sense of urgency. You are always in a hurry to get that machine working. RV and Harlin Dean were each working on their combine down in the bottom of the hopper trying to get it repaired. It was hot and sweaty work. When they needed a three-eighths-inch box-end wrench, they would each call to his son to hand it down. After a while, they might need a flathead screwdriver. Then they might work for twenty minutes or more before they called for anything else. Their sons wouldn't have much to do but sit up on top and wait for a tool to be called for. Sometimes, waiting around and doing nothing is hard to do. Sure enough, the call went out to hand down the big pry bar. Nothing, so they called again, a little louder this time. "Hand me the big pry bar," and still nothing. Dadgumit! Where is that boy? Here they came, crawling out of the bottom of the hopper, hot and aggravated.

RV got his head above the side of the hopper and looked around for his son, Reggie. "Where could he be?" He couldn't see him anywhere. "Where could he be? Wait a minute, what's that sound? It sounds like a piano!" Oh, boy. RV came boiling out of that hopper and headed for the sound. It was coming from the house. Yep, he found Reggie at the keyboard playing away. He just couldn't stand waiting around, doing nothing, while his dad was working. Surely one or two songs wouldn't hurt. I guess that might have been the day RV knew that Reggie wasn't going to grow up to be a farmer. Reggie has since taken his love for music and a good work ethic learned while farming and has developed a great career singing.

When Harlin Dean came up out of the hopper and looked around, he saw his son Robbie right away. Robbie was a grown man farming on his own, and he and his dad helped each other all the time, but he had gotten tired of sitting and waiting in the hot sun for his dad to ask for something. He couldn't resist getting his fishing pole out of the truck and going down to the pond; there were some good fish in that pond. Harlin Dean just shook his head. "Dan," he said, "he went off fishing while I was sweating down in that hopper, and, to top it off, it wasn't even my combine. It was his dang combine!" To this day, if Robbie runs into a tough mechanical problem, it is his dad Harlin Dean, in his 80s, who he calls. Robbie has worked hard, raised a fine family, and built a good business, but if he gets a chance, he can often be found hunting or fishing.

THEY ARE ALL MY CHILDREN
BY DONNA WADE

I had one son born to me, Tyler. This is the tale of all my nephews and a couple of nieces who seemed like my children as well.

Of these children, I can remember two boys, Thomas and Roy. I held Thomas in my arms soon after birth, and I thought, *What a beautiful baby!* His brother Roy was two weeks old when I first saw him; he was being carried by their dad, my brother Jerry. I thought, *This baby looks just like his dad, and he is only two weeks old.* These two boys were with me so much that they felt like children of my own, and I can remember their begging me, "Aunt Donna, please don't ever get married and leave us."

Max, Jerry's youngest son, Waylon, my brother Wallace's son, and April and Josh, my brother Dan's children, were born while I was working in Alaska and Seattle, so I missed out on their first few years, but they soon became part of my group. My nephew Max was five years old when he traveled with my mother to my sister Jenny's house in Aspen, Colorado. They went there to pick up me and my new baby, Tyler, when we were moving back to New Mexico in 1980. Weston, Wallace's youngest son, was born just four months after we moved back. His mother, Nancy, called and asked me to take her to the hospital when she went into labor with Weston. I was afraid to drive. I had not driven a car for the ten years I had been in Alaska. The roads had a little snow on them, so Nancy drove herself to the hospital with me as a passenger. My mother happened to be sick and in the hospital when Weston was born. I can remember going to her room and telling her about her new grandson. My nephews Waylon and Weston and my son Tyler were often thought to be triplets when they played together. All three had white blond hair and were close in age.

My brother Dan's children, April and Josh, spent a lot of time with me when Dan was working, as well as spending many weekends helping me care for their grandfather. April came with Tyler and me on vacations for several years. We drove over big mountain passes. She was afraid of those high passes and does not remember any of the beautiful scenery because all she saw was the floorboard where she curled into a little ball until we hit level roads again. I helped April pick out the dress she wore on her first day of kindergarten, and I loved fixing her hair into braids or curls; she was so good about that.

My brother Dan and I were there when our sister Jenny's daughter Alaena was born. We were the first family members to see and touch her; she came early and weighed only three pounds. She was brown with dark kinky hair. We were told to pet her and let her know she was loved. Alaena and her younger brother Ryan seemed to love coming to visit Tyler and me. I can remember going shopping and Ryan hiding under some clothes racks, scaring the rest of us so bad. I can see him as a wee one, sleeping under a coconut tree in Hawaii, and I see Alaena (Squirt) turning cartwheels whenever we came to an open space in a store.

I also remember Josh and Max camping out on my land early one winter and my going out in the middle of the night to check on them. I still see Tom and Roy as skinny little boys riding bareback on their old horse, Yankee, holding on for dear life. I have memories, too, of Dan, April, Josh, Tyler and me camping in the San Juan Mountains: it's raining, and we are all in the same tent; Dan and I are taking turns reading a Louis L'Amour book out loud; and will April remember her aunt wanting her to go skinny-dipping in that cold mountain pond?

I can still see and hear Jerry's daughter Alicia Ann telling me that she was hungry as we rode the sled down a snow-packed road. I remember her brother Terry in diapers, playing peek-a-boo with me while I stayed a weekend with them in White Rock, New Mexico.

These special children will never know how much joy they brought to my heart—each and every one of them.

I was thirteen years old when Alicia Ann was born and about thirty-five when Ryan was born, the oldest and youngest of my parents' grandchildren. This is a statement of love between siblings—Jerry, Wallace, Jenny, Dan, and me. We loved and trusted each other enough to share our children and to love each other's children. All of these children are grown now, scattered around the country, and many have children of their own. Jerry has passed on, but I know he would join the four of us—Wallace, Jenny, Dan, and me—in hoping our children all know that they and theirs are special to us; we are family. In life's twist and turns, some of us have moved and drifted apart, but we each hope that they all know that our porch lights on and the latchstrings out.

TORMENTED BY MY OLDER SISTERS
BY DAN WADE

There is photographic evidence that I was abused by my sisters as a child. I was the sixth child born to our parents, and I think by the time I came along they had pretty much lost interest. As a youngster, my care was mostly left to the tender mercies of my sisters, Donna and Jenny. They seem to have had trouble deciding whether I was a play doll or a pet. Either way, my life consisted of being tormented in one way or another. They did not seem to see caring for their younger brother as a responsibility so much as an opportunity. Even to this day, they gleefully gloat over pictures that clearly display my humiliation in various types of torture.

This torment continued into my early teens. An example of this cruel treatment is what I endured during supper. Here is a description of a typical supper growing up with my sisters. We each had assigned seating: Dad sat at the head of the table, and I was directly on his left with Mom to the left of me. First on Dad's right was Jenny, then came Donna, and, before he left home, Wallace sat at the end of the table opposite Dad. Notice that I sat directly across from Jenny, and Mother was across from Donna.

Our meals varied, but potatoes, pinto beans, and cornbread were almost always part of the meal. That was a problem for me. For some odd reason that I still don't understand, both of my sisters thought it necessary to mix all three together and then add ketchup to the mix. How gross! This concoction of different foods seemed to have caused a condition with a reaction that was the bane of my existence. The condition was that, whenever they both had a mouthful of that disgusting mixture, they would find something funny; usually something that only the two of them understood. At first, their mirth was just a small giggle, then giggling with a full mouth made them giggle harder, and soon the urge to laugh out loud was apparently irresistible. That is when the eruptions occurred.

When it became inevitable that an eruption was coming, they had to decide a direction. For some reason, I seemed to be the target of choice. Well, really I was the target of least resistance. They couldn't spew that vile mix on Dad, Mom, or Wallace. So I was the one who got covered with that special blend, and what didn't get on me got on my plate. I went hungry many a time because of my sisters' cruel propensity to spray me with chewed food! Even on nights when I didn't get sprayed, I had to worry that I might. This situation caused a lot of stress and anxiety for me.

As tough as that was, it wasn't the end of my suppertime torment. After supper was all done and I had wiped the cornbread and beans off my face, it was time for the dishes to be washed and dried. That was always Donna and Jenny's job. It had to be started right after supper, and nothing else could start until the dishes were washed and put away. If any two human beings ever washed dishes more slowly, I would be surprised. One washed, the other dried, and they both talked like they might never get the chance again. The dishwater would get cold, they would run some more, and talk and talk. While they talked, whatever we had planned to do after supper had to wait. I had to wait and wait. If I had a nickel for every time my sisters kept me waiting, well, I would have a lot of nickels.

And Jenny had a special way of torturing me: she forever had to finish something. Sometimes it was some knitting project. "Let me finish this row" is a phrase I hope never to hear again. While Jenny is the princess of forever finishing something, Donna is the queen of "we." There is no telling how many rocks were hauled and wild irises transplanted that "we" did without her ever touching a stone or a shovel. It can only be a testament to my resilience that I survived and grew up to be a fairly well-adjusted man.

MY MOM'S MIRROR
BY DAN WADE

When my mom got into her teenage years, it became important to dress a certain way to be accepted by the "in crowd" at school. Grandfather was a hard-working man, but fancy dresses just weren't in the budget. Mother never said a lot about it, but she said enough for us to understand that it hurt her to be excluded and slighted by the "in crowd." That was a large factor in her quitting school and going to work at the "creamery," I think after her junior year. I believe that is where she and Dad met.

It was about that time that Grandmother scrimped and saved to buy a few new pieces of parlor furniture so that her daughter Betty Sue (my mom) could have a nice place to entertain young gentleman suitors. I don't know how that worked out. Mom and Dad eloped to get married, so I am not sure how much time he spent in the parlor.

Even though she eloped, my mom treasured that little parlor set. My sister Jenny inherited a piece of it. It is a small bureau with an oval mirror. Both the mirror and the bureau look every bit of their eighty-some years old. Jenny keeps saying that she wants to refinish that old bureau and make it look like new.

But even after this many years, she still hasn't been able to bring herself to start that refinishing project. Because whenever she looks at that chipped, scratched, and faded mirror that really needs replacing, Jenny starts thinking of our mother and how she looked into it as a young lady long ago while dreaming of her future and brushing her hair on a warm afternoon.

VOICES IN THE DARK
BY DAN WADE

I don't remember my parents having conversations. When they talked, it was about day to day things like, "We're low on butane. I'll warm up the car," or "I'm going to the store. Do you need anything?" No discussions about politics, religion, or local news. They had conversations, just not around us kids. They talked after we were all in bed.

The house we grew up in didn't have hallways. The kitchen, dining area, and coal stove were all in one room in the middle of the house. My bedroom and Donna and Jenny's room were on one side of the great room, and our parents' room was on the other. Until he left home, Wallace stayed in a separate little house we called the "bunkhouse." Because of the location of the coal stove, we didn't close our doors. Actually, Mom and Dad's bedroom didn't have a door. Their room was a nice addition that was never completely finished. Isn't there an old saying about a carpenter and his house?

For much of the year, that old coal stove was the social center for the family. We would stoke it up till it glowed and stand around it, talking about the day's events and plans for tomorrow. While standing, we would all rotate. As our fronts got warm, we would turn to the side, then to the back, going around and around. We looked like a Wade rotisserie. Invariably someone would get too close and get burned. Blisters were common. When Mom and Dad decided it was time to bank the stove for the night, it was time for bed. Usually that would be about nine o'clock. To bed we went, hoping a little heat had snuck into our bedrooms through our open doors. None of us tossed and turned. We couldn't; the blankets were too heavy. I can't recall a time when I didn't read a book after going to bed. If told to turn off the lights, I would sneak a flashlight and read under the covers. Mom and Dad finally let me read as late as I wanted, but the time to rise and shine didn't change.

After the coal stove was banked up for the night and everyone was in bed the house quieted down. That was when Mom and Dad talked. The distant sound of their voices was reassuring to me. I couldn't understand a word that was said and didn't try to. The deep rumble of Dad's voice and Mom's smooth, clear tones let me know that, whatever problems we had, they would talk them over and have a plan to deal with them. Dad would learn how things were going with all of us and our activities. Mom would learn how his work was progressing. Sometimes we could hear soft laughter and be comforted by their joy. For years, Dad worked out of town, and I would look forward to the sound of their voices when he came home. Often I could hear Donna and Jenny talking as well until Mom or Dad would say, "You girls need to go to sleep." They would giggle, but then pretty quickly all was quiet. It didn't matter what was going on in my life; as long as I could hear those voices, all was right in my world.

CHAPTER 2

YOU CAN NEVER HAVE TOO MUCH FUN

FISHING AT OLIVERS' POND
BY DAN WADE

I left the house about an hour before dark. It would take me about that long to set the irrigation water. I needed to reset the irrigation water in a pasture near the house and hay field. We flood irrigated and had a lateral ditch beside the main ditch. When I reset the water, I took out the old dam in the lateral, reset a new one about one hundred feet downstream, and cut openings in the lateral about every six feet so that the field would be evenly watered. When finished, I would end up about a half mile from the house on the gravel road. My older brother Jerry planned to pick me up close to dark. We were going fishing!

I got the water set and reached the fence at the end of the hay field a little early. All I had to do was cross it to get to the road and wait for Jerry. It would have been easy to open the gap in the fence that was right there; just squeeze it open and walk through. At the time I was about thirteen years old, just starting to feel my oats. Opening the gap seemed like way too much trouble. On the side of the gap was what's called an "H brace." It is two posts set about four feet apart with a crossbeam about three feet off the ground. My plan was to grab a post, jump up on the crossbeam, and from there jump over the barbed wire to the other side. It was a good plan, but it didn't work out well. When I leaped up on the crossbeam, it gave way, and I fell—hitting the top of the barbed wire fence with my windpipe and it flipping me over. All of a sudden, I was flat on my back thinking I was dead. I couldn't breathe! I'd never had the wind knocked out of me before. In a bit, my breath started to come back, and I thought maybe I would live. Then I felt my neck. There was blood, a lot of blood. Holy cow, the fence had cut my throat. I was going to bleed to death! I tried to stop the bleeding with my shirt tail. Finally, deciding I wasn't going to bleed to death, I got up, squeezed the gap open, and stepped through. It wasn't all that much trouble after all.

Jerry pulled up as I was closing the gap. When he saw the blood all over me and the front of my shirt, he jumped out to see what had happened. He took a bandanna and wiped the blood away. That barbed wire had ripped my neck pretty good for about three inches, but it wasn't very deep. The bleeding had slowed, and I acted tough to impress Jerry. We decided that almost getting killed shouldn't stop a fishing trip. Jerry cleaned my neck the best he could with ditch water, tied the bandanna around my neck, and we went fishing.

We were going to Olivers' Pond. It was a five-acre, private pond stocked with big, fat trout that were fed once a week. The whole neighborhood knew their feeding schedule. We happened to be going the day before the fish got fed. They would be hungry. There was no road to the pond from our side of the river. The Olivers' driveway came from the other side of the river; they had their own bridge. We had to park on the side of the road, cross the fence, and walk through about three-quarters of a mile of their pasture. Sometimes there was more than one car on the side of the road. The pond could be crowded.

The Olivers were people who nobody knew. They were just known as rich people from Texas who lived in a huge, white, two-story house with a beautiful pond and the river. I don't really understand why it was that we didn't consider catching their fish stealing, but we didn't. None of us thought taking a fish or two from people that had so much was wrong. We knew they might see it differently; that's why we went at night.

It was dark by the time we parked and crawled over the fence into the pasture. Parts of the pasture were subirrigated and very uneven with tall grass. In the daylight, it would not have been fun to walk in; at night, carrying a fishing pole and tackle box, walking was difficult. Of course, it would have been easier with a flashlight. Since we were not invited, that wasn't an option. We were using their porch light to guide us to the pond. The night was dark but not pitch black. Our eyes adjusted just enough to walk without falling down.

Since their porch light was our guide, we came to the pond at the nearest point to the house, some sixty or seventy yards away. We could practically watch TV through their living room window. Jerry said this was a good spot, so we squatted down in the cattails, got our poles set and the bait on the hook. We were ready to fish. We had to whisper and close the tackle box real easy, careful to be quiet. When we cast our lines, the sinkers hitting the water sounded like a boulder. We crouched lower in the cattails and waited for a bite. It wasn't long before Jerry hooked the first one. That three-pound trout put up a fight. We were sure the people in the house would hear the splashing at any time. It would have been exciting to catch those big trout on a regular fishing trip, but in the dark, crouching amongst the cattails, in danger of getting caught at any moment, it was twice the fun and excitement. In less than an hour, we had as many as we wanted to carry. It was time to go home. We quietly loaded up and set out across the pasture.

The farther we got from the house, the more we relaxed. There by the pond, we'd practically been holding our breath. Now we could finally talk, a little above a whisper. We couldn't wait to get home and tell everybody about our trip. It had been fun!! We were walking along quicker than we'd come in when, all of a sudden, we stepped right in amongst some ducks. It was like an explosion! Whap, whap, whap! Those birds came right up from under us! Aheee!!! They could have heard us shout from the big house and a lot farther than that, but it really didn't matter. Nobody was going to catch us. As they say, "we were picking them up and putting them down all the way to the car."

Since then, Jerry has done all kinds of fishing. He's caught croppy by the bucketful, snagged salmon, and been deep-sea fishing. I've never asked him, but I'll bet he's never had more fun fishing than that night on Olivers' Pond. I know I haven't.

BACK ROADS TO ASPEN
BY TOM WADE

Here is a Colorado story. I think it was 1981 or 1982 that we took a trip to see Aunt Jenny Chilson. We went from Durango to Aspen without ever driving on pavement. All the way, backwoods four-wheeling and camping out. We went over a mountain pass where the old mining road was so narrow that one tire was half off the road, and the other side of the truck was scraping the side of the mountain. Many aspects of this trip have been lost, but I remember this road very well. I also recall how unhappy my mother was about going over that pass, and she let Dad know exactly what she thought! Then she got out of the four-wheeler and stomped down the trail. I am sure Dad was a little concerned, but he did not show it. He folded the passenger side window on the Jimmy and let her rip! I still can hear Dad laughing at the bottom as my mother confronted him again on his intelligence. It took a few minutes for her to calm down enough to get back in so we could continue on our journey.

I did not realize how special that trip was until I was in my twenties.

CITY SLICKERS IN THE COUNTRY
BY KEARNEY MORGAN

My cousin Jerry Wade was a fun-loving guy who loved his immediate and extended families very much. He was great to be around. I think back to when we were boys; James and I were *city slickers* visiting our cousins in the country. I remember the time we visited Jerry and Wallace at their farm in Mississippi. Time has faded a lot of details, but boy do I remember having a blast. There was the visit when we killed and skinned a water moccasin from their pond—a new experience for city boys! Another thing that Jerry thought was fun was to tease the bull in the pasture until he chased us, then run for the only tree in the pasture and see who was the last to climb up.

Aunt Betty Sue and Uncle Heber were so good to us. I can still hear Aunt Betty Sue's laugh after all these years. One warm summer evening, we all went to the drive-in movie in Uncle Heber's pickup truck. He parked the truck with the rear end facing the screen, and we all sat in straight-backed chairs to watch an *Our Gang* (Little Rascals) movie. The main plot of the movie was for the Gang to figure out their "secret sign." It consisted of their placing their wrists under their chins, palms down, and waving like the hands were attached to their chins.

We thought that was hilarious, so we made the "Hi Sign" to every car we saw and to each other for days after that.

Of course, all of the cousins know about my infamous ride with Jerry in a canoe down the creek at one of the Reunions many years ago. When we were not tumping (southern for turning canoes over) others, he was tumping us. A sure sign that this was about to happen was when he would say, "I'm getting hot!" Then I knew I was about to get wet again. There is no doubt that he enjoyed hearing me plead, "Not again, Jerry, not again!" I looked like a drowned rat in the video cousin Bob Kidd took of us coming out of that creek, and Jerry was laughing and having a great time.

COUSINS OFF-ROADING
BY WAYLON WADE

Weston has a thing he always says about dogs: one dog has one brain, but two or more dogs still have only one brain. If you've owned multiple dogs, you know what he means; you get a couple of dogs together, and, whatever one dog wants to do, the other dogs just go along. Usually this leads to mischief. Well, I suppose the same is also true of the Wade boys, particularly in the case of myself, my brother Weston, and our cousin Tyler. Just like with a group of dogs, we pretty much went with whoever had the funnest idea until one of the other two thought of something to top it.

The three of us grew up together and were close in age. We also grew up in a time and place where "outside" was an acceptable answer for parents to give when asked where their children were. It could mean the backyard or, in our case, miles off into the open, high-desert mesa that made up a lot of the area we grew up in. I've forgotten more adventures we had than there is time to tell them all. In my opinion, we may have saved the best for last.

It was about 2006, plus or minus, on one of those middle-of-the-year holidays that is pretty much there just to give people a three-day weekend. I can't recall which one. Weston and I went up to Bloomfield, New Mexico, to visit Tyler. He had a job driving a water truck in the oil fields. Now when people hear the term "oil field," images come to mind of sand dunes in the Middle East or maybe the flat expanses of west Texas. Well, those weren't the types of oil fields he was familiar with. The oil and gas fields in northern New Mexico are in some of the most beautiful wild New Mexico land you can imagine. Running through Carson National Forest and into the Jicarilla Apache Reservation, these oil and gas fields were in a seemingly endless expanse of rugged ridges of sandstone boulders, which formed canyons covered with juniper, piñon, and, in some places, ponderosa pine. Truly beautiful and wild country, and, thanks to the oil and gas fields, it could be accessed by anyone with enough guts to brave those rutty forest roads.

Weston and I met Tyler at his house and visited with Aunt Donna for a while. Tyler showed us the newest changes to their ever-evolving homestead. It didn't take long for Tyler to start telling us about how cool the country was that his new job was taking him through. At this point, the adventure began, and the thinking stopped. Weston and I had driven up in his four-by-four Jeep Cherokee Sport that was his pride and joy and a superbly capable vehicle for handling rutty dirt roads. Weston had driven up from Albuquerque, though, so Tyler insisted that he drive and that we take his truck, an old two-wheel-drive GMC with bald tires, one functioning headlight, no dashboard light, and remarkably little ground clearance for a full-sized pickup. Without a questioning thought, Wes and I jumped in the cab and off we went.

We saw some incredible country that day—gorgeous canyons, amazing views, and wildlife. We searched for antler sheds and saw mule deer, elk, and wild horses! I don't mean horses some guy has out to winter pasture; I mean real deal, descended from horses that escaped from conquistadors in the 1600s, wild-west-mustang wild horses! They were shorter than normal horses, with tails and manes that seemed twice as long as they should be and trailed behind them as they trotted along with the stallion of the group, who was nipping at the mares to herd them all together.

It was late in the day when we decided it was getting about time to head back. I have no idea how far away from civilization we were, but none of us had cell phone service for at least an hour. As we were looking for a spot to turn the truck around, Tyler pointed down a rutty dirt road and said, "I don't think I've ever been down this way," and then he turned down it, hoping to find a spot to flip around. What we found instead were ruts made by big oilfield water trucks and equipment haulers. With an unnerving thud, the old GMC hit those ruts and shuddered to a sudden stop. We all looked at each other knowing exactly what had happened. We were high centered in the middle of nowhere on a holiday weekend with fading daylight. Looking at the truck, it was pretty impressive: we had managed to get all four wheels off the ground with the two back wheels at least eight inches up in the air.

We did a quick inventory of what useful items we had, and it wasn't much—no food, no water, no coats, no blankets, one ten-foot ratchet strap, and a Leatherman Multi-Tool between the three of us. So we went on a scavenging mission. We searched for anything that might help us get out, and we had our imaginations in overdrive. The first item we came across was truly a lucky break. It was a heavy chain about twelve feet long running across the entry to a forest road. In all my years of driving through the boonies of New Mexico, it's the only time I've seen a road blocked that way, and, man, was I glad to see it then. We bashed the lock with rocks like cavemen until it finally broke, and the chain was free for us to utilize. We also found a road sign that was on a four-inch-by-four-inch post. Our final scavenged item was a pretty long length of barbed wire that had been used to fence off a sinkhole. We headed back to the truck and tried to figure out how to use our scavenged treasures to get that truck unstuck.

The arrangement we finally came up with was as brilliant as it was life threatening. First we put rocks under the front tires so the front end wouldn't dip. The nearest tree was a long way off, so we had to attach the chain to that tree; then we doubled up and twisted the barbed wire, which we attached to the chain on one end and the tree on the other. The ratchet strap was attached to the other end of the chain and then to the bumper of the truck. Finally, using a rock as the fulcrum, we wedged the post of the road sign under one of the rear tires. Now, with this set up, the plan was simple. I was in the driver's seat of the truck, Tyler was working the ratchet strap, and Weston was on the sign. The plan was that I would gun the engine, causing the one tire not in touch with anything to spin like crazy, at which point Weston would jump on the sign which would then act like a teeter-totter of death and lever up one side of the truck, forcing the spinning tire to touch the ground and the truck to lurch backwards. Tyler would then frantically work the ratchet to take up the slack before the truck rocked back and was once again stuck, having only moved an inch or two.

As dangerous as that sounds, it was worse. The barbed wire was god-only-knows-how old and rusty. We were constantly afraid that it would snap and whip back at us. To prevent losing and eye, Tyler actually had his t-shirt wrapped around his head. Plus, every time Weston jumped and landed on that sign, the entire truck moved, and that sign would twist out from under his feet so he was falling right as the truck was jumping backwards. It only took us about three good hours and probably two or three dozen repetitions of the jump, ratchet, and hope-no-one-dies routine before we got the truck back with four wheels on the ground.

The drive home was an adventure in itself, what with nearly hitting several elk in the dark and listening to Weston desperately try to explain to his wife Cristy what had happened and why he was still in Carson National Forest when he should have been home in Albuquerque (a four-plus-hour drive away) two hours ago. But that was all still pretty unremarkable when compared to what the rest of the day had been.

Sometimes you go on an adventure knowing that's what you're doing, but, in my experience, most adventures happen when you get three people together and just go with whoever has the funnest idea at the time.

OLD-FASHIONED FIREWORKS
BY DAN WADE

Dad used to tell us about a Fourth-of-July celebration tradition that has somehow fallen by the wayside. Every family had a big chopping block where they split their firewood with an ax. It was a big solid stump of hardwood. Early on Fourth-of-July morning, they would hollow out a hole in the chopping block and fill it with black powder. Then they would put their blacksmith anvil on top of the chopping block over the powder. That anvil weighed about one hundred pounds. After that, they warmed up with a sixteen-pound sledgehammer, then slammed the top of the anvil as hard as they could with that big sledgehammer. If they hit it just right with enough force, the compression would set the powder off, and the explosion would blast the anvil a hundred feet in the air with a loud boom. Then you would hear the blasts from all over the neighborhood as each household let the hammer down on their anvils. Can you imagine seeing a one-hundred-pound anvil flying in the air with an ear-splitting blast? Then hearing the big booms from the neighbors? Now that's fireworks!

SCARED, SO SCARED, BUT TRYING TO ACT BRAVE
BY DONNA WADE

Picture this: two sisters maybe fourteen and sixteen years old, both tall and thin. One sister is known as "The Pretty One"; the other one is known to have talent—she could sew, knit, play piano, and ride wild horses. They lived on a ranch in beautiful southwest Colorado. The sisters worked hard, played hard, and one day they decided to each invite a friend to go camping about a mile or two from the house. The site was a little patch of meadow grass surrounded by tall pines, known to the family as "The Clearing." The one condition was that little brother, eleven-year-old Dan, had to stay home. This was to be a girls-only outing.

I remember cooking food over a little fire—talking and laughing as it got dark—and thinking camping out was so much fun. I really don't like marshmallows, but, when you put them on a stick and hold them over a fire until they are charred, they become pretty good. Well, it got dark, and we began to hear sounds back in the trees. At first it was just a little sound, nonetheless loud enough to make everyone stop and look around. The pretty sister tried to let everyone know that it was just some of the cows moving around, nothing to worry about. Then a little bit later in the night, a louder sound came from a different area; it sounded like a branch breaking. The talented sister and friends began to doubt it was the cows. We all gathered a little closer, armed ourselves with big sticks, and began to make sounds loud enough to scare away the biggest of spooks. Now we were scared, very scared, but we could not pack up and go home; that would not have been the brave thing to do. Over the next several hours, the sounds would come and go—first from one side of The Clearing then the other. We put more and more wood on the fire; finally, the sounds seemed to stop; and we may have gotten a little sleep.

Morning came after a long night, and we went home and were proud to tell our story of being brave in the night. While telling our story, we noticed little brother Dan laughing. Then we knew that our one big, very big, mistake was not inviting him to come with us in the first place. We should have known to keep him close. Can you even imagine an eleven-year-old sneaking out of the house and walking in the pitch-black night a couple of miles through the hills and woods to go and scare his sisters and their friends camping out? Can you imagine how much fun he had? Well, folks, that's what happened. It was not cows. It was not spooks in the night. It was little brother Dan!

DAD GOING TO SINGS
BY DAN WADE

Dad told us of hand washing, starching, and ironing his best white shirt for Saturday night after doing a day's work plowing behind a mule. That's when he'd get ready and go to what he called a "sing." I think a "sing" consisted of a number of groups of young men from miles around taking turns harmonizing and quartet singing. Dad loved music and enjoyed singing with a group who understood how it should be done. These "sings" would be big social events with young people and families all having a good time. He said it was not uncommon to walk up to twenty miles for a "sing" and walk home the same night. How's that for cruising on a Saturday night?

A TRAIL RIDE AND A HORSE RACE
BY DAN WADE

In my experience, if you put two kids on horseback, pretty soon there will be a horse race. While my sisters, Donna and Jenny, and I were growing up on our ranch in Colorado, if we weren't working, we were riding horses. Jerry and Wallace joined in when they could. Donna and Jenny barrel raced just down the road from the house at a spot we called "the barrel spot." It was a clearing right outside our property line on the road. We didn't know who owned that piece of land, but I think they lived out of state. I did everything I could think of on horseback, from jumping logs and gullies and trying to lean down in the saddle and pick my hat off the ground while at a gallop to roping cattle. We all broke and trained horses. We also worked cattle on horseback and spent a lot of time just enjoying riding the horses.

There were several trail rides that we liked to take. One was a long loop on the north side of our place. The first part of the ride was up the road about half a mile, then we cut off through a clearing, and then we got into the trees. All along the way, we would walk the horses and visit or gallop along, just depending on how we felt. After about a mile or so of riding through the forest and hills we would come to a long valley.

This was why we went that way. Our neighbor Mr. VanCamp farmed that valley. He planted it in oats or wheat every year. We never rode in the field until he harvested in the fall, but after that it was our favorite racetrack.

We had many exciting rides there in that field. There is nothing more exhilarating than being on a good horse and asking it for all it can do. One time that sticks in my mind is when Jerry was riding his quarter-horse mare Peppy, Jenny was on Little Red, I was on Firecracker, and Donna was on her big black horse Gander. Peppy and Little Red were both fast, and, for a short distance, they could stay with Firecracker but not for very long. Gander was a great big horse, pretty and high spirited, but he was no race horse. On this day, when we got to the field, we all agreed that the finish line would be about three-quarters of a mile down the valley at a big dead tree. So we lined up, and someone said, "Go!" Off we went, whooping and a-hollering. The horses were as excited as we were. They knew the race was on. Jerry, Jenny, and I went flying through the field neck and neck, pushing those horses to go as fast as they could. Before we knew it, we passed the tree.

I don't even remember who won, but we were all laughing with sheer joy as we pulled our horses to a stop and turned to watch Donna come racing to the finish line. We had left her far behind. Here she came, galloping towards us on that big black horse; she had the biggest grin in the world. When she got close to us, she pulled the reins. Ol' Gander wasn't fast, but he sure could stop. Donna just meant to slow him down, but Gander thought she meant to stop, so he stopped. Donna didn't! That horse's sliding stop caught her by surprise, and she just kept coming. It was amazing to watch. She did a perfect somersault in the air coming off that horse and landed on the ground sitting up, smiling at us. Gander was right at her side. If they had practiced that fancy dismount, they couldn't have done it any prettier.

We laughed and talked all the way home. That was a great ride!

There was another ride we took that was longer and rougher. We'd leave the house and cross the valley, already looking forward to the trip. We rode single file up the steep hills that were our southern border. Topping out, one of us would get down and open the gap in the boundary fence. When we crossed through, we were on a large block of BLM (Bureau of Land Management) land where there were a few long-abandoned homesteads and traces of old wagon roads. There was almost an eerie feeling about the area. It seemed so big and empty. We never saw anyone there, and it felt like our secret place. Once we passed the fence and rode down from the hill, our trail swung out into the foothills. Then it turned north through arroyos, brushy flats, steep little hills, and long flats with open and brushy parts. For a lot of that stretch, our trail followed an old wagon road. We could see traces of the wheel tracks in the brush.

Mr. VanCamp's wheat field made a perfect racetrack for

speed, but this long, rough, brushy trail made a perfect "Wild West" racetrack. Racing over hills, jumping across arroyos, going out of our way to jump fallen logs, and taking shortcuts through steep rocky places made for a wild ride. All was fair in this race which went on for almost two miles. We would cut each other off, try to force the others off the trail, or scare their horses by screaming and waving our arms. By the time we got to the finish line, our horses were lathered and wild-eyed. All of us were wet with sweat and thrilled just to have survived that wild ride. The finish line was a tumbled-down, old homestead. We would stop there to rest, talk about our race, and kick around the old homestead wondering about those who had lived there. On one ride that stands out in my mind, all five of us kids were there—Jerry, Wallace, Donna, Jenny, and me. Dad was also riding with us on his mare Little Red. He didn't get to ride with us often, so this was an extra special day. Jenny went rummaging around the homestead and discovered an old, enameled coffee pot. It was a little bent up, but the lid was still attached. Of course, she had to take it home. As I remember, Jenny was riding Donna's mare that day because Dad was riding Little Red, which was the horse she usually rode. Donna's mare Etta was a good horse, but she had sometimes been known to buck.

After we all rested up and the horses had cooled down, it was time to go. We all mounted up and waited while Jenny tied the coffee pot to her saddle. She got finished, jumped aboard, and kicked her mare to take the lead up the trail at an easy lope.

It wasn't long before her horse had to jump a small arroyo, and that is when the coffee pot lid started clanging. That was all it took! The rodeo was on! That mare put her head down between her legs and started bucking. The more she bucked, the more the coffee pot clanged; and the more it clanged, the more she bucked. Jenny rode her with one arm in the air just like the pros. It took a bit, but she finally got the mare's head up and pulled her to a stop. We tied the coffee pot to my saddle, and we tied the lid open this time. Jenny rested for a minute, and then we were ready to go again. Dad didn't say much about Jenny's ride on the bucking horse, but you could tell he was proud of her. Dad and Mom didn't raise any sissies.

From there, it was back up the hill and over the ridge where we crossed the fence back into our ranch. Riding down off that ridge and through the trees, we would usually jump some deer. When we got down to the valley, it was about a mile and a half back to the house, but we all looked forward to stopping at an old windmill just a little way down the valley. The windmill tower was still there, but the mill was long gone. Someone had put a hand pump on that well, and after pumping that handle up and down for a while to get it primed, we would get the coldest, clearest water in the world. At least it seemed like that to us after four or five miles of hard riding. We would drink it, splash in it, and stick our heads in the cold water. It was great to get a drink and cool off. Then it was an easy mile's ride back to the house. We unsaddled and tended to the horses, then headed to the house. Jenny was glad to show Mom her coffee pot. We all had fun telling stories about the ride and Jenny's rodeo. That day really was extra special, especially because Dad had been riding with all five of us kids. He didn't take time to ride with us very often, but, when he did, he had as much fun as any of us. That was a great ride!

ZIP LINE

BY ROBBIE SMITH

This story is one that I vaguely remember. The details are hard to recall, but it is a memory worth sharing. My siblings and I were at Uncle Noel's and Aunt Minnie Lee's. I was about eight years old. Back then, we spent a lot of time there. Aunt Minnie Lee watched us while Mom and Dad went to see a man about a dog. (Funny thing is that they never brought a dog home.) We had wandered off down behind their house, exploring. Then one of the older brothers found a homemade zip line. I found out later that Wayne and Robert Walters had stolen Aunt Minnie Lee's clothes line and cut a piece off a bicycle's handlebar to make it. Well, you know what happened next: we took turns at flying down the hill. We laughed at each other, trying to time our dismount. We had a blast until we were exhausted and too bruised up to continue. It is a good memory, a time in our lives when we all had fun together.

BULL IN THE HOLE

BY WALLACE WADE

I was probably eleven or twelve years old, and we were living at "the old place" in Roswell. Back then, there wasn't cable TV, video games, social media, or much in the way of anything beyond books that were readily accessible and designed to occupy your time. It required a little imagination for a young person to keep from getting bored. One day, to keep myself entertained, I decided I was going to dig a hole. I picked a spot where the ground was soft and went to work digging. After the first day, I had it deep enough that I needed help because I couldn't toss the dirt out of the hole. So I enlisted Donna and Jenny to help. I would scoop the dirt into buckets, and they would haul the buckets up out of the hole.

With all the work we had put in, we had that pit about eleven feet deep after the second day of digging. To prevent accidents, I did intend to take certain safety precautions. After we were done working on operations for the day, the plan was for me to push a trailer over the top of the hole. But at the end of the second day, I was pretty tired and just didn't feel like pushing that trailer over the hole; so I just didn't.

I woke up on the third day with a plan. I would tunnel

from my current hole over to the barn because, to my young mind, having escape tunnels was important. As I walked up and looked in the hole, my plans instantly changed. One of Dad's prize bulls was down in the hole! To my amazement and relief, the bull was still alive.

My mind was racing: how on earth was I going to get this huge animal out of that shaft? Terrified, I went back into the house to talk to Mother. I told Mom what had happened. She knew where Dad and Jerry were working and drove into town to get them. Once they got home and assessed the situation, the solution was pretty obvious: we had to dig a way out of that hole for the bull. Dad, Jerry, and I set to work digging a ramp down to the bull. When the ramp was completed, all we had to do was to get that bull to walk out. It wasn't as easy as it sounds. Apparently, the fall had taken a lot out of the bull. It was lying down in the bottom of that pit and wouldn't get up. Dad knew a trick; he took a bucket of water and poured it into the bull's nose. That bull snorted, coughed, gagged, and jumped to its feet. From there, it was easily led up the ramp and back to the surface.

After the bull was out, Dad handed me the shovel, looked me in the eye, and told me, "I want this hole filled in by the time I get home." For the rest of the day, I worked my tail off because, come hell or high water, I was going to have that pit filled in before Dad got home. To my surprise, that was the only punishment I ever got for nearly killing one of his prize bulls.

That experience did teach me to find other ways to keep myself entertained, although most would argue that shooting off homemade rockets isn't any safer than digging holes. But that's a story for another day.

SLEDDING WITH MY SISTERS
BY DAN WADE

My sisters, Donna and Jenny, and I grew up having a lot of fun snow sledding. There is a lot more to sledding than just sliding down hills. Good sled runs have to be built, and we learned to be expert sled-run builders for all kinds of sleds. We knew our business! Our older brothers Jerry and Wallace joined in whenever they could, but the three of us were really the experts. We did all kinds of sledding—western flyers with steel runners, toboggans, plastic sheets. They were all great, but our all-time favorite was the saucer sled. Saucers were made of sheet metal and shaped like their name. With most sleds, you can choose to either sit or lie down on them, but not so with a saucer sled; sitting cross-legged and gripping the rope handles on each side as hard as you can is the only proper way to ride a saucer. There is virtually no control on these sleds: you can't steer, slow, or stop them. All you can do is hang on for dear life!

Since they have no controls, we had to build a special run just for our saucer sled. The hill right next to our house was the best place. Our house was built on the side of the hill. The driveway was cut into the hillside, and it came to the house from the side, so that it was level. The uphill side of the drive was steep, and on the downhill side there was a pretty good drop-off with an irrigation ditch at the bottom. After a snow, Dad would clear the drive by pushing the snow to the downhill side of the driveway with the blade on his John Deere tractor, making a snowbank on that side of the drive. That bank would grow taller with each snow; after two or three good snows, it would get up to five feet tall. Then we would have a good steep hill on the upper side of the drive, and a large embankment on the lower side with a twelve-foot drop over the top of the snowbank.

This is how we built the run. First, we would walk up the hill breaking a trail, carrying the sled to the top of the hill above the driveway. Then, one of us sat on the saucer with our legs crossed holding onto a strap handhold on each side. The other two would then push and pull it down the hill through the deep snow to the driveway. We would do that over and over until we had a well packed run. Right before dark, we would sprinkle it with water. We sprinkled it pretty heavy. Overnight it would freeze, and then we had a run that was pure ice. It would be fast! The driveway was already icy. Flying down the hill, we would cross the rough, frozen driveway and hit the snowbank on the downhill side. That was a sudden stop, but we would ramp the snowbank a little bit with a shovel, and each run we would go up it a little higher, and pretty soon we'd go over the top of the snowbank. Each ride was a little faster. It wouldn't be long before we were flying over the embankment fast enough to get airborne for ten or fifteen feet before landing in the deep soft snow at the bottom. It was a great ride! We all took turns.

Watching each other come screaming down the hill, bouncing across the icy drive, then catapulting over the embankment, and flying through the air was sometimes more fun than doing it ourselves.

Even Dad would take the ride. One time he had a really great run and went flying up and over the embankment. After getting high in the air, for some reason he turned completely upside down and fell head first into the deep snow at the bottom of the hill, still holding tight to the saucer sled. He was totally buried; the only thing we could see was the bottom of the sled. We were afraid he was hurt. But, when he came up out of that deep snow, he still had his hat on, his glasses were full of snow, and Dad was grinning from ear to ear. He had, as they say in gymnastics, "stuck his landing."

There was one other way we used that sled. It was, as far as I know, our own invention. I had a little Shetland pony that I named Apt, 'cause she was apt to do anything. (I'll tell you more about that pony another time.) Riding the sled, screaming downhill, across the icy drive, over the embankment, and then flying through the air just wasn't enough excitement for us; we needed an even more exciting way to risk our lives. So, we decided to try using my pony Apt to pull the saucer sled with a rope. Since I rode Apt bareback, there wasn't anything to tie the rope to. Without a saddle horn to tie the rope to, what we needed was a horse collar; of course, we didn't have one. We overcame this problem by making one. Using what we had, we took an old pair of jeans, tied the bottom of the legs together with baling twine, and stuffed each leg full of hay; then we tied the belt line tight. Presto! We had a horse collar. We'd tie one end of a thirty-foot rope to the collar (jeans) and the other end to the sled, and, when we put our new horse collar over Apt's head, we were ready for a ride!

Our place for "horse sledding" was a fairly flat pasture in front of the house. Ideally it was covered with eight to sixteen inches of snow; it could be a little deeper, but then it would get too deep for little Apt. One of my sisters would get on the saucer, and we'd take off. I'd get Apt to a full gallop and ride in a big circle, then go in smaller and smaller circles. I won't even try to explain the physics of it, but the smaller the circle I rode, the faster that sled flew. When that pony and I got down to a tight spin, Donna or Jenny would be airborne and hanging on for dear life. I don't know how fast you have to go to get a teenager on flat ground, riding a sled, to be airborne, but it is fast! They could get more than two feet off the snow. Apt and I would try to make them go faster. First one sister, then the other. We had a great time!

I had a blast riding Apt and giving rides, but one day Donna decided it wasn't fair that I never got to ride the sled. She insisted on giving me a ride on the saucer while she rode Apt. I was leery about her riding Apt because at that time Donna was a good six inches taller than I was, and Apt was small. Donna was sure it would be fun, so I reluctantly got on the saucer. Donna got on Apt, and off we went. This was her first time riding that pony, and her legs were too long to wrap around

Apt without dragging in the snow, so they were straight out on both sides. She got Apt up to a gallop, but she couldn't grip the pony with her legs. That was a big problem. She soon started leaning—just a little at first, then more and more—until, just as they were crossing a frozen ditch, she fell off Apt. It was a hard landing on the ice. I'm pretty sure she was still bouncing when we ran right over her with the sled. Apt hadn't stopped running! Before I could yell, "Look out!" that sled and I ran right over Donna! After that experience, we decided that I would be Apt's only rider. It was a short sled ride for me, and that was just fine.

Riding that little pony and getting my sisters airborne was more fun than a barrel full of monkeys. Since we've been grown, we've all been to big amusement parks and ridden big fancy rides. They're all great, but I don't think anything has ever even come close to that old saucer sled—either screaming down the hill and flying over the embankment or being pulled on the sled behind that little Shetland pony with the horse collar made of old jeans stuffed full of hay. We didn't buy tickets; we didn't stand in line; we did it all by ourselves.

MOM, PROFESSOR OF PLAY

BY DAN WADE

When I was a boy, I got an advanced education in playing. My mom was the professor, and Dad was the assistant. She taught us to make kites using tree branches, newspaper, a little string, some fabric scraps, flour and water. We flew those paper kites for hours. When they crashed, we would repair or rebuild them. All we needed were some new sticks, newspaper, string, and flour, and we were ready to go. As kids, we weren't skilled enough with a knife to make a top, so Dad would help us. He'd take a wooden spool from Mom's sewing basket, a stick about the size of a pencil, and his sharp pocket knife. In a couple of minutes, he'd carve that spool to a point, then sharpen and shape the stick until it would fit in the spool. Presto! We had a spinning top. We learned to wrap string around and around the top, tie one end to our finger, and, if we threw it just right, it would spin and spin. Of course, we had top-spinning contests to see who could spin it the longest.

Mom taught us to take a forked tree branch, an old inner tube cut into strips, for the rubbers, a little kite string, and the tongue off of a pair of worn-out boots to make a slingshot. I think the most damage I ever did with a slingshot was putting dents in tin cans. I sure spent a lot of time trying to hit a bird, but the best I ever did was scare a few. Mom also taught us to make a one-rubber slingshot. You use a straight stick and one rubber tied so that it would go over the top of the stick before releasing the rock. I have never seen one anywhere else, but they work pretty well.

Dad showed us to how to make a push-stick by taking two sticks or small boards—one about three feet long and another one about eight inches long—then nail the short one to the long one, making a *T*. After that, all we needed was an eight- to twelve-inch steel hoop, and we were ready to play. Gripping the push-stick with the T down, then standing the hoop on the ground, we'd begin pushing it with the push-stick faster and faster, as far and as fast as we could. We called it "chasing the hoop." Whoever could keep the hoop rolling the longest was the winner.

I learned from Dad how to make a trap for small animals and birds by using a bunch of straight sticks and a little string. He taught me to whittle a figure-four trigger that, when the bird or squirrel touched it, the trap would fall.

Jerry and Wallace learned to play the baseball game of "flies and skinners" from Mom, then they taught Donna, Jenny, and me. We would all chase that ball for hours. We played hide-and-seek, tag, hopscotch, and jacks. We built stilts for ourselves from scrap lumber and straightened nails. We had sack races with real gunny sacks, we held wheelbarrow races, and we spent hours playing the basketball game of "Horse."

We played the game of horseshoes with real horseshoes. Then at night, we played checkers, dominoes, tic-tac-toe, hangman, Wahoo, and—best of all—Monopoly. If we weren't sleeping or doing chores, we were playing. And if we were playing, we were competing with each other.

I think Mom and Dad believed that their job as parents was to raise their children to work hard and to be respectful, kind, truthful, and God-fearing. They showed us how to get started playing, but after that they left us alone. I don't think it even remotely occurred to them that they were responsible for entertaining us. If we wanted to be entertained, it was up to us. Our parents joined in our play whenever they could, but for the most part we were on our own.

I am pretty sure that all five of Heber and Betty Sue Wade's children will always remember the first movie we ever saw (for me it was Gone with the Wind), the first time we ate in a sit-down restaurant (Western Steak House), and maybe the first merry-go-round we rode on, but none of us can remember a time that we didn't take great pleasure in small things.

MAGIC MOMENTS
BY MELITA WADE THORPE

The Moselle School Halloween Carnival had been on Friday night, and Mom, Beatrice Wade, had created for me the best-looking witch costume out of crepe paper (black). I was one proud spook. The thirty-first fell on Saturday, however. To continue our "eight-year-old" fun, Dad, Vardaman Wade, suggested that we build a bonfire in the yard and roast potatoes and tell our favorite ghost stories. This was going to be thriller, magic, and horror.

Dad and I gathered the wood while Mom got some potatoes ready to cook among the coals. I could not wait for Dad's story to begin. He said that we could not start the story until the fire was blazing red and the potatoes were roasting. The anticipation was intense.

Though a full harvest moon was over Walters' Woods, darkness seemed to close in. There was a nip in the air, and, once Dad began his tale of graveyards, goblins, and things that go bump in the night, I found the night chill a good excuse to snuggle in his lap and strong arms. Mom was still getting things ready in the kitchen.

As the story developed, Dad's eyes were wide with drama,

and his voice elaborated on every word's villainous sound. Nobody could tell it better. My eyes widened, too, with every eerie noise. Just as his voice began its high tremolo to announce the ghost's appearance, out of the darkness a white figure appeared! The hair on my neck pricked. I tried to crawl right into Dad's jacket.

His story continued, and the ghost came over close, raised its arms, and began to make sounds! I wanted to scream, run, close my eyes, and make it go away, but I was frozen in eight-year-old terror! Dad, sensing my horror, stopped his story and asked, "Beatrice, is that you?" Mom laughed and said, "Boo!" We all had a good, relieving laugh. The potatoes never tasted to so good.

There are so many special, close family moments that Dad, Mom and I shared together. Everything always centered around our tiny world. We always supported, applauded, and enjoyed each other's achievements.

Dad's work in the 4-H Club brought many honors which Mom and I shared with him. His New Orleans Chamber of Commerce Award in 1958, his Outstanding Award in 1963, and—the one he's the proudest of—the 50 Year Award in 4-H. We celebrated with him and proudly sent him off to the club's Congress in Chicago—its National Convention.

Mom was a leader in the Methodist Women, and, when she went to her summer sessions at the Seashore Camp Grounds in Biloxi, Mississippi, Dad and I always went along with her.

During her free time, we'd go out to Ship Island or on the beach. As my fourth-grade teacher, Mom inspired in me a deep love for geography and a fascination for faraway places.

When I received two Best Actress Awards from University of Southern Mississippi (USM) they were there, laughing, crying, and applauding.

These were the gladdest of times, with the grandest parental support anyone could desire. Mom and Dad's ethics and strengths are incredible. And our special moments have been magical, purely magical.

ROCKET LAUNCHES AND GRANDMOTHER

BY WALLACE WADE

As a little boy growing up, I was always fascinated by rockets. It started when Dad and I got stopped at a roadblock at White Sands Missile Range. They had the road closed because they were testing a new rocket; I believe it was a test of the Viking rocket. We watched it lift off and shoot straight up out of sight from right there in the truck. Years later, the United States was in the space race with the Soviet Union and was playing catch up. The Soviets had already put a man in orbit, and the National Aeronautics and Space Administration (NASA) had started the Mercury program to get an American into orbit.

Coincidentally, this was going on during the few months Grandmother Wade was staying with us. I would tell her about the latest missions by NASA. She would listen and smile. In 1962 when the Mercury missions were set to launch, I desperately wanted to see them on TV. With the launches taking place at Cape Canaveral (now Kennedy Space Center) on the East Coast, I'd need to wake up at three o'clock in the morning to watch the countdown. The big problem was that I didn't have an alarm clock and was worried I couldn't get myself up in time. Grandmother Wade was amazing; she had the ability to just decide when she was going to wake up. She didn't need an alarm. If she told herself before going to sleep that she wanted to get up at a certain time, she would just wake up at that time. I told her of the historic launch of the Mercury spacecraft and how worried I was about missing it. She said she'd get up with me and watch it.

The thing about rocket launches is that they need a very specific type of weather to go off smoothly, and checking and double checking every system is required, or the launch is called off or "scrubbed." Grandmother Wade and I got very familiar with the term "scrubbing the mission." Nine times she woke me, and nine times we watched them scrub the mission. It got to be a joke with us. She'd wake me up at three in the morning with, "Get up, Wallace! It's time to watch them scrub the mission," and laugh. On the tenth morning, that's how she woke me, and we watched the black and white image on the screen of the rocket and the little clock in the corner counting down. We watched in silence as the countdown went to zero and that rocket lifted off taking John Glenn into orbit. The first pass of his three orbits even went over our house, since its path took it over White Sands!

I lost a lot of sleep getting up those mornings with Grandmother Wade, but I still remember her laugh. The lost sleep was well worth it.

HIGH COUNTRY TRIP
BY DAN WADE

Two or three years after we moved to Colorado, Jerry got to talking about a trip to the high country. I'm pretty sure Jerry lived in Albuquerque at the time and worked with our dad building houses. He came up to the ranch as often as he could. My sisters and I sure looked forward to his visits. Even when we worked hauling hay, Jerry made it fun. He was twenty-six or twenty-seven years old and full of life; we all looked up to him. He kept talking about taking a pack trip to the high county. It sounded great! We picked a date about a month out. Even Dad was planning to go.

In preparation, Jenny took some visqueen plastic we used to cover the hay with and sewed a nice rain coat. Prudent people would have used that month to get ready. They would have gotten their horses shod, secured a good lightweight tent—as well as a lightweight camp stove and cookware—rounded up a pack saddle, and found some protective rain gear. A well-prepared group would certainly have a first-aid kit, maybe a safety flare, an air horn, and a flashlight, along with food for three days. That's what prudent people would do. We did none of that. Heck, Jerry's horse wasn't even broke to ride yet. We would do that the day before our trip.

The day before we left was a busy day. That's when we did all of our preparations. We rolled up our sleeping bags and grabbed some eggs, bacon, potatoes, bread, and tomato soup. I think the last thing we packed was our fishing gear, fifty feet of line, and a few hooks. If we needed a pole, we would cut one in the mountains. Along with our preparations, we also broke Jerry's horse. He would be riding a high-powered, quarter-horse mare named Peppy. Peppy was a big four-year-old bay that Jerry had bought a year or so before, but we had never touched her until we caught her that day. We broke her to lead and ride using our one-day method. Peppy didn't get quite as much breaking as usual because we had to get ready. After getting her working pretty well, Jerry pronounced her ready to go. We got busy loading the truck with saddles, tack, and supplies, and we didn't forget rain gear. Jenny had sewn herself that nice raincoat, and, at the last minute, the rest of us made our own, too. We cut eight-foot-by-eight-foot squares of visqueen, put a hole in the middle, and—presto!—we had a poncho. After hooking up the trailer, we were all set. I couldn't wait to leave early in the morning. We were excited!

Dad decided not to go after all. I think he'd already taken his day off for that year. At the last minute, Jenny decided that she couldn't go either. She had some dang 4-H project that had to get finished by a certain time. Taking time for the trip of a lifetime just wasn't an option. She had made a commitment and wouldn't be dissuaded. We were all disappointed and tried to talk her into going, but she wouldn't budge. Jenny was a stickler for finishing what she started; she still is.

Early the next morning, we got the horses loaded and headed out. Dad drove us high up in the San Juan Mountains to the trailhead where Vallecito Creek flows into the lake. Our route would take us up Vallecito Creek and cross over the mountains to the Pine River, then go back down to the lake on the other side. It would be a pretty hard, three-day ride that none of us would ever forget. That morning we got to the trailhead, unloaded the horses, saddled, and got packed up way before daylight. After saying goodbye to Dad, we mounted up.

It was the first time Jerry had ever been on Peppy. I had been riding her while we broke her to ride the day before. She was pretty frisky, we had to tie her to the horse trailer to get the saddle on, and Jerry had to spin her for a while before he could get on. Spinning a horse is a way to tire them just a bit, making them a little easier to get on and handle. Here's how you spin a horse. Take the reins with your left hand, pull the horse's head around and grab the saddle horn; then, with your right hand, grab the back of the saddle skirt; then you step on the horse's back foot. The horse will move; then you step on his foot again. Pretty soon, the horse will be spinning fast enough to lift you off the ground. A few minutes of that will usually take the starch out of a horse.

Donna was riding a big black gelding that Dad had traded for. He was one of the few horses that were broke when we got him. He was broke, but he needed to be reminded. It sure took an experienced horseman to ride him, and the rider had better be paying attention. Donna loved him. She did not like to ride any horse without a lot of spirit. His name was Gander. I rode a bomb-proof mare named Jubilee.

We hit the trail. It was just starting to get light. Jerry was in the lead, then Donna, and I brought up the rear. It was just a few minutes before we came to a rock bluff that a trail had been blasted into. For my money, they could have used more powder. That trail might have been wider than three feet, but not much. As we rode, we had a rock wall on one side and a cliff on the other side. That cliff dropped off no less than 150 feet. I think that cliff trail was about seventy-five yards long, making a couple of turns along the way. We were into the first turn when Jerry's mount Peppy "broke into." What I mean is, she started bucking. As soon as Peppy started, Gander went to bucking as well. Those horses didn't have a chance in the world of throwing Donna or Jerry off; they weren't coming off! The question was: could the horses stay on the trail? Jubilee just kept her pace. I couldn't do anything but watch, thinking I would see my brother and sister plunge to their deaths any second. They didn't. Instead they were putting on a bronc riding show, while those horses did their best to throw them. It seemed like forever, but, in reality, it probably wasn't more than twenty seconds or so. When they got off the cliff, Peppy stopped bucking, then Gander did, too. Both horses acted like nothing had happened. They wanted to start grazing. We all got off our horses. I hadn't been in danger, but my knees were shaking. I don't know about Donna and Jerry. Giving up the trip and going back was not an option; we'd have to cross that cliff again if we did. So after a good break, we mounted up, and Jerry led us up the trail.

The sun came up, and it sure felt good. It's pretty cool up there in the mountains, even in the summer. As we rode into the canyon, the sun disappeared. It would appear and disappear at least seven times; it was a special morning. When we stopped for lunch, we were still in the canyon bottom. On the bank of Vallecito Creek, we ate lunch. What a morning it had been: excitement, terror, relief, awe, and anticipation. What next? We couldn't rest long; we needed to make Flint Lake before night to stay on schedule. So, after tying our coats to our saddles, we mounted up and headed out. The country opened up the higher we went. We would follow Vallecito Creek until it was joined by Flint Creek, then we'd turn and follow it to Flint Lake. After we turned at Flint Creek, the country opened up to a wide mountain valley with craggy peaks on both sides. We were below timberline but not far below. It was beautiful.

Jerry was setting a fairly fast pace, for two reasons, I think. One, we needed to make camp at the lake before dark; and, two, I could see he was worried about some thunder clouds that were starting to gather. Once they started gathering, they came on quickly. Lightning started to pop. The lightning was all around us; we could smell it. The thunder was so close, it felt like we were being hit. Then the hail started. Jerry had us at a high trot; those horses were as scared as we were. Our visqueen ponchos were flapping in the wind, but they were helping until that hail got to be the size of golf balls. It was beating us to death. We stopped and huddled under our poor horses, but we still got pounded. The only shelter was the trees. The lightning was why we had stayed in the open, hoping it would hit the trees and not us. Jerry said we could stay there in the open and get beat to death or get under the trees and pray. Donna and I didn't have any trouble deciding; we voted for the trees. Jerry led us out, whipping and spurring his horse. We had about a quarter of a mile to go to the trees. Those horses had their bellies to the ground the whole way; that was a fast ride! We crowded up under the trees, finally safe from the hail. The lightning was still popping and cracking all around us, and the thunder was booming. I think even Jerry was a little frightened. Like in foxholes, I guarantee, there are no atheists in a lightning storm. It seemed like the storm lasted forever, but it was probably less than an hour. It left as quickly as it came, and the sun came out and started warming us up. The horses were steaming while they dried. We were just glad to be alive. Jerry was still focused on getting to Flint Lake to set up camp. So we set out, riding through the fallen hail; it was turning slushy as we rode. Sooner than we expected, there it was—Flint Lake. We'd made it!

We were happy and exhausted, but there was camp to set up. The first thing was to care for the horses. We unsaddled and staked them out, so they could graze in the melting hail. Then we gathered rocks for a fire ring. Dry wood was hard to find, but we gathered enough for the night. Donna got supplies out of the saddlebag: a pan, a pot, some pork and beans. That was about it; we had packed light. Our planned entree was fish; that was Jerry's and my job. With our little camp shovel, we found some earthworms, got our line and hooks, and walked over to the lake. After crawling up on some big rocks, we dropped our hooks in the clear water. Peeking over the edge, we could see those mountain trout grab the worms, and we'd jerk the hook and pull them up. It was that easy. Soon there was plenty for supper. Pork and beans and trout seemed like a meal fit for a king, there in the high country. After supper, we didn't stay up long; all of us were really tired. We crawled in our sleeping bags and looked up. It was a pitch-black night, and the stars were huge! Then the show started, falling stars or meteorites by the hundreds. They were right on top of us. Wow! What a sight! "Look at that!" one of us would say. "No, look at this!" another would exclaim. We'd all seen plenty of falling stars, but this was a storm of meteors, not just a shower. After the show, we slept like babies on that cold wet ground.

We woke early. Jerry made a fire and cooked breakfast—scrambled eggs cooked in bacon grease and a piece of bread. It was great, but the best part on that cold, high country morning was the tomato soup. We drank it like hot chocolate, and it was the best hot drink any of us ever had. After saddling up, we wondered what this day would bring.

Jerry warned us we had some miles to cover to stay on schedule. Our three-day trip would have been a comfortable four-day ride, but we only had three days to spare. By riding hard, we packed four days of fun and adventure into three days. The route that day would take us by Rock Lake, then on to the Pine River. With the craggy peaks on both sides, we rode in awe of God's work. Lunch would be at Rock Lake, and, with some hard riding, we'd get there by noon. The horses didn't act up, and we made good time. Rock Lake is aptly named. It is surrounded on three sides by sheer rock cliff. The reflection in that clear water was ever changing. Making lunch there, we were all sort of quiet; being loud seemed irreverent. It was that kind of place. The meadow we were in started to narrow after we left the lake. By the time we reached the Pine River, the trail wound through giant fir, spruce, and pine trees. It was shady, cool, and quiet with only the sound of the breeze in the trees to be heard. Turning downstream, the trail was right next to the river sometimes and up to a quarter of a mile away at others. Jerry kept us moving pretty well. We had to push the horses; they were a little tired after being ridden so hard. We were a bit tired, too, but still enjoyed the magical afternoon, the sights and sounds of the breeze through the trees, and the roar of the river. We might not have been in heaven, but we were sure next door!

Jerry finally decided that we'd traveled far enough to make camp. We planned to meet Dad at the trailhead where the Pine River runs into Valerio Lake around three o'clock the next day. Setting up camp went quickly; we all knew our jobs. Supper was a little skimpy, but we all got our fill. We had packed light; tomorrow's lunch wasn't looking good. After supper, we were looking forward to another meteor show, and the stars were large and bright, but they didn't fall. Before I was ready for it, Jerry was cooking breakfast and calling a cheerful good morning. It was still dark. Donna and I got up and helped out. Again, the best part was the tomato soup. Fifty years later, I can still taste it; it was that good. As we headed down the trail, Jerry tried to boost our spirits. The greatest trip we'd ever even imagined was coming to an end. He got us to thinking about what our next trip would be—maybe the trail along the Continental Divide, or we might just go all the way to Silverton.

Our poor horses were worn out and foot sore. We just let them pick the pace. Jerry said we'd meet Dad on time. At noon, we stopped to rest the horses and us, too. We were down to a couple of candy bars for lunch. It helped to know that Mom would have a big supper for us at home. Dad was there to meet us at the trailhead. After loading up, we headed home—a tired and happy bunch. Boy, did we have some stories to tell!

The years have passed, and life happened. Despite our intentions, we never rode the high country together again. We hoped to, meant to; it just never got done. All of us have been back to the high country, just not together. Thanks to Jerry's insistence though, we have that trip in our memories. It really was a once-in-a-lifetime experience. Donna and I have talked many times of taking another high-country trip. By the way, Jerry is still focused on staying on schedule, and Jenny is sorry she stayed home, working on a long-forgotten 4-H project. You know what? We all just might get back to the high country yet.

ରେ   ରେ   ରେ   ଟେ   ଟେ   ଟେ

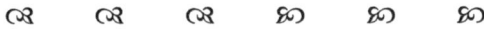

Jerry, don't think, just because you've gone on, that we won't ride together again. Whenever I mount up on a good horse on a cold clear morning, you'll be with me. Whenever I close on a good deal, you'll be with me. Whenever I figure out a better way to do a project, you'll be with me.

Jerry, I never told you thanks for all the good times we shared, and they were all good times. Save a spot for me, buddy. I'll be there soon.

Author's Note:

Our older brother Jerry died suddenly on November 8, 2015, after a struggle with cancer. He was seventy-five years young.

CHAPTER 3

CHARACTER(S) REVEALED

THEY CALLED HIM MISTER WADE
BY DAN WADE

His name was James Heber Wade, but about the only people I ever heard call my dad by his name, Heber, were relatives. He was James to some business associates. Otherwise, he was "Mister Wade" to our neighbors and friends. Even though he asked to be called James or Heber, they continued to call him "Mister" out of respect. He was known as a man of his word, and he was often turned to for settling disagreements. Dad was plain spoken, but not outspoken. When the situation called for it, he could say things in a way that would not be misunderstood. Here are a few examples.

Dad was working as a carpenter, tying top plates together on some twelve-foot walls when he heard a coworker talking to their foreman below him. He did not know Dad was there. "I borrowed this handsaw from Wade, and it is the sorriest saw I have ever seen. You can tell he's not much of a carpenter, if he owns such a sorry tool," his coworker said. Dad responded in a strong voice from above, "I keep that saw to loan to sorry blankety-blanks like you who have to borrow a saw since you don't own one." At the time, Dad was working away from home with hundreds of men, building a top-secret military facility in Oak Ridge, Tennessee, during the Second World War. Like a lot of big jobs, there were two ways not to get laid off. One was to ingratiate yourself to your boss, and the other was to be good at what you did and hope it was noticed. Dad chose the latter.

I was about thirty years old and had gone broke in my contracting business, losing our home and everything I had except a truck with payments on it and a few tools. I was visiting with my dad, trying to put the best light on my failure. Explaining that while I had failed, at least I had tried, and all the "bullet holes" were in front. Dad got real quiet, then said these words that I will always remember: "You are the second son of mine to tell me that, and I will tell you what I told him. That is one of the stupidest things I have ever heard." Then raising his voice, he said "THE IDEA IS NOT TO GET SHOT."

When Dad was in his sixties, multiple sclerosis, melanoma, and bad surgeries had ravaged his body to the point where he had use of only one arm, but he was grateful that he could still sit on and operate a scooter. We had made a trip with him to visit family in Mississippi. Dad was visiting with his brother Haskell. Like a lot of older people, Uncle Hack had aches and pains, but he was still very able and active. He started telling Dad about some of his health problems—this little thing and that little thing. Dad was sitting there on his scooter, with a big lump on his head from melanoma, unable to turn his head or move his legs, and was in pain most of the time. Dad listened quietly for a while, then said "Haskell, if that was all the problems I had, I don't believe I would even mention them."

For a number of years, Dad contracted concrete work, pouring foundations and slabs for a big developer. Working concrete is hard work, and, once you start, you can't stop until it is finished. If you don't get it finished right, it will set up hard, and you have to break it up and do it over. One November morning, Dad and his crew poured a house slab. They had just got it poured out of the truck and screeded flat when a cold front came in. It was blowing snow and bitter cold, and they still had to finish the concrete, first the jitterbug, then the bull-float, then hand-trowel to a smooth finish, and edge that slab. That is a lot of work on a nice day and is much, much harder in those conditions. Dad went to his truck, pulled his coveralls out from under the seat, put them on, and went back to work. His crew came to him and said they didn't have coveralls, and it was too cold to work. Dad told them, "Maybe this will teach you to be prepared. But cold or not, we are going to finish this slab." No one froze to death, and they got the job done.

I subcontracted framing houses for a builder in my early twenties. I had a good crew, and the builder kept us pretty busy. This builder was pretty demanding and insisted that I attend meetings once a week after five o'clock. These meetings sometimes lasted for hours. He had the fancy car, the pretty girlfriend, and was one of those men that seemed to think the world revolved around him and wanted you to think so, too. As a young man, everything about him irritated me. Even though his work fed my family, I made sure he knew that I was not impressed by him. I guess I was jealous of his success.

Even when he tried to be friendly, I made a point of keeping my distance. One day when I was visiting with my dad, I told him about that builder seeming to want to be friends, but I was having none of it. Dad said, "Son, I have never thought I was so rich that I didn't need another friend. Some of the best friends I have are men I have worked for."

In April 1974, I was starting my adult life with a wife and a baby. I was driving a big, beautiful 1972 Ford truck that got about fifteen miles per gallon of gas. I was earning 500 dollars a month for a sixty-hour week and working a part-time job on my day off. Money was tight, and gas was up to seventy-five cents a gallon. I decided I needed to save money by trading in my big gas-hog truck for something that got better gas mileage. The Ford dealer had just the truck for me: a little bright yellow Ford Ranger. It got twenty-five to thirty miles per gallon. We made the deal, and I drove over to Mom and Dad's house to show them my new truck. Dad looked it over real good, then said, "That is a nice little truck. It will be good until you need a real truck, then you'll have to borrow one."

Growing up, I do not remember Dad correcting me, and I do not remember him raising his voice. What I do remember is wanting his approval and dreading his disapproval. He taught me many things, and for the most part I never knew that I was learning. We worked together on the ranch. Work is almost all Dad and I did together: irrigating, haying, fencing, working cattle and horses, and building whatever was needed. Whatever we were doing, I tried to keep up and do my part. When I was eight years old, I went with him to irrigate the pasture and hay fields. We flood-irrigated out of a ditch. Dad saw that a full-size shovel was too big for me, so he cut the handle off of a good shovel to just my size. I was proud to have a shovel of my own. Working with Dad, I learned how to set the water and when to move it. I learned to check the water and make sure there were no dry spots. It was a proud day when I was trusted to irrigate the fields by myself. I was eleven. I would also go with Dad to the feed store to buy grain for the stock. They sold corn in one-hundred-pound burlap sacks. Dad, who weighed one hundred and sixty pounds, would easily pick up a hundred-pound sack, put it on his shoulder, and walk to the truck. I had to drag and wrestle mine. It was another proud day when I could put that hundred-pound sack on my shoulder just like Dad. I was thirteen.

Years passed. Mother died in 1984, and Dad's health continued to decline. In 1988, we as a family had to put Dad in a nursing home. He never complained, not one word. But it was hard for that proud man to be there. I finally got enough money together for a down payment on a house. It needed some work, but it would be big enough for Dad, a caretaker, and me and the kids, April and Joshua. And it was yet another proud day when I could get him out of the nursing home. Truth be told, I have spent a good part of my life trying to live and work in a way that Dad, or "Mister Wade," would be proud of. It was a very proud day when he told me, "I'm proud of you, Son." I remember both times.

UNCLE NOEL'S UNSOLICITED ADVICE
BY DAN WADE

Uncle Noel told us of going to the grocery store with Aunt Minnie Lee while they lived in Roswell. With him being such a coffee lover, it's not shocking that Uncle Noel got distracted on the coffee aisle, studying all the different brands of coffee. He had lost track of Aunt Minnie Lee and didn't know that she was just on the other side of the aisle from where he was admiring the coffee. While he was standing there wondering how he could go about tasting all the different coffees, he noticed a small, well-dressed, mature lady also studying them, apparently having difficulty choosing just the right brand. Thinking he could be of assistance, he lifted a can of Folgers, held it out towards her, and said in his deep rumbling voice, "Ma'am, Miss Olson on television highly recommends Folgers coffee, and I can tell you that I myself find it enjoyable."

The little lady squared up on Uncle Noel, who towered high above her. She shook her finger in his face and responded, "The Bible tells us that television is the tool of the devil, and those who watch it are on the road to hell, and I'll thank you not to offer advice unless it is asked for."

Uncle Noel didn't know how to respond to that. So

he simply set the can of Folgers back on the shelf, said, "Yes ma'am," excused himself, and walked away, unaware that Aunt Minnie Lee had heard the whole exchange. She had found it very entertaining, and, after they left the store, she asked Uncle Noel if he had learned a lesson about giving advice to ladies he didn't know. He knew right away that she had heard that little lady giving him "what for," and of course he wasn't surprised when she asked him how he felt about being on the road to hell. I know that Uncle Noel is enjoying a good hot cup of Folgers in heaven right now.

NOT JUST A HORSE STORY
BY DONNA WADE

Sometimes people ask you which teacher you had that made a difference in your life. I cannot think of any teacher who helped me in that way. For me, it was horses and sports. I was a very, very shy girl; I wouldn't talk even if a teacher called on me in class. Around family, I was comfortable, but there were so many things in life that passed me by because of my shyness. I was always wanting to do things, but I was completely unable to make myself get out and do them. I was good at sports, though, and loved horses.

We were living in Roswell, and I was eleven years old when Daddy brought home an old horse named Cactus. He had been trained as a cutting horse in his younger days, but that did not mean anything to us until we rode him. We weren't allowed to use a saddle, so we had to learn to ride bareback, and, sometimes when I got him running, he would suddenly make a sharp turn and off I would go. Being too small to simply leap onto his back, I would have to lead him up to a bucket or a fence and use it to climb up on his back. He was the first horse I ever loved. I had found my passion—horses.

Then Dad brought home a younger, more spirited horse

named Soldier, and I got my first horse upgrade. It was while we had Soldier that I started sneaking the saddle on him while dad was at work, then I would ride all day. When I was fourteen, we moved to live and work on the Colorado ranch. Dad and Jerry bought several horses.

One of the horses Jerry bought was a very beautiful, tall, black horse named Gander. He was another one that I started riding without permission whenever I could. Gander was wild and full of spirit. If he did not try to throw me off, it was a very disappointing ride.

One day I was out riding in the mountains and came upon a neighbor doing some tractor work. I stopped to say "hello." Mostly I wanted to show off my wild horse. This neighbor is one person I remember who made a difference in my life. He told me in no uncertain terms that I should not be riding such a wild horse. He said that, if I were his daughter, I would not be allowed to ride such a wild, crazy horse; it was too dangerous. This made me feel about ten feet tall. Not only was I riding that wild, crazy horse, I rode him very well! This is a story of feeling exceptional, invincible, and special. Something we all need once in a while. This is a story of a wonderful childhood.

MOM AND MAYNA
BY DAN WADE

As a kid at school functions, I never worried about getting separated from my mom. All I had to do was stop and listen. Pretty soon I would hear her voice or laughter. In crowds of several hundred people, it never failed. She wasn't loud, but her voice sure carried, and she loved to visit. Mom was everyone's friend, and she loved to be in the middle of everything. When my sisters and I joined 4-H, she was right there with us. For years she directed plays for 4-H competitions, and her teams won every year. No one knew that unless they were in 4-H. She never mentioned it. Helping young people was all that mattered to Mom.

She had lots of friends but only one best friend—Mayna. Mayna was a little younger. Her second oldest girl was in Donna's class, and her oldest son was in Jenny's. Their dad, like ours, worked away from home a lot. Mom and Mayna would trade visits to each other's houses.

The first time Mayna came to our house was shocking. My sisters and I had never heard anything like it: Mayna cussed! She cussed in our house! We had heard a few cuss words but never, never in our house. Mom acted like it was normal. We knew Dad wouldn't stand for cussing in our house. What would happen when our dad heard? Pretty soon we found out. He acted like it was normal, too. I was confused. I had already gotten my mouth washed out with soap for saying "damn." Why was this allowed? "Why did I get in trouble for saying the same words Mayna said?" I asked. "Mayna is an adult," Mom said. "She is free to talk any way she wants." Mom continued, "She is also free to meet all her obligations, to be honest and forthright with her neighbors, and to be a good wife and mother. We are free to decide which traits we think are the most important."

She let that sink in for a moment, then added. "I don't get to choose to be friends with part of Mayna. I'm her friend because of who she is, not how she talks." Mom's words were a lesson to me about friendship, priorities, and separating what matters from what doesn't. Thinking back, Mayna's rough talk wasn't rough at all by today's standards. It didn't take much to shock us in 1966.

NEW BRITCHES
BY DAN WADE

In the summer of 1964, I was going into the fourth grade. Our mother made many of my sisters' clothes and most of my shirts. She was always busy in August getting clothes ready for school. Donna and Jenny were often standing on chairs, so Mom could get the hems just right. The three of them seemed to enjoy the whole process: picking the pattern and material at JCPenney's, cutting the cloth out on the table, and Mom's sewing it together. For them it was fun. Not so much for me. Trying shirts on to check the sleeves or something just wasn't what I wanted to do with my time. In no way did I appreciate Mom's hard work, and I was no help at all when it came to picking out patterns or material. That may have been why she seemed to enjoy making dresses for my sisters more.

Mom always bought my britches, though, usually from the Sears, Roebuck & Company catalog. That summer, Sears had a package special on a set of three pair. I think one pair was blue, one tan, and one brown. Each pair had a matching belt sewn into the waist line. I can remember Mom showing them to me in the catalog to see if I liked them. They were fine with me. Even as a boy, I can remember sensing Mom's disappointment when I wasn't as enthusiastic as she was about the good deal and nice britches she had found. She placed the order for the britches, and they arrived before school started, but I wasn't allowed to wear them. They were special for school.

The day before school started, Mom laid my new clothes out and cautioned me to be careful to not fall down and tear the knees out of my new britches while we played at recess. Of course, I told Mom that I would be careful. I was careful, and I didn't take both knees out of my new britches during the first recess. It happened in the second recess. Mom's disappointment was plain even to me when I came in the house and she saw my scraped knees. She talked sternly to me while cleaning the pavement out of my knees. I was sure Mom used some extra Mercurochrome while she talked. "Do not tear another pair of britches. They have to last all year. You must be more careful not to fall down." I promised to be more careful and told Mom it had been an accident. I explained that I had tripped while trying to get to the ball first.

In my defense, schools back then built playgrounds out of material that would last and hold up to kids and the elements. They did not worry about scraped knees or kids' clothes. Our playground was asphalt pavement. Good to drive on, not so great for playing. After Mom's stern warning to be more careful, I was, but it was hard. The next day I wore my second pair of brand new britches. During the last recess, right before the bell, it happened. I fell. It wasn't bad, just one knee scraped, and it wasn't a bad tear. I still dreaded going home. Mom had warned me to be careful. I was going to be in big trouble. I was right. Mom was mad! She barely spoke to me, and that was worse than being chewed out. I really felt bad. It was terrible to have Mom angry with me, and I promised myself not to fail her again.

The next morning, I put the third pair of britches on, determined not to tear the knees out. And I didn't, that day or the next. In fact, I made it through the week. The following week, I wore neatly patched britches. When I tore the patch, Mom didn't really seem upset. She just patched them again. Several weeks passed with just a few new patches on old patches. I think Mom was proud of me. Then it happened: I was wearing the unpatched britches, and, in the middle of a great game of kickball, I took a bad spill and got both knees bloody. They hurt pretty badly, but I was more worried about my mom. I had torn my only untorn pair of britches. What was she going to do? I found out when I got off the bus and slowly walked in the house. When Mom saw the torn knees in my britches, I saw shock and hurt in her eyes, and, before she turned away, I saw a tear. Oh, no! Mom was crying. I was stunned. I don't think I had ever seen my mother cry. I ran to her, pleading, "Mom, don't cry. I'm okay. You can patch the britches. They'll be fine. Don't cry!" "Oh, don't worry son. I'll be all right," Mom said as she wiped her eyes with a tissue. "I just had my heart set on you having at least one good pair of britches."

I would have children myself before I really understood how Mom must have felt. Like all parents, she wanted the best for her children. At the time, those patches were like badges of honor for me. They didn't always match, but they were always straight and square, and the stitches were tight. Before the school year was over, even my patches had patches, but they were well done, and my clothes were clean. My mother did the best she could with what she had.

POLITICS IN MY LIFE
BY April Wade Turk

So today, election day 2016, I thought I would write a story.

I honestly cannot remember a time growing up that my dad, Dan Wade, and I didn't talk about politics or history. It has always been our thing.

I remember in high school that he encouraged me to think about my opinions and not just lead with "I feel." He also encouraged me to read and experience things, so I could get a better understanding about how the world works. It was important to understand the issues and to vote.

I turned eighteen in 1992 and was able to vote in my first presidential election. I proudly voted for George Bush and was so disappointed when he lost to Bill Clinton. My college roommate could have cared less about politics and thought I was nuts as I yelled at the TV during the debates and likely had a few tears on election night. In fact, most people did not understand my passion about politics.

In 1995, Dad suggested that I leave the small school I was going to in southern New Mexico and move home. The thinking behind the decision was that I would be able to get involved with the Republican Party and work as a volunteer. It was the year before the election, so I would have the opportunity to see a presidential election firsthand. I'm not sure either of us understood what that would mean for my future.

I started working as a volunteer, and they soon were paying me. I wasn't making much money, but I was so proud of the work.

Soon I was organizing all the volunteers and met some of the most amazing people. I loved my work and enjoyed every day. Now, some days were harder than others, but at the time we were considered the best state Republican Party in the country. It was an amazing team; I am still in contact and work with this group today.

One of my goals was to attend the 1996 Republican National Convention, and I was able to go as a page. At the 2000 Convention, I was one of the youngest delegates to attend.

I have made get-out-the-vote calls, knocked on doors, coordinated events, and stamped millions of pieces of mail, and I have been present at some very important events, raised money, and met some amazing people. Getting my picture taken with elected officials was never my thing, but I do have a few such photos. I was always more about the "win."

Today, Dad and I still talk politics and about what is going on in the world. This 2016 electioneering cycle, we have found ourselves on opposite sides for the first time. In fact, I have been pretty quiet in my opinions. (Some of you would say that is a first.) We have stayed away from the topic, but a couple of weeks ago we did talk. I listened to his views, and he listened to mine. We agreed that it was okay to disagree and laughed.

We may not always agree, but I am so thankful that he encouraged me to make that one call to volunteer. It has provided me a career and experiences that I may never have had otherwise. Today, we took our kids to vote and hopefully planted the seed on how important it is to participate in the electoral process.

Tonight, I am sure there will be a family gathering at my Dad's house to watch the results. It will likely be like a Super Bowl party—everyone watching the returns with anticipation. There will be some laughing, yelling at the TV, sighs of relief, and *some* debate (well maybe more than some debate).

I hope everyone voted, and, if not, the polls are still open!

MEETING JERRY
BY KEVIN JUDICE

My story of Jerry is small, but that is the only thing small about Jerry. I just remember meeting this bear of a man when I was nineteen years old at one of the family reunions in Mississippi and being crushed by his giant hug around my shoulders and that amazing laugh at my obvious discomfort! He later overturned me in a canoe, and I remember the laugh again, as I went down the creek and over a waterfall without said canoe. He will be missed. I hope God isn't a canoer, otherwise he will get wet quite a bit!

MY BROTHER JERRY
BY DAN WADE

My first clear memory of Jerry is of my running across the yard as hard as I could, trying not to get roped and thrown to the ground. He was a better roper than I was a runner, but somehow he got me to keep trying and trying. Another favorite pastime was playing catch with a football. We played catch a little differently than most. I would get into a three-point stance; at six years old, he insisted I keep my butt down, back straight, and head up. I ran post, button hooks, slants, flag, and hook-and-go patterns. It seemed to me that he threw the ball as hard as he could, and the rule was that, if I could touch it, I should catch it. If I didn't, we would try again and again until I did catch the ball. Looking back, it was all about doing things right and trying as hard as I could.

I remember once when I was a teenager, my Uncle Harley, our mom's brother, had a temporary job stocking sheetrock in an apartment building. He was explaining to Jerry and me that he was able to do the work by pacing himself. Jerry had no patience with men who didn't do their best, and he didn't want me to think it was okay to pace myself or loaf on the job. These were the same thing to Jerry, and he told Uncle Harley that in no uncertain terms. Uncle Harley disagreed; he saw it differently.

Jerry and I were both taught that all work was honorable if you did your best, but only if you did your best.

Before I was strong enough to load the hay wagon, I was the stacker. Jerry and Wallace would compete to see which one could knock me down or off the wagon by throwing sixty-pound bales at me. I learned quickly to deflect or dodge those hay missiles. When I was nine or ten, Jerry was putting me on the back of unbroken horses and dragging us across the country with a six-foot lead rope tied to the saddle horn on the big stout horse he was riding. Hanging onto the saddle for dear life while on the back of an unbroken horse is exciting and will sure help you sharpen your focusing skills. We all played tag on horseback, through trees, over gullies, up and down hills, and around rocks. If there is a more exciting or dangerous game you can do on horseback, I've never seen it. We worked hard and played harder, and I loved every minute of it.

As I grew into a young man, a little bit of a distance seemed to come between Jerry and me. I really don't know why, but it seemed like, if the two of us were in the same room, it got crowded. Neither one of us could bridge the gap, but I never doubted for a minute that we were brothers. I knew he had my back, and I had his.

Both our lives were affected by President Jimmy Carter and our own decisions. We both hit a low point about the same time. When interest rates passed fifteen percent, our world changed. People couldn't afford to build or remodel homes.

Jerry had worked hard and had become a nationally recognized builder. I had worked and studied. I was as good a carpenter and small contractor as I would ever be. We both went broke. Jerry packed up and moved his family back to Albuquerque where he and Dad had worked years before. He still knew a lot of people there who would realize that he might be down, but he sure wasn't out. There was no work in Colorado where I was, and I knew I had to go somewhere, but I hadn't decided where. Jerry and I happened to meet at our dad's home one Sunday and got to talking. He was finding a little work in Albuquerque and hoped to find more. The upshot was that he asked me to go down and work with him.

I probably thought about it for about a half second before I said, "Yes," and we shook on it. The first couple of years we were there were pretty grim. We tried several things: concrete work, framing, and building a few houses that didn't sell very well. When we had work, he and I worked together. When we didn't, I found work where I could. It was tough times in construction.

Jerry found a subdivision that was ready to be built in. I think the developer had gone bust, and at that time no one else saw any potential in selling houses there except Jerry. Because no one else wanted it, Jerry was able to tie the entire subdivision up with a deal to pay for each lot when we sold the completed house. Jerry was able—by the force of his personality and reputation—to put a complete team of subcontractors together from financing to final clean who all agreed to the same deal.

Everybody would get paid when the house sold. Not only did he get everybody to wait for closing to get paid, he also got the developers to cut their prices so that we could sell a 1,300-square-foot townhouse for $55,000. Even in 1985, that was unheard of. That first year, we built and sold fifty houses. We were on our way. We weren't out of the woods yet, but we could see a little daylight.

For Jerry and me, it was a case of what to do when you come to the end of your rope. Our answer was: tie a knot in it, and hang on! At a state auction, Jerry bought a little truck, so he could haul appliances and supplies. His young sons Tom and Roy and even eleven-year-old Max did sprinkler systems and landscaping after school and weekends. Their mother, Donna Jean, did the books. My children April and Joshua worked with me on weekends even when they were young. I did the trim, cabinets, hardware, shelving, counter-top installation, fencing, and the scheduling after the house was framed. We built those houses on a twenty-eight-day schedule, start to finish. We did that for a long time. Jerry kept finding distressed subdivisions and developing new plans. I kept pushing the houses. For years, we battled shoulder to shoulder and back to back. It was us against the world. As more time passed, Jerry quit hauling appliances, and I hired help and developed a business within a business. We were still hungry, but we weren't desperate anymore. Things had changed. We had office staff, superintendents, CPAs, and lawyers. Jerry and I started to find the room crowded again. We slowly evolved to where Jerry and I were each running our own business, still side by side, still working together, and watching out for each other but not stepping on each other's toes. Our companies continue to work together to this day.

It really doesn't seem possible that it has been thirty-two years since we shook hands there in Dad's family room. During that time, Jerry became a national hall-of-fame builder, and he liked to say he had never worked a day of his life; Jerry loved what he did. Jerry Wade was a home builder right down to his roots, and he was proud to be one! He admired anyone who was among the best at whatever they did. He understood what it took to be the best in his field. Jerry had few peers in home building. He learned the building business from the ground up, working with Dad; then he took it to another level. Dad was sure proud of Jerry. Mom and Jerry had a special bond; she probably knew him better than he knew himself. For Wallace, Donna, Jenny, and me, he was our friend, teacher, benefactor, co-conspirator, and much-loved big brother. For others he was a father, grandfather, husband, co-worker, employer, competitor, mentor, supporter, friend, and—for a certain few—an enemy with a long memory. We all miss him.

MEMORIES OF MY COUSIN JERRY
BY LaGuewn Wade Wilson

I asked my sister Rebecca a few weeks ago, when Dan started asking for stories, what would she write about her memories of family gatherings at our Grandmother Wade's? Without taking a breath, she said, "It would start with, 'Oh, shit! There's Jerry!'" I knew well what she meant! He would terrify us as much as possible, laughing the whole time. He chased us by himself or with his bike, threw fireworks at us, and did anything else he could get by with. It didn't end there. When we went to the creek, pushing us underwater was also amusement! Between our cousin JR Smith and Jerry Wade, I didn't learn to swim until late in life. I was forty when I first jumped off a diving board (not dived, jumped). You might think we should have told on Jerry, and we did—believe me, we did. It did us no good. We were told, "Oh, you know, that is just Jerry."

Time moved on. We moved to New Mexico. Jerry was hardly home; by then he had gone on to college. When I saw him, it was no longer torture, just teasing. I could live with that. Years went by. We all had our own families, but we stayed in touch.

After our first family reunion in Moselle, Mississippi, Jerry came back to Daddy's with us. We were all in Mom and Dad's (Noel and Minnie Lee Wade) room, sitting and lying across the beds talking to Mom. We were reminiscing about old times. Mom said to us that we should start making new memories, instead of always talking about the old ones. That thought stuck. So right there was how our current day reunions came to be. Never again to be an only one day affair; make it fun, and make it last with lots of good food and laughter. Game on! We planned the next reunion and have been having a lot of great times ever since. It has been more than twenty years. Our children looked forward to and loved every minute of each reunion. Now their children enjoy it as much as we did and still do. It must go on!

When we lost JR, it felt like we could never be the same. We are not, but we continue on because we are still family with everyone as important as those we lost. We have great memories, and we will make many more. Take comfort that Jerry and JR are with our beloved family members who have gone before us, planning—only Lord knows what—for that wonderful day we are all together again. I'm looking forward to that.

Back to Jerry, he was someone we learned to love and respect. He did it all—worked very hard, won and lost, and won again, never giving up. He played college football, started his business, learned to fly a plane, then owned his own plane, bought and built a ranch, bought a Harley, and rode it all over the country. Jerry was not afraid of marriage; he tried it many times, enjoyed the respect of all his wives, and was very proud of it. In his older age, he learned to dance, so he could dance with his beautiful sister, niece, and granddaughters. What was there not to love about Jerry? He made you feel so special. He loved his family. He loved us all. I, for one, will miss him and cherish the memories—the good with the bad.

The last comment that Rebecca and I want to make is, "Oh, no, Jerry will not be with us! Not in this life. I know he will be in the next!" As Dan said, it is about the journey, and, oh, did Jerry journey well! I love you all.

TRAVELING WITH POP
BY APRIL WADE TURK

When I was little, Mom and Pop (that's what we called my Grandparents, James Heber and Betty Sue Wade) would sometimes take me to Roswell to spend time with them at their house. I don't remember a lot about those trips.

One time, Pop was taking me from our house in Farmington to Roswell to stay with them for a week or two. Uncle Jerry was driving us. I guess that I wasn't clear on the plans, but, when we pulled up to the airport, it was a shock. My reaction wasn't good. In fact, I acted like most four-year-olds and threw a fit. I don't remember what happened next. I am sure they tried to reason with me, but that doesn't always work with a toddler. Somehow, we ended up on a bus. At this point, I believe Pop had a walker, maybe a cane, but I know he had something to help him walk. At one point, we stopped somewhere, and he bought me a piece of pie. I remember Mom standing next to her red Buick waiting when we finally arrived in Roswell.

I don't remember Pop being cross with me or being impatient with me. It has always been a memory I treasured, and it was our little adventure.

HOW ROBBIE AND KAYE MET
BY ROBBIE SMITH

It was at the Moselle Fall Festival 1973 where I first met the love of my life. She was with her mother and looking very good. I had broken up with my last girlfriend a couple of months before. A few friends were with me, and one of them knew her and introduced us. Her name was Kaye Knight. Well, I couldn't help myself; I asked her out. I don't know why, but she said she would go; and her mother let her go with me and three others whom she did not know. We went bowling, and I took very good care of her. After bowling we went BACK to her house, not a minute late.

After that we dated regularly. We were not serious for a long time. It was just having fun. I thought of myself as her protector and friend because she was so fragile and so sweet and vulnerable. After about nine months, I was thinking about how I would feel if we broke up, and I realized that I was in love with her. We talked, but we knew she had to graduate before we could make any plans. After we had been dating for two years, we got engaged. The engagement would be until June because she wanted to be a June bride.

Well, something went wrong with her because sometime

in April she got cold feet. She just said, "I think I need some time. Maybe see some other people." I didn't know what to say or do, so I said "okay." After a week, she came to see if I would take her back. I was the happiest person on the planet! During that week, I did not sleep much. Then on June 25, 1976 we got married. I was so nervous that I needed help to put the ring on her finger.

Well, we have had our share of ups and downs, but we have never lost sight of our wedding vows. I love her more now than ever. After knowing her almost forty-two years, the excitement is still there. With the two perfect children she gave me and our six grandchildren, I am a very blessed man! We have always held onto our Christian values and morals and taught them to our children. How time flies!

UNCLE VARDAMAN WAS A JOYOUS MAN
BY DAN WADE

Uncle Vardaman, my dad's oldest brother, seemed to me to be a truly joyous man. He is one of the few men I've known for whom the word "joyous" seems like an apt description. For him, life was great, and he liked it that way. He enjoyed life and a chaw of chewing tobacco more than anyone I've ever seen.

I remember Mom, Dad, and me having supper at my aunt and uncle's house; it was always a good meal. My dear Aunt Beatrice took a lot of pride in her fried chicken; justifiably so, it was great. After supper, Aunt Beatrice and my mom would clean up and visit while Uncle Vardaman took Dad and me out to the backyard. He and Dad would take a big chaw of Beechnut tobacco. They would take a minute and get that chaw softened just right and fitting between their cheek and jaw, then start visiting. Whatever they talked about—politics, work, or old times—they would find a humorous way to look at it. Those two brothers would have a good time. Uncle Vardaman was a big man with a wide "Wade" jaw and big square chin. He's the only man I ever saw who really chewed tobacco; I mean he *really* chewed. When he got to going, his chin would practically hit his nose. I can still picture that big man, chewing his Beechnut with great enthusiasm. Then, when he found something funny, throwing his head back and laughing. A great, booming laugh that came all the way from his belly. It was a joyous sound! You couldn't hear it without feeling joyful, too.

THE LEGACY OF THE EIGHT-DOLLAR SHOES
BY WAYLON WADE

My dad, Wallace, is a big man. He's six feet two inches tall and is the tallest man that height I've ever met. It's the perfect height for a man to be—tall enough to be considered tall without being so tall that life becomes difficult because of your size. Somehow Dad has always seemed taller than the measuring tape said he was. Every time I met a fella that said he was six feet two inches tall, I'd think "that's my dad's height, but he's taller than you." He wasn't just tall, though; he was big. For most of his life—especially in my childhood—my dad was heavy. He is also big in personality; he has never been a man who you had to ask what was on his mind.

When I was six years old going on seven, Dad turned forty and declared that he was going to do something about being "a fat man." He went to K-Mart and picked up a pair of plastic running shoes. I would bet a kidney he didn't pay more than eight dollars for them.

We lived on a short, flat, little dirt road that ran parallel to a paved country road. We always said the dirt road was a quarter mile long. (Having run it myself hundreds of times, I can tell you it's about 60 yards short of that distance.) Dad started out running down that dirt road and back. Wearing a white cotton t-shirt, polyester shorts, those classic 1980s socks that came most of the way up the calf with the three stripes of blue-yellow-blue at the top, and those eight-dollar K-Mart shoes. At first, he couldn't make it all the way to the end of that quarter-mile(ish) dirt road and back without walking. Slowly— over months—he got to where he could make it a full lap down the dirt road and back without walking. Eventually the lap turned into laps.

I don't know how big my dad was when he started, but he had a significant spare tire around his middle. At a tall six feet two inches and carrying that much weight, he sure wasn't built like a runner. What's hard to grasp today is that he didn't have any information about running. There was no internet to watch YouTube videos about running, no Google to search articles about how quickly you should try and increase your runs, not even Instagram or Facebook to take inspiration from other people's posts about exercising. He never got a subscription to *Runner's World* or *Men's Health* and, as far as I know, never even checked a book out of the library about the subject. None of that deterred him.

I remember when he graduated off that little dirt road and started trying to run on the paved country road that our little dirt road ran alongside. The first time he tried, I was surprised to see him walk back in the house a lot earlier than I expected. Almost exactly even with where our little dirt road ended, that country road started going uphill. That paved road had a lot of hills, and—as anyone who has ever run will tell you—every hill is steeper than it looks when you're trying to run up it.

Just like he did with the dirt road, Dad took on that paved road, and, little by little, month over month, he nibbled his way farther out and back each time. He'd walk in the house, red faced and sweaty. Weston and I would ask him, "Did you have a good run?" "Oh, yes," he'd say. "The fat was just falling off me. I could hear it go splat with every step. They're gonna have to get a snowplow to come along and scrape it off the roads."

Dad had a funny way of keeping himself accountable. As anyone trying to maintain a fitness routine knows, starting the workout is the hardest part. Well, he and our cousin Bill Bryant worked together, and Bill lived a few doors down from us, so they would carpool. In the morning as they were driving to work, Dad would tell Bill, "After work, this is where I want you to drop me off." That afternoon, Bill would stop the truck at that spot, and Dad would run the rest of the way home. He never gave himself the option of cutting a workout short.

That method worked. In spite of his eight-dollar shoes, complete lack of information or guidance in fitness, and planning only as far in advance as which landmark Bill was going to kick him out of the truck at that evening, he got results. Just like I don't know how heavy he was to start out with, I don't know how light he got at his peak. I do know he got lean and flat bellied.

Dad never ran a race. I don't even know if back then there

were races in our little, dusty, rural corner of New Mexico. At the time, if you asked him what a 5K was, I doubt that a foot race would have been his answer even if you gave him a dozen guesses. To me, that's the most amazing thing about my dad's time as a runner: he never wanted to race. He didn't want to do it so that he could post pictures about his workouts on Instagram. He was married with two young boys, so he sure wasn't doing it to impress the ladies. He just ran because he wanted to be healthy, and he liked it with no ulterior motives.

As Weston and I grew older, we would wait for him, and we'd run the last few dozen yards with him as he was coming in. One day when I believe I was nine, I asked if I could go with him on a run. He said, "Sure, but you have to stay right behind me, and, if you get tired, you'll have to wait and rest. And when I come back, we'll run home together." I stuck right behind him, and—to both his surprise and mine—I made it two miles out and two miles home right behind him.

I ran with him a handful more times. On the last one I asked, "Dad, you're going kind of slow. Can I pass you?" He had a surprised look when he said, "Sure, if you want to run faster that's okay." I went around him, and that was that. I was probably five minutes ahead of him getting back to the house.

After that run, we had a little talk about how, if I wanted to run without him, I had permission. He told me that I should always run on the left shoulder and watch out for drunks on that curvy little country road.

Not long after that, Weston and I reached the age when children get into extracurriculars. Things like Little League, Boys Club basketball, and numerous other things that put demands on a father's time. Dad's running waned, but it had been passed on to his sons. We both have gone on to be runners still to this day, and we've shared our enjoyment of it with family like Jenny, Alaena, Ryan, and many others.

Dad didn't know it, but lacing up those eight-dollar plastic shoes and getting out there because he wanted to had a positive ripple effect that is still being felt thirty-five years later.

CONFAR HILL
BY DAN WADE

Confar Hill is south of Pagosa Springs, Colorado, just over the line in New Mexico. When it's dry, you might not even notice it—just a long grade with a steep drop off on one side. That changes when it is snow-packed, icy, and about zero degrees. My mom, dad, and I discovered that in November of 1963, when l was about eight years old. Our family had moved from Roswell, New Mexico, to Bayfield, Colorado, earlier in the month. I think, after we got settled a few days, Dad and Mom needed to make one more trip to Roswell and back and thought I was too young to leave behind in Bayfield.

We must have gotten a real late start leaving Roswell to return to Colorado because I know they would not have planned to hit those high elevations late at night. That winter was our first in snow country. I'm pretty sure we were pulling a trailer, and Dad didn't have snow tires, much less tire chains. That old pickup started fishtailing about half way up Confar Hill. It kept getting worse, and finally Dad came to a stop about two feet from a good one-hundred-foot drop-off. Here was our situation: it was snowing pretty heavy, zero degrees; we hadn't seen another car for a while; we were not at all prepared to stay the night in the truck; and we needed help.

Through the snow away off in the distance, we could see a yard light. Perhaps it was a ranch house, maybe someone was home, maybe they could help, maybe! Dad said he would go, but Mom said he needed to stay with the truck and me, in case anything happened. She was right, and he knew it. They got her bundled up the best they could, which wasn't very good, and I know her shoes were a long way from snow boots. She had to walk down that icy hill and spot the turn-off in the dark. We didn't have a flashlight. Then she had to walk about a mile through six or eight inches of unplowed snow, hoping someone would be in the ranch house.

Dad found some rocks to block the tires because the truck and trailer were sliding a bit. We had some rope and cord in the truck, and Dad set out to make some tire chains. He was good with knots, but the rope was frozen, and his hands were so stiff he could hardly use them. After some time, he got a pair built that looked like tire chains. I helped the best I could as he tied them on the tires. Those frozen-rope tire chains worked at first, but they started coming apart after maybe ten feet. By the time Dad quit trying, we were even closer to the drop-off. He hurried to get the tires blocked again. Mom had been gone a long time. Dad kept looking in that direction, hoping to see headlights. Meantime, he started to rebuild the rope chains. Finally, after what seemed like forever, we saw lights headed our way. Mom had made it there and found the rancher at home. He had left her warming up by the stove while he started up a big tractor. She was standing on the side of the tractor when they got to us. The rancher and Dad got a chain hooked up and away we went to the top of the hill. They got the tractor unhooked, thanked the rancher, and he went home. We somehow made it to Bayfield without trouble, and it sure was good to get home!

NEIGHBORS

BY DAN WADE

After moving to Colorado, we were welcomed to the neighborhood. Our new neighbors made a point to stop by and meet us and let us know that they were glad we had moved into our new home. Stopping by and greeting newcomers to the community was customary at that time. We had new friends before we had really unpacked. They would all be special people in our lives. There were other neighbors that moved in over the years: the Campbells, Guests, Millers, Kugells. Hagaes, and a few others. I bicycled to all their houses, selling raffle tickets and candy for school fund raisers. They all watched out for us and we watched out for them.

Here is an introduction to some of the first people we met in Colorado. They were some great people and great characters.

Mrs. Ruby Bowers was truly one of a kind. The first time we saw her, she came roaring into the driveway on a big old John Deere tractor—POP, POP, POP! We all ran to see what the noise was about and found a little, bitty, five-foot-tall lady wearing a baseball cap, flannel shirt, and jeans tucked into her knee-high irrigation boots. She climbed down off the tractor and welcomed us to the community like we were her long-lost friends. She and Mr. Bowers were the sweetest people in the world. They had a beautiful farm by the Pine River. I fell in the river there once while we were fishing, and the water was tumbling me like a doll. I was terrified, and I couldn't stop rolling. Dad rushed out in the river and pulled me to the bank.

Mr. Bowers was a real quiet man who had spent so much time on a tractor that his pants just sort of drooped on the back side.

The Snows were a long-time mountain family who grew most of their own food and hunted elk and deer for meat, and they also trapped beaver and bobcat. Mr. Snow worked at the sawmill. They were the first people I had ever heard who used use the word "purtenneer." That means "pretty near" or "almost," as in: "Hey Joe, did you catch a fish?" Joe replied, "Purtenneer did, but the line broke." In 1963, Mr. Snow's car was twenty-five years old. It still ran like a top and was as clean as a whistle. He was a man who took great care of his possessions. He made his own bullets, tied his own flies, and made his own snowshoes. I spent a good deal of time in their house. Mr. and Mrs. Snow were good to me, and I considered their son Ron a close friend.

Whenever the Snow family went away from home for a few days, they adhered to an old mountain custom. They would leave their house unlocked with the table set. The plates and glasses were upside-down so they wouldn't get dusty. There would be a pot of stew in the fridge and canned goods in the cupboard. This old custom was from a time when a passing traveler, friend, or stranger was welcome to a meal and a night's rest if they needed it. In exchange, it went without saying that they would clean up and chop some wood before they moved on. This custom had been carried on by their families for generations. It was a sad day in 1972 when their hospitality was abused, and the house got vandalized. A real sad day.

Mr. **Homer Oliver** was a quiet, gentle giant who wore boots that had the sole on one boot about two inches thicker than the other; he had been born with one leg shorter than the other. As a boy, I couldn't help but find that amazing. He was always friendly and kind to me. His family had come to Colorado in a covered wagon. He drove our school bus for years. I guess he must have had a lot on his mind because, fairly often in the mornings, my sisters, Donna and Jenny, and I would be standing by the road waiting for the bus, and Mr. Oliver would go right past us. Then he would hit the brakes until he got that big bus stopped and slowly back up to get us, while we ran laughing to catch up.

A couple of times when Jenny was a high school cheer-leader, she would be running late getting to a ball game and would leave the house but forget to get her tennis shoes off the top of the car. The reason her tennis shoes were on top of the car was because she had been late washing them, and she put them on the car so they would dry faster. In a rush, she would jump in the car and go. The tennis shoes would fall off the roof of the car somewhere on the four-mile trip to town. When Mr.

Oliver was driving to town, he would see them on the road. Figuring they must be Jenny's, he would stop and pick them up. The whole gymnasium paid attention when great big Mr. Oliver—in his overalls, hat, and boots—came walking across the gym floor holding a pair of little white tennis shoes high in the air. Jenny was always glad to see him. It meant she didn't have to slide around the floor in her white socks. Mr. Oliver always got a hug. Jenny still runs late, but she usually has her shoes on.

The Lafoes stopped by to welcome us, too. Mr. Lafoe's back was bent, and he sort of looked up all the time. Mrs. Lafoe dressed and acted like a man. We did see her in a dress once when they came to our house for a cook-out. It looked like it had never been worn and had been in style thirty years ago. All of their furniture was covered with plastic—not like plastic slip covers, but sheet plastic draped over everything but the kitchen table and chairs. Some of their turkeys had the run of the house; they were the reason the plastic was on the furniture.

Their hayfields were right on the road, and they were often bothered by poachers shooting from the road and killing deer and one of their cows or goats every so often. One evening, Mrs. Lafoe caught two men coming out of their hayfield dragging a poached deer. She stopped her pickup, pointed her .30-30 lever-action rifle out the window, and told them, "I've called the game warden. You men will just wait right where you are until he gets here." Both men were armed and didn't know how to take this old lady pointing a gun at them. One of them decided she was probably bluffing and said to his friend, "She's just one old lady. She can't get both of us. Let's take her!" "You're probably right," said Mrs. Lafoe, cocking that rifle. "but I'll sure get you." Those men were still waiting there an hour later when the game warden arrived.

Mr. Lafoe, bent back and all, once trailed two poachers who had killed a deer about five miles through the hills before he caught them. They had dropped the deer after about two miles. Mr. Lafoe marched two armed men, half his age, back through the hills, made them pick up the deer, and drag it to the road. Then he turned them over to the game warden.

These good people finally sold out, retired, and moved to town. Some trust-funder-wanna-be-hippie bought their place and brought a bunch of friends. Suddenly we had hippies in the neighborhood with long hair, wild clothes, and VW vans. Those folks were as strange to us as a bunch of leprechauns. They didn't farm or ranch. We heard that they planned to sell peat moss, but mostly they just kept to themselves. We missed our neighbors, but not everybody had their own hippie commune next door!

THE UNCLES
BY DAN WADE

Towards the end of my dad's life, he lived with me and my kids, April and Joshua. He required a lot of care. We had a service that provided caretakers twenty-four hours a day. Even though he suffered a great deal, he tried to keep a good attitude. The kids were both involved in his care. He always tried to visit and be cheerful. He and I would often visit after everyone went to bed. Even at this point in his life, he wanted me to try "therapy" on his legs. I would work his legs back and forth and massage his muscles. Sometimes he thought it felt better. If he ever gave up on getting better, I didn't know it. Never, not once, did he say, "Woe is me." He was, he said, "Smiling Jim." His favorite saying was, "When it's too tough for the rest of them, that's just the way we like it." Well, he had plenty to like: MS and melanoma, together with other common ailments and side effects from drugs.

Dad's first trip to the hospital after he moved in with us seemed serious, and we let his brothers know. Uncle Vardaman couldn't come. I don't think he could leave Aunt Beatrice. Uncle Haskell and Uncle Noel probably could have found a reason not to make the trip; they were both in their eighties and had their own health problems. The plane trip from Mississippi wasn't easy on either of them. They came anyway and stayed with me. I had some concerns. How was I going to deal with my elderly guests, along with my kids, my dad, and my work? These good men made it clear that all they would need from me would be a ride to the hospital and back, but, if that was a problem, they would take a cab. They could find their way around the house if they needed something, including the kitchen, if that was okay with me. It was, but, about the hospital, when would they want to go and when would they want to be picked up? They looked at me like I had lost my mind. "What time do visiting hours start?" they asked. "Eight o'clock," I answered. "Will that be OK with you?" they asked. "Of course it would. What about in the afternoon?" "Well," they said, "what time do visiting hours end?" "Nine o'clock, but you don't want to stay that late," I replied. Of course they wanted to stay. That's what they were here for, to see their brother Heber. Seeing Heber is what they did. When Dad was able to visit, they would visit; when he wasn't able, they would wait until he was. The only time they left his side was to get a bite to eat; otherwise, all they wanted to do was stay with their brother. They knew it might be the last time they saw Heber, and they didn't want to waste a minute.

We did get them away from the hospital one evening to eat out. I picked a decent restaurant, and we all went in. The kids and I thought it was a pretty good place. It had a salad bar I thought they would enjoy. After seating us, the waitress brought water and menus. It didn't take long for me to notice that there was a problem. Both uncles acted like the menus were written in Swahili. I was perplexed. What should I do? Offer to help with the menu? Make a suggestion? Suddenly I had an inspiration. Would they rather go to Furr's Cafeteria? "Oh, yes!" they replied enthusiastically. I left a couple of bucks for the water, and we had a great meal at Furr's. I don't know why I didn't think of Furr's in the first place. My mom and dad loved Furr's, too. I think being able to see the food and pick the portions is what they liked so much. Dad slowly got a little better. After about four days, both brothers went home. Soon Dad came home too. I think that was the last time my dad ever saw his brothers, but I know he treasured that time with them.

I've never ceased to be grateful for the love Uncle Haskell and Uncle Noel showed my dad. We all need heroes, people to look up to, and these brothers filled the bill. The term "natural gentleman" was invented to describe men like these.

CHAPTER 4

PASSING DOWN

SURE I CAN [BUILD A WINDOW]
BY DAN WADE

As an employer, I have always been a little forgiving of exaggerations and "lies" on job applications. Partly because I might have exaggerated a bit on a few myself and partly because of a story Dad told me. Dad must have been in his early thirties when he found himself needing a job and heard about a home builder who was hiring carpenters. Dad had done some carpentry around the farm, but he was years of hard work from being a carpenter. When he was asking for a job with the builder, he embellished that experience a little bit, and, when the builder asked if he could build windows, he said that of course he could. They agreed on a rate of pay, and he hired Dad and told him he could start the next day. Dad had told the builder that he "could" build windows, and he figured he could, but he had never actually done it before.

The next day, he was assigned the job of building a window as his first project. Luckily, he was working next to an experienced man who was working on another window. Dad got his tools laid out and tried to see out of the corner of his eye what the other man was doing and did the best he could to copy him. When it came noontime, the other men headed outside to eat lunch. Dad said he wasn't hungry and stayed in the house.

As soon as he was by himself, he rushed over to where the other man was working and studied how he was doing his window, then rushed back to his own and made his look like what he saw. By the end of the day, he had learned to build a "sash balance" window. He hadn't exactly lied when he told that builder that he "could" build a window. He was sure that he "could," and, given a chance, he did.

Dad worked for that builder for several years and had great respect for him. The builder had such a good reputation that all his work was done on a "cost plus ten percent" basis. The entire time Dad worked for him, they addressed each other as Mister or Sir. None of the crew was allowed to be on a first-name basis. Everyone was required to be respectful when speaking to each other.

That job was Dad's start in learning carpentry and home building. He went on to work many jobs and studied construction through an Audel correspondence course. After a number of years, he became a contractor and made homebuilding a lifelong career.

BIRDS AND BEES
by Tom Wade

It is an exciting time at the Ranch. Our mares have started foaling. On Monday, we had three colts on the ground with several mares looking like they could drop foals anytime. As we were watching them and taking pictures, my wife, Carla Huish Wade, mentioned how excited my dad, Jerry Wade, would have been. Dad did enjoy foaling and calving season. He really got a kick out of watching the foals run around trying to get used to their legs.

Back in 1980, Dad decided that we would start raising Appaloosas, so he went and bought each of us boys a mare. I really enjoyed learning about raising and breeding horses and still do. Dad even sent me to a Ray Hunt horse training clinic. It was a really fun time for me. Unfortunately, two years later was the beginning of the Jimmy Carter recession, which changed everything. Dad was not able to spend as much time with us and the horses as he had been, but, when he did, he always wanted to make sure we were learning something.

By then, I was thirteen going on fourteen and was a full-blown teenager, and by that I mean I was becoming a management headache. One day, Dad told me to hook up the trailer and load the mares and foals; it was time to take them to be bred. In years past, we would drop them off and come back two weeks later to pick them up.

This time went a little differently. Before we put the mares in the pens, Dad had me hold each mare while they brought the stud out to see if they were in season. That was my first time seeing this interaction in person. Afterward, we put the mares and foals in the pen and headed home. As we were driving, Dad started talking about what we saw. This turned out to be his "the Birds and the Bees" talk with my brother Roy and me. He finished by stating that a stud was only useful as long he did two things: one, produced good foals; two, behaved himself. Dad then looked at me and said, "Do you know what happens to a stud when he does not do what he is supposed to or has an attitude problem?" I replied that I had no idea. Dad looked back at me and said, "We castrate the SOB, and, young man, you might want to start changing your attitude before that happens to you!"

A lesson I never forgot and a memory that comes back every time it is breeding season.

UNCLE HASKELL AND SPINNING ROPE

BY DAN WADE

Uncle Haskell and Aunt Willie Mae came to visit us in Colorado several times. We always enjoyed their company. I remember several good times with Uncle Hack. One year my parents had gone to some sort of sales promotion and came home with a couch, a chair, and a Super 8mm movie camera. The couch and chair were really like lawn furniture with cushions, pretty light. This was the first new furniture that I can remember. The movie camera was amazing. We really enjoyed it—lots of movies of kids on horseback and kids going to proms. The film must have been expensive to develop, though. Mom acted toward the movie camera the same way she did about long-distance calls: just a little at a time, keep it short. We were very careful to use the movie camera sparingly.

Uncle Hack loved to spin a rope, and he was pretty good at it. I was probably about eleven years old, we were in our yard, and he decided to show me some rope tricks. When he got started—spinning the rope on one side and jumping through to the other side—I got the inspiration to make a movie. When I asked Uncle Hack what he thought about it, he was agreeable. Then I asked my mom if I could. She thought it was a good idea, but she was adamant that I keep it short. I had a fresh roll of film, but Mom made it very clear to me that I wasn't to use any more than fifteen minutes of film. When I got outside with the camera, Uncle Hack combed his hair, tucked his shirt in, and got started. This time was different though. He told me what he was going to do next. "Dan," he would say, "I'll start off with a flat right-hand spin, then I'll make it into a tall right-hand spin." That's the way it went. He would describe the trick, do it, then ask if I had gotten it on film alright. Uncle Hack was having such a good time and working so hard to do his tricks well, I never had the heart to stop filming. It was a thing of beauty. We finally ran out of film, and he was about worn out. I had to explain to Mom why I'd kept filming. She wasn't very happy, but she understood. As gentle as Uncle Hack was, he was a force to be reckoned with when he got going on something.

(Sad to say, those Super 8mm films didn't survive. What I wouldn't give!)

SAVING THE BOYS

BY DONNA WADE

You might guess from some of the other stories that I had a wonderful childhood. A mission of mine as a single mother was to pass on some similar good times to my son. My son Tyler and I went camping and fishing many times when he was young, and we had some great trips. After he turned twelve years old, it wasn't as much fun to be with Mom. Understand that I personally never fished or did any hunting; I just enjoyed being outdoors. When I took my son fishing, I always had a book and looked for a place where he could fish and I could read under a tree. Someone told us about a beautiful small lake, north of Durango on the very top of the mountain, almost straight up the mountain from the Bar D Chuckwagon show. It sounded like a great place.

So one day, when Tyler was about eleven, I came home from work one Saturday and told him to start loading up; we were going to find that lake, where I could sit and enjoy being there, and he would be close by fishing. We loaded up our two dogs—one small dog named Little Eddie and a big very protective dog named Rusty. In went the tent, sleeping bags, and food, and off we went. It took about one hour to get there. Driving to the top of that mountain was slow going. It was a narrow winding road, but, when we got there, it was all we had hoped it would be. We chose a campsite close to the water's edge, got our tent up and a fire going, and Tyler went off fishing while there was still a little light. I started cooking dinner on the fire.

It was almost dusk, and I was looking forward to a great evening with my son. Suddenly, from out of nowhere, two teenagers with helmets and knee pads pushing dirt bikes came rushing into our camp, out of breath with bloody noses and bruises. They were frightened and excited as they told us that a bunch of older boys had jumped them, beaten them up, and poured dirt in their gas tanks. Both boys were afraid that the older boys would find them again. They were right because, no sooner than they told us what had happened, a Toyota pickup with four almost-grown young men standing in the back drove up. The biggest of the bunch jumped down and started toward us. Those young boys were in my care once they came into my camp, and my son was there. As the big guy approached us, I grabbed a big limb and put one end in the fire holding it like a club. I pointed at him with my other arm and, in my toughest voice, said, "Stop right there." And he did! Our big dog Rusty sensed trouble, and Tyler was holding his collar to keep him back. I whispered, "Let him go." "No," Tyler whispered back. "They might hurt him." Between Rusty's growling and my holding that burning club, the big punk backed off, but, as he did, he warned us not to sleep too well; they might be back.

As soon as they were out of sight, I told the two boys and Tyler to start putting everything into the truck. We just threw things in the truck bed without even taking time to take the tent completely down. The dirt bikes and the two kids and dogs held the tent down while Tyler rode shotgun and I drove off that mountain as fast as I could. It was pitch dark by then, and, even with the headlights on, I was straining to see the curves in the road ahead. Tyler was keeping watch for headlights behind us. We finally made it all the way down the mountain to a small store where the young boys called their parents. I was able to leave them in the care of the storekeeper, and Tyler and I headed back home. We had just gotten home about midnight when I remembered that we had left camp in such a hurry that we forgot to put out the camp fire. Oh my gosh! I prayed that it did not start a forest fire. Luckily, it didn't.

About a week later I was telling a neighbor this story, and she said to look at the Sunday paper in the personal section. There was a man looking for the woman with a young boy who was at that lake and helped his son. I waited a few days before I called because I thought it could be the bad guys wanting to get even; but, when I called, it was the dad of one of the kids we had helped. He thanked me for helping his son. He also said that he was a lawyer and wanted to take the bad dudes to court because this was part of an ongoing thing with that group bullying his son and his friend. After that call, I never heard from him again, and we have never been back to that beautiful lake.

RETIREMENT

BY WAYLON WADE

Most of the time (at least for me), life lessons are things that dawn on you over time, and they take a while to really wrap your head around. Often it can take years to completely internalize and understand what they're all about. But, every once in a while, someone tells you something that just strikes you. It lights up part of your mind in a way that makes you aware on the spot that you just got a profound bit of knowledge that you will carry with you forever.

Family get-togethers are something I like to think we do bigger, better, and more often than most. It was at one of these that happened in either 2013 or early 2014 where Jerry and I ended up sitting next to each other. He was still actively working, running a construction crew which—for a man in his seventies—is uncommon, to say the least. I hadn't had as much interaction with Jerry as I did with a lot of other folks in the family over the years. Because he and I didn't really have a lot of history to fall back on, most of the time our conversations revolved around gently ribbing each other about one thing or another without getting into anything really deep. In that spirit, I asked him jokingly, "Jerry, what on earth are you doing out there running a construction crew at your age? When are you going to retire and leave that stuff to someone else?" He looked at me with a twinkle in his eye and said, "Waylon, I'm never going to retire. Women can retire; they do fine with it. They join book clubs, go to bible study, and grow beautiful gardens when they retire. When men retire, all they do is they sit down. They sit down, and they die." And then he repeated, "I'm never going to retire."

I can't think of a time when anyone said anything to me that resonated as truly as those words did. As on point as his words were, it was how he lived that really gave weight to them. Here was a man who, in addition to working full time and providing jobs for people for most of his adult life, had ridden a motorcycle to each of the lower forty-eight states, taken up dancing in his seventies, and really and truly understood that "life" is a noun, and it's something that we all have, but "live" is a verb, and it's really what matters.

In reality, there are men out there who can retire and do fine, but, as soon as Jerry finished speaking, I knew I wasn't one of them. He wasn't either, and he'd figured it out on his own. I was blessed to have him to share this wisdom. I don't know if I would have learned it on my own. It's easy to say that you're never going to retire while you're in your thirties, but, based on the chord that his words struck in me and the way they still resonate, I don't believe I will. Our conversation was actually the catalyst for my return to school, so that I can get the skills that I hope will enable me to be fully in control of when or if I retire. Regardless of whether or not that comes to pass, the underlying message of his words—that not living will kill you and that you need a reason to get up and live every day—won't ever leave me.

UNCLE VARDAMAN AND COON HUNTING
by Dan Wade

One summer before my junior year in high school, I stayed a few nights with Uncle Vardaman and Aunt Beatrice in Mississippi. I don't remember how this came to be; it is one of the few times I remember spending time with relatives by myself. Of course, they made me feel right at home. I enjoyed spending time with them. It was late summer, and I wanted to get in shape for football season, so I ran on the neighborhood streets in the evening. Uncle Vardaman encouraged my running. I think he ran as a young man. At that altitude, it seemed I could run forever. When I got back to Colorado, I found I wasn't in such great shape; there was just more air in Mississippi.

Uncle Vardaman decided one day that we needed to go coon hunting. I think he remembered great coon hunts as a young man and wanted to share that experience with me. I was a bit doubtful. I didn't think he'd been hunting in forty years, and I was pretty sure his old beagle had never been out of town. Uncle Vardaman, though, was confident. He was sure that old dog was a natural coon dog and the coons were out there waiting for us. I was still a little leery, but his enthusiasm was infectious.

We got prepared—gathering flash lights, boots, bug spray, and his shotgun. I don't know why, but it seems you can only hunt coons at night. We got to the woods near Grandmother Wade's right at dusk. When we got out of the car, the first thing that beagle did was go chasing after a rabbit. That set the tone for the hunt. Uncle Vardaman called his dog back, and we set off into the woods—or tried to. Those woods had changed since he had hunted there as young man. As a young man he could walk through those piney woods without a care. Now they were so overgrown with brier and brush that we needed a machete just to move. A lot of the overgrowth had thorns and stickers, and, even with flashlights, we could barely see ten feet in front of us. After fighting our way through the woods for an hour or so without even a glimmer of a coon, pulling stickers out of that beagle's feet, and both of us getting scratched and poked from head to toe, even Uncle Vardaman's enthusiasm began to wane. That's when we decided to just enjoy each other's company out in the dark woods, despite the stickers, thorns, and bugs. We didn't get a coon, but we had a great hunt.

JERRY EXACTS JUSTICE
BY WALLACE WADE

When we first moved from Mississippi, we lived in Dexter, New Mexico, for a short time. We lived right across the street from the gymnasium. On Saturday nights, they would use the gym floor as a roller-skating rink. We were the new kids, and I had a little bit of a mouth on me, and for some reason a couple of the other boys didn't like me. As I was skating, they intentionally tripped me, sending me crashing first into a barrier and then into some cabinets next to the concession stand. I ended up with a black eye and a bloody nose. My big brother Jerry was there and helped me get home.

Daddy and Mother took care of me, stopping my nose bleed and putting a cold compress on my black eye. I didn't see Jerry for the rest of that evening. Monday, I showed up at school sporting my shiner, which wasn't terribly out of the ordinary. What was unusual though was the condition of the two boys who had tripped me. They were battered and bruised a lot worse than I was and wanted nothing to do with me at all. It turns out that Jerry had gone back to the gym and gotten revenge on my behalf and taught them a lesson to boot. He never said a word about doing it; he just did it.

UNCLE HASKELL AND SOUTHERN HISTORY
BY DAN WADE

Uncle Haskell was a self-taught historian about the Civil War. He had been to many battlefields and could tell you the details of troop movements in many of the major battles. He had a passion for that history and was very knowledgeable and well-read.

In my teens, I thought I was pretty well-read as well. After reading a book called *Andersonville* by MacKinley Kantor that detailed the horrible conditions the captured northern soldiers endured in a southern prison camp, I was more than a little disgusted and ashamed of Southerners—of us—for treating prisoners so horribly. I basically confronted Uncle Hack. How could our people have committed such atrocities against our fellow man? He said he didn't support it and wouldn't defend it. However, he said, I should understand that while the prisoners were starving at Andersonville, so were the local people and the southern soldiers as well. He continued explaining that practically the whole South was burned out and turned upside down. He stated that it's not really an excuse, but there just wasn't enough food left in the South for everybody to eat. General Sherman's march to the sea had just about destroyed the South.

Then he gently gave me a book about a northern prison camp that was not nearly as popular as *Andersonville*, and no movie was ever made of it. It was the story of a northern prison camp in Elmira, New York, an area untouched by war. No crops had been burned, the local people had not been terrorized by war, and they had plenty to eat. The prisoners there endured at least as deplorable and wretched conditions as were suffered at Andersonville. Southern prisoners were the only people starving in that area. The crops were plentiful. They never made a movie about the Elmira prison camp. My uncle gently taught me that a little knowledge wasn't always the whole story.

WATERMELON, STORIES, AND THE FRONT PORCH

BY DAN WADE

These days when I eat watermelon, it is usually cut into bite-sized pieces and placed in a bowl. I put a little salt on it and enjoy a good melon. They are never as good, though, as the watermelons I remember as a kid. Those were especially good and were grown by my Uncle Noel and his family. The family would gather once a year at Grandmother Wade's—all four brothers: Vardaman, Noel, Haskell, my dad Heber, and their families. As I recall, sometime in the afternoon, the brothers would set up a table—really a couple of planks on sawhorses. Then with the ceremony of carving a turkey, one of the brothers would begin slicing the melons with a huge butcher knife. This would take place under that big tree in front of the house, just past the drive on the fence line. I was in my twenties before I realized that a melon had more than eight pieces. I can still see those big melons being cut; there would be gasps of amazement as the halves were laid open; and we could see how ripe and pretty they were. First, they cut the melon in half, then cut the halves into quarters, then split the quarters into eighths. That's all a melon had was eight pieces. There would be a salt shaker on the table. All the cousins would line up and get a piece and find a grassy spot in the shade.

It seems to me that the brothers would all use their pocket knives to cut their melons with. The rest of us were left with the old face-to-the-rind method. I'm here to tell you those were some good melons! Later in the day, we would have supper that the ladies would have made. They would still be in good humor after letting Aunt Beatrice tell them all how to cook. We would all have a good supper after grace was said. After supper, the ladies would clean up. The brothers would gather outside on the porch to visit. Us kids would do kid stuff—chase fireflies, play tag, or go hide and seek. It wouldn't be long, though, before the real entertainment would begin. It would start like this: "Heber," one of his brothers would say, "Do you remember that time?" They would be off then, one story after another, us kids just soaking it up. Soon the ladies would be out, and they would visit and listen to the stories as well. The stories were of living, loving, good times, and bad. All were told with great humor and no malice. I'll bet I only had six or eight of those days, perhaps less, but they sure are great memories.

UNCLE VARDAMAN AND HARMONICA SALES
BY DAN WADE

Mom and Dad were living in Bloomfield, New Mexico, when Uncle Vardaman and Aunt Beatrice drove out from Mississippi to visit. At the time, Mom was sick and weak, and Dad didn't feel great either. They were glad to have Uncle Vardaman and Aunt Beatrice visit, but they both tired easily. I believe that's why Donna and I took our aunt and uncle to Durango, Colorado, for a day trip. We planned to show them a good time and let Mom and Dad rest a little.

Durango, as many of you know, is a fun place to walk around in. Main Street has a lot of interesting shops. As we left Durango, we stopped at the mall. Donna and Aunt Beatrice went one way, and Uncle Vardaman and I, the other. As we were walking past a music store, a young man was asking the salesman questions about harmonicas. Uncle Vardaman stopped and listened to a couple of answers before very politely interjecting himself into the conversation. It was quickly apparent that Uncle Vardaman was the expert; the salesman was smart enough to just be quiet and stay out of the way. That young man shopping for a harmonica probably learned more about harmonicas than he ever wanted to know. Uncle Vardaman schooled him on all the various types of harmonicas, then recommended one in particular that would be just right for him. The young man took the recommendation, bought the harmonica, and thanked Uncle Vardaman sincerely for his help; so did the salesman. Uncle Vardaman took joy in sharing his knowledge to help people.

VISITORS ON HORSEBACK
BY DAN WADE

When we were growing up on the ranch in Colorado, we often took visitors horseback riding. Some people enjoyed it. Wayne Wade and his bride Gail had a good time, I think. They came to visit on their honeymoon. Gail was experienced, and Wayne never lacked confidence or courage. A few people could have probably skipped our ride and been okay with that.

Wallace and Nancy had been married for a little while when we all decided it was past time to take her riding. I don't think Nancy really looked forward to riding, but she's a good sport and was willing to give it a try. She had been raised on a farm and ranch, and they had horses, and Nancy rode some around their place. Wallace was around twenty-two years old at the time—a big, powerful man. Our mother had always said he was the best horseman of all of us. She was right. We could all ride, but Wallace was a natural horseman. He looked like he was one with the horse.

We put Nancy on Jubilee. She was a real gentle mare that none of us liked to ride. We could trust her not to hurt anyone, but sometimes she would take advantage of an inexperienced rider, acting like she was the boss. Unfortunately, that day with Nancy was one of those days Jubilee wanted to be the boss.

The group of us saddled up. There were five of us: Wallace, Nancy, Donna, Jenny, and I. As we left the corrals, everything was going well. Nancy was doing great. We had planned an easy ride; there was no need to worry. It was a beautiful day. Laughing and talking, we started across the pasture. It wasn't far before we came to an irrigation ditch that Jubilee had crossed a thousand times. She didn't plan on crossing it this day. We crossed between a small pond and an irrigation box. It was the best place to cross because the banks weren't steep, and it was only about four feet wide. All of us crossed, expecting Nancy to be right with us, only she wasn't. Jubilee was being stubborn, acting like she had never seen water before. Of course, we all gave Nancy helpful advice: "Don't let her get away with that. Don't let her have her head. Pull the reins! Kick her!" That mare would spin away every time Nancy got her to the ditch, and somehow our giving advice louder didn't seem to help. Nancy was trying, but we could see that she was getting frustrated with the horse's acting up and all of us telling her what she should do.

What we should have done was have Nancy get off and walk across the ditch on the irrigation box. It was only twenty feet away. One of us could have gotten on Jubilee and ridden her across the ditch. Then we could have gone on with our ride and had a good time. It would have been easy. Of course, that's not what happened. I had the bright idea to ride back across the ditch and take the reins from Nancy and lead Jubilee across. This was old Jubilee; I never dreamed she'd give me any trouble. We were about half way across without any problem when she suddenly reared back and jerked the reins out of my hand. Then gentle old Jubilee spun like a cutting horse and took off at a dead run back to the corrals with the reins flapping in the breeze.

Wallace was the first to react. He took off after them. Nancy was hanging onto the saddle, racing across the pasture. She would be okay until they got to the corrals; but then there were gates, corners, and a barbed-wire fence—plenty of opportunities for something bad to happen. We were all scared but Wallace most of all. He was racing to save Nancy, and, man, could he ride! Jubilee had a head start, but Wallace was on a faster horse, and he gained on them quickly and caught up just a little over half way back to the corrals. There are very few men in the world who could do what he did next. He rode up alongside Jubilee, and, with one arm, reached over, grabbed Nancy's upper arm, and lifted her up from the saddle. Even from a distance we could see Nancy's relief. Everything was alright; she had been saved by her new husband from the real dangers of a runaway horse. Holding her by her arm, Wallace drew her close to his side and slowed his horse. He'd saved Nancy, she was out of danger, so he wasn't scared anymore. Now he was mad, I mean real mad, at the horse that had put his bride in danger. After slowing his horse down to a lope, he leaned over, so Nancy wouldn't have so far to fall, straightened his arm out, and unceremoniously dropped her to the ground.

With Nancy safe, now he could punish that horse that had put his wife in danger. So in anger, he spurred his horse to catch Jubilee. When Nancy hit the ground, I swear she rolled like a Navy seal, came to her feet, and started chasing Wallace, who was chasing the horse. Wallace caught up with Jubilee, grabbed the reins, pulled her to a stop, swung down to the ground, and, holding her by the bridle, reared back to hit that horse with a big right hand. He might have killed that horse if he had let that punch go. It never landed. Just at that moment, Nancy caught up to him. She was fighting mad—we could not hear what was said—but suddenly Wallace forgot all about that horse, dropped the reins, and gave his new bride his full attention. She kept it, too. Continuing to express her feelings as they walked through the corrals and across the yard to their car, we could see that he was paying strict attention, but he wasn't saying a word. They left without saying goodbye.

CHAPTER 5

A DIFFERENT TIME

AIRSHIP

BY DAN WADE

Uncle Noel Wade was a truly good, hardworking, God-fearing man. He was also the best story teller I have ever heard, maybe the best anybody ever heard. His expressions, inflections, hand motions, and timing just couldn't be matched. His family was smart enough to get some of his story-telling sessions on video. If you get the chance, dear Grandchild, watch one of those; you will see a true master at work. I am going to write one of his greatest stories. I will do the best I can to capture the essence of his story, but, at the very best, it will be an imitation. I mean it to honor that good man.

In about 1916, my grandparents Jesse Felix and Minnie Ozella Wade and their children had a farm in the Cracker's Neck community near Soso, Mississippi. Their house was set on the back side of their farm, about a quarter of a mile off the road. At that time, the six kids—Vardaman, Lola, Beulah, Noel, Haskell, and Heber—ranged in age from five or six years old to the early teens. Automobiles were new to that area. They had heard of them and had even seen one or two pass on the road. One Sunday afternoon, they were all at the house just messing around in the yard like kids do. Suddenly, they all stopped what they were doing.

What was that noise? They could hear something in the distance go "pop, pop, pop." It was getting louder. Oh boy! They were going to see an automobile, and it must be a big one. Now the roar was getting even louder and louder. The whole family was straining to see it on the road. It sounded close. It had to be there soon! The four boys couldn't stand waiting, so they climbed up on the shed to get a better view. Their mom and dad were on the porch, and the girls were in the yard. All of them were straining to see the automobile. As hard as they tried, there was no auto to be seen. Where was it? The sound was right on top of them! Where could it be? Then the roar wasn't on top of them, it was past them! Past them? Yes, the roar of a motor was going away. What in the world?

They all knew what was in back of the house: a forest and a swamp. Those boys knew it well, and no auto could go there. The entire family was stunned. What had just happened? Something had been there, and then it wasn't, and where it went it couldn't go. They talked about it. Even their dad was mystified. It just wasn't possible. The whole family was a little worried. The next day, a neighbor came by. He was all excited and wanted to know if they had seen the airship. Airship? What was that? They had looked and looked, everywhere but up.

That was the Wade family's first experience with what they called an "airship."

DAD WAS A BARBER
BY DAN WADE

They say that Mom cried after I lost my curls. Dad gave me my first haircut at two years old. From that first haircut until I was twelve years old, Dad cut my hair about every two weeks. He called it a flattop, but it sure looked like a buzz cut to me. After I started noticing girls and they weren't noticing me, I decided that a flattop wasn't for me. I could see that girls liked guys better who combed their hair. I wanted to start combing my hair.

Dad had always cut my hair. He was a skilled barber, at least he was if you wanted white walls and a flattop. That style was his specialty. Dad had professional electric clippers, a barber's comb, and scissors. He told me that he had started cutting hair as a young man. First his brothers, then most of the young men in his community. They would show up at the home place on Saturday afternoon and wait their turn. He said he would often give eight to twelve haircuts on any given Saturday. Dad didn't charge anything for haircuts, and he figured that might have been the reason for his popularity with the neighbors. He didn't charge for his haircuts, but he would accept payment if offered. One young man always paid Dad a nickel for his haircut. No one else ever offered. He thought that was a true testament to human nature.

We had a kitchen stool which got me high enough for Dad to cut my hair comfortably. Comfortable for him, for me not so much. Of course there was no back on the stool. I perched on top of the stool with my feet dangling in the air. Dad expected me to sit up straight and be still, and I mean as still as a rock. No matter how hard I tried, I was never able to sit still enough. Dad had a solution for that. He would grab my head like a bowling ball with a talon-like grip. Of course that grip hurt, which would make me squirm more. Squirming would bring a stern admonishment to "sit still" and an even tighter grip. That tighter grip made me squirm even more. It was a vicious circle: the tighter Dad gripped my head, the more I squirmed, and the more I squirmed, the tighter he gripped my head. I dreaded haircuts. The relief I felt when they were over was the only thing I liked about them.

It was great day for me—a milestone on the way to growing up—when I was finally allowed to let my hair grow out and get my hair cut at the barber shop. Just to be different, I decided to part my hair on the right. Boys were supposed to part it on the left. I guess I was a young rebel. Even as a youngster, I was treated like a customer at the barbershop. Mr. Hickman, our town barber, was a businessman. He tried to make getting a haircut at his shop a pleasant experience. He would engage me in conversation and regale me with wild stories about cowboys and the old days. He wanted me to come back for another haircut. (I went back to his shop once after I had graduated and had been gone from town for ten years. Mr. Hickman said, "How are you doing, Dan?" just like he'd seen me yesterday.)

Dad wasn't concerned about my having a pleasant experience when he cut my hair. He didn't worry at all about my wanting to come back. After a hard day's work, he just wanted to get the job done, and the quicker the better. When Dad cut my hair, I felt more like a victim than a customer. Wallace always told me that I shouldn't complain. He said that, when Dad had cut his hair, he used old-time, hand-operated clippers that seemed to pull as much hair as they cut.

Looking back, I'll bet Dad was happier than I was when I started going to the barber.

COTTON HOER
BY WALLACE WADE

These days, it seems like there are a lot of people out there on the internet who are sensitive about terms and phrases. I've been told that some folk even take exception to the term "cotton-picking." As in "wait a cotton-picking minute" or "keep your cotton-picking hands to yourself." Apparently, they think it's racist. This seems a little inaccurate to me because I've spent more minutes, hours, and days than I can count picking cotton, and I'm pretty sure that means I literally have "cotton-picking" hands, and I am just a little less white than the cotton I picked. I spent many hours working in cotton fields. As a younger man, I picked cotton, chopped cotton, and planted cotton.

This is a story about chopping cotton and being given a label no one would ever expect. Back in 1959, we were living in Roswell, and Noel Wade and his family also lived in New Mexico. Most summers, I would work for Dad helping him build houses. Well, Wayne Wade and I were thick as thieves back then, and we both knew that working for Dad and Jerry was going to be hard work. Wayne has always been a guy who was on the lookout for an opportunity, and that was as true back then as it is today. He found a local farmer named Mr. Payne. Mr. Payne was looking for strong young men to work in his cotton fields chopping cotton, which is something both Wayne and I had a lot of experience with, and the job paid really well: fifty cents an hour!

Chopping cotton means taking a hoe and using it to chop the weeds out of the cotton rows. Wayne and I met up with Mr. Payne the first day, and he wanted to try us out to see how we did. He was a little taken aback that we didn't want to use the hoes he offered, which were big heavy square things. Wayne and I both had our own personal hoes that we'd customized. They were goose-necked and shaved down on one side to save weight, making them easier to get at the weeds in between the cotton plants and lighter to lift, thousands of times a day.

That first morning Mr. Payne started off chopping with us. Cotton is planted in long rows, and the way Wayne and I did the job was to straddle one row of cotton as we worked. That way you could get the weeds in that row as well as the row on either side, doing three rows at a time. Mr. Payne had never seen people use that method and was impressed. His family would only hoe one row at a time; so seeing us handle three was revolutionary to him, and we were hired on the spot.

Mr. Payne had contracts with several farms around the Roswell area to chop their cotton that summer. Wayne and I worked all of them. Mr. Payne held us in very high regard. One day Wayne and I were finishing up our last rows of cotton, and, as we approached the edge of the field, we got within earshot of Mr. Payne. He was talking to the farmer who owned this cotton patch. We heard Mr. Payne proudly tell the other farmer, "You see those two? Those two Wade boys are the best hoers I have ever had!"

I've been called a lot of things over the years, and I imagine so has Wayne, but that's the only time anyone's called either of us a "hoer" and meant it as a compliment.

A NEW MEXICO CHRISTMAS

BY JENNY WADE CHILSON

"Oh, no, they don't have any trees either!" Dan, Donna, and I all said at the same time. It was about 1961, and we were all pressing our faces against the backseat car windows hoping to spot a Christmas tree that we could take home. It was a week before Christmas, and Mother and Daddy had driven us into Roswell, New Mexico, in a yearly Christmas tradition, one which was excitedly anticipated and important for us. Getting our tree each year officially kicked off the fun family days of Christmas—days when we would decorate and make cookies and fudge, and the whole family would be happy and play a lot of games. And, of course, Christmas brought hopes that Santa Claus would bring us something special and leave it under the Christmas tree. Daddy drove us from tree lot to tree lot all over town, and every lot was empty; all we saw were other cars with families looking for a Christmas tree.

Finally, Daddy started driving us out of town—without a tree—and we couldn't believe he would do that. We begged him to keep looking, but Daddy told us that we had checked everywhere; that Roswell had just not gotten enough Christmas trees that year, and we needed to go home. To us, that meant that there would be no Christmas because, without a tree, it couldn't be Christmas! Mother turned around to us and said, "Don't worry, it will be okay." The three of us just looked at her and wondered how she could possibly think "it would be okay." It was a sad ride home, and we thought the worst thing in the world had just happened to us. Sitting and worrying in the backseat, the three of us didn't say a word. We just kept looking at each other, communicating with each other through our eyes, the way all close siblings learn to do. Even worse, Mother and Daddy didn't seem very concerned.

Once we got home, Mother and Daddy got busy with their normal chores, and they told us to go play. We pretended to go play, but we stayed close to keep our eyes on them, hoping we were going to see them come to their senses and put us back in the car to go find a Christmas tree somewhere! Jerry was still off at college, and Wallace was a teenager who got to stay home alone if he wanted. After being at home for a little while, Mother called Wallace into the house and took him into a room to speak to him privately. We thought the day had just gotten worse. We didn't have a Christmas tree, and now Wallace was in trouble! Soon, they both came out of the room and just walked by the three of us. Neither was speaking, and Mother went about working in the kitchen. We watched as Wallace went out of the house, thinking he was mad about being in trouble.

The front of our house faced the county road, and across the road was just open prairie land for miles and miles. But the land had slight hills, so a person walking out there could not be seen after about 400 yards. Wallace often headed out into those fields and hiked for hours, exploring land that none of the rest of us ever saw. Daddy always said that his brother Noel and Wallace were the best hikers he had ever known. He said the two of them could hike forever and never tire. Wallace enjoyed nature and exploring and being out by himself. So, it wasn't unusual at all when we saw Wallace cross the road and head off into the wide-open field. The three of us were left to despair all by ourselves. We tried to distract ourselves—playing some games and trying to figure things out for ourselves—the way only six-, nine-, and eleven-year-olds can do. Not only had we discovered that we weren't going to have Christmas, but we had a Daddy that didn't seem to care, and we had a Mother that actually said everything would be okay! "How could she say that? Has she gone crazy?" we asked each other. And, of course, we were debating how Santa Claus could possibly come to a house with no Christmas tree.

We were keeping our hopeful eyes on everyone. After a couple of hours, we spotted Wallace way out in the field, returning from his hike. We ran into the house to tell Mother that Wallace was coming home and that he was dragging something! To our surprise, this made Mother happy, and she put her kitchen towel down and hurried out the front door to stand with us as we watched Wallace returning. Once he got near the yard, Mother ran to him and put her arm around him, telling him that he had done such a good job! Mother called us over to see what Wallace was dragging. It was the biggest yucca cactus plant we had ever seen! The bottom of the plant had extra-long green blades, and, on top, the yucca still had tall spikes from several blooming seasons. Mother then said, "This is going to be our Christmas tree!" She said that this was going to be a special year because we were going to have a unique New Mexico Christmas tree. Instantly, our world changed. We had a tree, and we were going to have Christmas after all!

Wallace and Daddy built a stand for the yucca-plant Christmas tree, and we put it in front of the living room picture window. It was just as big as a regular Christmas tree. Mother sprayed the whole plant with a thick coating of artificial snow. Then, we decorated it with lights and shiny red, green, and gold bulbs. The sharp points on all the blades were perfect for holding all the shiny ornaments. The yucca plant that had been dragged for miles across the field was suddenly a magical Christmas tree! It was beautiful! Our upside-down world had quickly reversed and was filled with more Christmas joy and love and excitement than we could ever have had if we had found a Christmas tree on one of those deserted lots in town. Our whole family was so happy, and Mother and Wallace loved their little secret plan and how they knew all along that we were about to be the happiest kids in the world.

We had a great Christmas! We all thought we had the best Christmas tree ever. And Mother's three youngest kids learned to trust her when she said, "It will be okay."

HONEY BAIT

BY TOM WADE

Two years ago, my daughter Brittany and I saw a crowd-funding ad for a newfangled beehive on Facebook. So we decided to order this hive and dive into the honey business. Because of the success of their crowdfunding campaign, we had to wait until this spring for our hive box. For anyone who wants to check it out, Google "Flowhive." It promises gallons of fresh raw honey!

Jerry Wade, my dad, was excited about this venture as well. He would always tell two stories about going into the deep woods of Mississippi with his dad, my grandfather James Heber Wade. All his grandchildren called him "Pop." In one story, they would always stop and sit in the car for a while, and, after making sure that no one was around, Pop would get out and walk to an old stump or fallen tree. There he would retrieve a jar of moonshine. On occasion, they might meet up with other men and sit around to drink the moonshine. One time, Dad ventured into the circle and, when the Mason jar was passed around, he took a swig and then passed it on. He said it gave him quite a jolt, and he was still trying to recover as he saw the jar headed back around towards him. Fortunately, he was skipped as the jar passed him. He said he had no idea how he was going to keep face among the men had the jar been given to him the second time. He always appreciated the men for doing that.

That wasn't the case the other times they would go out into the woods. These were the times when they went for honey. The men would get the smokers ready and then proceed to the hive.

They would make Dad stay a ways back. Dad said he could never understand how the other men hardly ever got stung while the whole time he would be being chased by bees. He said that years later he read that, when a hive is disturbed, the soldier bees set up a perimeter around the hive and patrol it and then work back towards the hive. He then realized that he had been the decoy!

Well, tonight Brittany and I had to add the second box to the hive, and, man, I wish Dad had been here as the decoy. I ended up getting stung several times and had bees in my shirt and up my pants legs!

SNAKE HUNTERS

BY WAYNE WADE

When I was in elementary school, we had long summer vacations or, maybe I should say, a long work holiday. There was a lot of work, but there was also a lot of play. We did not have TV, record player, phone, and, of course, no computers. We slept with our windows propped up with window sticks and fell asleep with the symphony of tree frogs, crickets, and whippoor-wills. We all drank from the same dipper from the water bucket that we drew from the well, and we shared a two-hole outdoor privy. What we did have were parents, Noel and Minnie Lee Wade, who loved us and encouraged us to develop our great God-given endowments such as "imagination."

It was during that time that my cousin Burney Morgan would spend the summer with me. The nights were particularly interesting; it was too hot to sit around the house and be bored, so we invented many exciting activities to fill our time. One of our favorite nighttime adventures was snake hunting. Somehow we had come up with a pretty dependable carbide headlight and an old machete.

The copperheads and dry-land snakes were normally taken out by my dog Tags. Tags was a border collie that I got from

Uncle Haskell as a puppy. Uncle Haskell didn't much care for dogs, so I got the pick of the litter. At any rate, Tags was good at treeing possums and squirrels, herding cows and chickens, and killing snakes. He was always close by in Burney's and my adventures.

The water moccasins and cottonmouths were a different matter. Burney and I would wade the creeks and pond edges at night until we found one. One of us would shine the light close to the snake's head into its eyes, and the other would hit it in the head with a stick or cut its head off with the machete. We would, of course, drag the snake home for everyone to see the next morning. Mother would get mad and chase us and the dead snake with the yard broom, and Dad would laugh.

However, there was one snake story that ended a little differently. At the far end of our property, there was a live creek that ran most of the time and a water hole that Burney and I enjoyed spearing bullfrogs in. When we worked that particular water hole, we would bring Dad's thirty-six-inch 16-gauge shotgun that was commonly called a "Long Tom." There was a huge cottonmouth that also enjoyed frogging in that same hole, and his reputation continued to grow each summer. One summer, my sister LeGuewn and I rode Ole George, our plow horse, down to the water hole to give him fresh water after spending a day of pulling a plow. The big snake was wrapped around a tree just out of the water. When Ole George started drinking, the snake slid into the water and headed for him. Ole George saw the snake, bucked both LeGuewn and me off, and took off for the house. To this day I don't know who got home first—us or Ole George.

Back to the event at hand. On this particular day, Burney and I were allowed to go frogging during the day. We had spotted a very large bullfrog that we would soon have in the skillet. However, for some reason, the frog disappeared. This was not the first time this had happened, and we knew exactly what to do. We jumped in and began to muddy the water with our feet, as we knew from experience that this would force the frog to surface. I had just stepped out of the water for some reason when I heard Burney yell, "Help! Get the gun!" I looked to see half of that huge cottonmouth's body raised out of the water with its head up between Burney's thighs. Burney then calmly told me to stick the barrel of the gun up close the snake's head and shoot. To say I was nervous would be a lie; I was plain scared. I picked the gun up, eased the barrel up close to the snake's head—aiming down so as not to hit Burney's legs or other parts—and pulled the trigger. I would say the fact that Burney is a parent and grandparent today is testament to a good clean shot!

Of course, we dragged the big snake back to the house for everyone to see. After cutting the snake's belly open to investigate the big lump in his middle, we found our frog.

HERDING PIGS
BY DAN WADE

A couple of years after moving to Colorado, Dad decided to raise four young pigs—or "shoats" as he called them—in the chicken pen. These were not pets. The plan was to sell what we didn't slaughter for ourselves. We had fixed the pen well enough so that it would keep them from getting out. It would be my job to feed them, and I knew from listening to my parents that the feed we bought at the co-op was expensive.

Around that time at ten years old, I was well started on a lifelong love of the written word. I had already traveled the world with Marco Polo. I had mushed to Alaska in a dog sled with Jack London and *The Call of the Wild*. In the story of *Old Yeller*, I had learned all about pigs and how a young boy could take responsibility to help his family.

Dad was working away from home, Wallace was already off on his own that summer, and being the "man of the house" weighed heavily on me. One morning when it was time for me to slop the pigs (you didn't feed pigs; you slopped them) with that expensive feed, I got to thinking that I could save the family some money. My idea was to let the pigs out of the pen to graze on the tall grass and sage brush just outside of the pen.

I figured they would still grow and get fat, but we wouldn't have to spend so much money on feed. So that is what I did. I opened the gate, and, once they were out of the pen, they went to eating the grass and brush just like I had read about in *Old Yeller*. During the day I checked on them a few times, and they were happy as clams and staying close to the house and the pen, just eating away. I was sure proud of myself and told Mom what I had done. She seemed a bit surprised and concerned while cautioning me that they would have to be back in the pen by nightfall. I wasn't worried about that. Putting them back in the pen would be easy.

A little before sundown, I went out to pen them up for the night. All four of them were scattered out eating within a hundred yards of the pen. I opened the gate and put out a little feed to tempt them in. Then I walked out past the farthest little pig and started getting closer and closer, gently moving him towards the others. I kept walking around real easy, slowly getting all four of them together. It was going really well; this was going to be a cinch. I soon had them gathered up and then started moving them slowly towards the pen. All four of those thirty-five-pound shoats got right up to the gate and just started milling around. I thought I'd give them some time, so I just stayed still and waited, thinking that at any moment one of them would see the feed I'd put out and go in the gate.

They didn't see the feed inside the gate, so I edged closer. No luck. They were still milling around. I waited again. Surely they would see the feed, but no. Okay, one more step, and suddenly they exploded in four different directions! One minute they were almost in the pen. The next minute those four thirty-five-pound pigs were GONE! Have you ever tried to catch a thirty-five-pound pig in an open field? Well, I am here to tell you it cannot be done, certainly not by a ten-year-old. It didn't take long for me to realize I was in trouble. Those dang pigs had headed for the hills, and it would be dark soon. I needed help! So I started running to the house, yelling for my sisters to hurry and come help catch those pigs. They rushed out to help.

Donna, Jenny, and I hurried up the hill until we got in front of them. Then we spread out trying to turn them back towards the house. That didn't work. They just ran between us, still heading deeper into the hills. It was almost dark, but there still might be time for one more try. Maybe we could catch just one at a time. The three of us ran to get ahead of them again, and, instead of trying to stop all four, we just focused on one little pig. We got him hemmed in between us. We had him stopped and surrounded, and all we had to do was grab him. You have probably heard of a greased pig. Well, this one wasn't greased, but he moved like greased lighting! When I jumped to grab him, all I got was a mouth full of dirt and a handful of air, and he was gone again! Right between my screaming sister's legs he went. Holy smokes! I was in trouble. How were we ever going to catch those pigs?

Mother didn't seem too surprised when we walked in after dark and reported our failure to catch those pigs. It was a long night, though. She had told me that, since I had let them out, it was my job to catch them. I had no idea how far those pigs would go or how I could catch them or find them. Finding them turned out to be easy. Early the next morning, we had calls from two different neighbors who had spotted some loose pigs. "Have you lost any?" they asked. Yes, we had. After we tried and failed again to catch them at the neighbors, it quickly became a community effort to round up those little pigs. It seemed like all of our neighbors were experts at capturing pigs. I got plenty of advice, and some even wanted to help.

There were a couple of cowboys in the neighborhood who thought they had the answer to catching pigs, and they would show us all how to do it. They saddled up, shook out a loop in their ropes, and rode out to hogtie them a pig. After many tries, they had about wore their horses out and discovered that pigs don't run in a straight line, and—guess what?—you can't really rope a pig.

Days went by and no pigs. Finally, a neighbor called to say they had one cornered. When we got the call, off we went. Mom drove me to their place, and I wrestled that bugger into a gunny sack and hauled it home. A few days later, we got another call, and off we went again. It was two weeks before we finally had them all back home in our pen. The last one had been almost five miles away! I had almost given up hope of finding them all.

I never got in trouble for letting the little shoats out. I guess Mom and Dad figured that chasing those pigs was punishment enough and thought that I had learned my lesson.

HORSE BREAKING
by Dan Wade

After moving to Colorado, somehow my family became "horse poor." We moved there with several horses, but for some reason both Dad and Jerry brought more home. It seemed like all of them were unbroken. Jerry would even bring other people's horses to be broken. Jerry came up with a method for breaking a horse that even he might not recommend, but it sure was effective and only took one day. Jerry was the horse breaker, and Donna, Jenny and I were his team.

This is how we did it. Please don't try this at home. The first job was to saddle the horse. Often they weren't even broke to lead; we would have to rope and snub them tight to a fence. It was always a fight, but, with the sisters and me helping as much as we could, Jerry would get them saddled and haltered. For the next step, Jerry would get on a good stout horse, grab the lead rope on the unbroken horse, get a tight dally (three wraps of the rope) on his saddle horn, and then take off. With Jerry pulling, Donna, Jenny, and I would be pushing from behind. That is, one of us rode right behind the horse, close enough to slap it on the butt if it slowed down, and the other two rode real close on each side. We rode as hard as we could, up and down hills, over ditches and logs. After a few hours, that horse was broke to lead and about wore out. We'd go back to the corral, tie the horse up, tend to our riding horses, and go have lunch. After an hour or so, we'd get back to it. It was almost the same plan; the only difference was that this time they put me on the horse we were breaking. That horse now had a bridle, as well as the halter, and my job was just to hang on for a while. (Did I mention I was about ten years old?) I wasn't to touch the reins yet. Off we'd go again, Jerry pulling, Donna and Jenny pushing, and me hanging on for dear life. It was the same program—up and down hills, across ditches over logs. After some time, Jerry would have me start using the reins while he pulled left and right and stopped and started. Soon he would give more slack on the lead rope, and Donna and Jenny backed off a little. I would be in charge of the horse—turning, stopping, going from a walk to a gallop. That's how we'd finish the day: Jerry always kept the lead rope; he just gave me more and more slack; and my sisters gave me just a little more room. When we got back to the corrals, we had a broke horse. A broke horse that just needed some training.

We had an unusual method of training. Of course, it was also Jerry's idea. When time allowed, we'd put the finishing touches on that horse, usually the next day. Training the horse was again a team effort. It didn't take long, and we had a blast doing it. You all remember playing tag as a kid, chasing and dodging each other. Well, that's what we did to train that horse. We all mounted up and played tag. Jerry rode the "green" or untrained horse, and at first Donna, Jenny, and I would be faster and quicker on our trained mounts. Jerry couldn't catch us going through and around trees, over logs, through and over gullies, and up and down hills. Soon, with work, Jerry's horse would start responding to Jerry's commands better. When he could catch us and we couldn't catch him, we had a trained horse. Playing tag on horseback is exciting and about as wild riding as you can do. One trick to playing tag on horseback is to race past a tree, then turn just past it, and your pursuer will turn to cut you off. You know the trick worked when they rode right under a tree branch and got scraped off the saddle. Horseback tag is good training for the horseman as well as the horse. I still wonder how it was that no one got hurt badly or killed. None of us would want to see our kids or grandkids play tag on horseback. It's crazy! I'll bet, though, that none of us have ever had so much fun.

I could also tell you about a ride when we didn't have time for the training day and how an untrained horse reacts to a 150-foot cliff. But that's a story for another day.

STRIP-DOWN AUTO

BY DAN WADE

As a young man, Dad worked hard—farming, trapping, and cutting stove wood—finally managing to buy himself an automobile. Not a new one, not even a complete one. What he got was called a *strip-down,* which was basically a frame with a motor, steering wheel, and gear shift. No body, no seats, nothing. It didn't even run. He pulled it home with a mule. I think it was the frame of a Ford Model A. After he pulled it home with the mule, he worked on the motor until he got it running pretty well. He tied a board to the frame to have a place to put his feet, and he tied a wooden bench to the frame just behind the floor board. Just like that, he had himself an *automobile.* He was ready to go. It wasn't much even then as cars go, but it was his. He'd paid for it, he'd fixed it up and got it running, and he was proud of it.

He asked a pretty young lady out for a date. She said, "Yes," and one Saturday night he went to pick her up,—all dressed up, just as proud and happy as he could be. He went inside and paid his respects to her parents, then he and his date went to leave. Her father came outside with them. When they all got out to Dad's *strip-down automobile,* her dad made a big show of walking to the front, then walking to the back, and studying it real close. Then he looked at Dad and started laughing. He said, "Where's the rest of your car?" Haw haw.

That hurt Dad's pride enough for him to tell me about it almost fifty years later. He never asked that girl for a date again, and he never was quite as proud of his *strip-down automobile*.

JERRY AND TOMATOES
BY TOM WADE

Everyone knows how much Dad loved tomatoes. In the fall of the year, all he wanted to eat was tomato sandwiches. A lot of mayo, a load of salt, and as many tomato slices as he could fit between two pieces of white bread. I know that Jerry's sister, Donna, has the same love for tomatoes, but I am not sure about the other siblings. In my household, it's me, my son Bryce, and my youngest daughter Brynn that share this affliction. Of my two brothers, Max enjoys them, but Roy does not like tomatoes in the least bit. At least the last time I checked, he did not.

I think this dislike goes back to when we were kids living in Bloomfield. Dad always planted a substantial garden and about half of it was tomatoes. Every fall as frost approached, Dad would have Roy and me line up sawhorses on both sides of the tomato rows and then drape tarps across them, covering the tomatoes. Every evening, we would light up the torpedo heaters for the night. In the morning before school, Roy and I would uncover the tomatoes. After school, we would go through and pick the good ones and get rid of any that were overripe or had gotten some frost on them. Then we would re-tarp and start the torpedoes. This would continue until the plants just gave out.

Every year, Roy would discuss the merits of adulthood, and growing tomatoes was definitely not going to be on the list. He swore that the smell of tomatoes actually made him ill. Dad's goal was to have the first tomato before the Fourth of July and the last at Thanksgiving. Rarely was this feat achieved, but that did not keep him from trying. He said that the best thing about sports and growing tomatoes was that you always have next year.

TRAINING COLTS AND JENNY'S TRAIN WRECK
BY DAN WADE

When my sisters and I were kids on the ranch in Colorado, we each got a colt. Dad gave Donna and Jenny each a yearling filly, but, being a young man at nine years old, I was required to buy mine. I paid twenty-five dollars for my filly and named her Jamboree. The three colts were about a year old when we got them. They were too young to ride, but they were old enough to start training. We had a blast training them to lead, lounge on a lead line at a walk, trot, gallop, and stop. "Whoa" was the voice command for stop. To change gaits, my sisters clucked like our dad and brothers did. Clucking is a sound made with your mouth slightly open, your tongue pressed to the roof, and somehow making a sound like a chicken. My sisters clucked like pros, but, for the life of me, I couldn't get the hang of it; so I substituted with a popping sound made by pursing my lips together, sucking in, and then opening my lips. I was humiliated that I couldn't cluck, but Jamboree didn't seem to mind. While those colts were too young to saddle, we tormented them in all sorts of ways. Somewhere we got a set of books on horse training. We taught our colts to say "yes," "no," and count, just like Roy Rogers's horse Trigger. Well, maybe not quite as good. By driving them with lines, we taught them how to plow rein;

pulling on the right rein, then the left, taught them to respond to pressure. We also got them used to saddle blankets, which would make saddling them easy later on.

Finally, the colts were old enough to break. First came the saddle, and, with work, they were soon used to being saddled. When they got used to lounging with the stirrups flopping around, it was time to get on! Yeehaw! Getting on a colt for the first time is exciting. You just don't know what might happen. Keeping a tight grip on the reins, with one hand on the saddle horn and the other on the cantle, we'd get one foot in the stirrup, get all our weight on that stirrup, then we would wait just a minute, take a deep breath, and swing our leg over the saddle. "Whoa now, easy girl, whoa now," we'd say softly while petting them on the neck. If they were pretty calm, we'd loosen up on the reins and make that clucking sound to get them to walk around the corral for a couple of turns. That was enough. We'd get off and tell our colts how good they were, pet them, and calm them down. Then we'd do it again, going a little farther each time, and then it was time to ride out of the corral and put some miles on. Soon we'd have a broken horse.

Donna and I soon got our colts working pretty well, but Jenny's colt, a filly named Honeycomb—a real pretty sorrel with a flaxen mane and tail—was a different story. She just wouldn't cooperate. Jenny could saddle and get on her without any problem, but, once Jenny was on her, Honeycomb wouldn't move. When we tried to get her to move, Honeycomb would lie down. We even tried our one-day breaking method, same result.

Jerry would lead her as I rode, while Donna and Jenny pushed from behind. That worked well until she sulled up; she would refuse to move and lie down. She might lie there for hours. We finally did get Honeycomb broke, but she sure wasn't any fun to ride.

Jenny started riding a good quarter-horse mare we called Little Red. She was fast and quick and suited Jenny well. Technically, Little Red was Dad's horse, but Dad didn't ride often. Donna's mare was called Etta. Donna got her broke well enough, but Etta turned out to be a horse no one wanted to ride at all. You couldn't trust her, and she just didn't ride well. Donna started riding a big black gelding named Gander. He was barely broke and half wild. Donna loved that big horse. Dad and Jerry saw that my colt Jamboree wasn't ever going to be more than a good kid's horse. They talked me into trading her for a yearling colt out of Lily of the Valley, a mustang mare from the mountains of New Mexico, and a big buckskin stud that belonged to our neighbor. Dad and Jerry thought that colt would be a good horse. They were wrong; he turned into a great horse. I called him Firecracker, and he was explosive. None of us ended up riding the colt we trained, but we all rode good horses.

Jenny never completely gave up on Honeycomb. She was probably the prettiest horse we had, and, as she got older, seemed to grow out of that sulling nonsense. All she really needed was some miles. Between one thing and another, Honeycomb didn't get ridden enough to be much more than green broke. What we all thought she needed was some miles under saddle to be a good horse. Jenny came home at Christmas during her first year of college and was really hoping to ride Honeycomb that next summer. She asked me to ride her whenever I had time during the spring. I said I would, and, during the next four months, I rode her quite a bit. She had turned into a pretty good riding horse. A good fast walk, a nice smooth canter, and a fast gallop. I got her reining and stopping pretty well. I rode her quite a bit and never had any trouble. I would soon wish I had ridden her more, a lot more!

Jenny got home for the summer and asked if I'd found time to ride Honeycomb. I said I had and told her how well she had been doing. Jenny could hardly wait to take a ride on her beautiful horse. We planned a morning ride, and, after saddling up, we took off. I was riding my horse Firecracker. We were going to ride in a big circle. We would stay on the road for about a half a mile, then we'd ride off into the hills. There was a good trail that would take us all the way around what we called "the big mountain" and back to the house from the other side. It was probably about a four- or five-mile ride with plenty of long open trails that invited us to see how fast we could go. It wasn't far after we turned off the road that we came to a great part of the trail. It was wide, straight, and slightly up hill. It was perfect. Honeycomb had been doing real good. Jenny and I had been riding along having a great time. We had absolutely no concern about her acting up.

We started in a trot, then we cantered for a ways. All was

going well. Jenny was riding in front of me, having a great time. Soon we pushed the horses into a nice gallop. Still no problem, so we eased into a faster gallop. It was going great when, all of a sudden, that mare that had never bucked before got her head down and bucked as high as I've ever seen. Jenny stayed with her, but it loosened her up on the saddle. She was still on after one more jump, but the third one sent her airborne. She went higher than I've ever seen anyone go. As Jenny came back down, it was like I was watching slow motion. Jenny was coming down horizontal, and that horse was still bucking. The horse's head was coming up as Jenny was coming down. Their heads met. The force of the blow knocked Jenny back up into the air spinning. I swear she did three complete revolutions before hitting the ground like a rag doll. I thought she was dead, but, when I got to her, she was breathing but unconscious.

I was scared to death! What should I do? I had to get her home! I picked her up. We were a little over a quarter of a mile from the road, and somehow I had the strength to carry her at a run, and I did. I ran as hard as I could. About halfway to the road, Jenny started babbling nonsense, and that scared me worse. I ran faster. Finally reaching the road, my chest was about to explode, so I thought I could set Jenny down and run for help faster. I put her down and sat her up against a tree. She was still babbling. I spoke sternly, "You have to stay right here. You can't move, stay here!" I couldn't tell what she understood. Still scared out of my wits, I started running for the house. Before I was halfway home, Mom and Dad met me in the pickup. They had seen the horses come running home and knew something was wrong. I jumped in the back, and Dad sped up the road to Jenny. She was still sitting against the tree. She was making a little more sense, but not a lot. We got her in the truck with Mom and Dad, and off they went. It was over twenty miles to Durango and a doctor. I stayed behind because there wasn't room for me in the pickup, the horses still needed tending to, and there were always chores to do.

It seemed like forever, but they finally brought Jenny home late in the evening. I was sure glad to see her. Her head hurt, but she wasn't talking nonsense anymore. The doctor said she had a bad concussion, and we had to keep her awake all night. We could finally let her sleep at dawn. After a day or two, Jenny was fine but just a little sore. No one, especially Jenny, ever blamed me for her almost getting killed.

I believe that, as pretty as that mare was, there was something not right with her. I couldn't help wondering, though. Could I have done a better job? Should I have ridden that mare more? Of course I could have, and of course I should have.

THE PUPPY, THE COYOTE, AND LADY
BY DAN WADE

In the summer of 1967, our dog Lady had a litter of puppies. I think Mom found a home for some of them, and I had taken care of the others. We kept just one to raise. That one puppy disappeared one day, and we had no idea what could have happened to him. He was too young to have gone far. Something or someone had to have taken him. We didn't know what it could have been. A hawk? A bobcat? It was a mystery. What could have happened to our puppy?

Four days later, we were all outside doing chores around the barn and in the yard when we heard a coyote barking. We looked across the valley and saw it, about 200 yards away. That coyote kept barking, yelping, and moving back and forth excitedly until it was sure that all of us were paying attention. Then it reached down and picked our lost puppy up by the back of its neck and held it up high in the air for a minute. When it was sure we saw the puppy, the coyote set it back down and trotted off.

Several of us rushed across the valley to get the puppy, and it was fine. How could that be? That puppy was only about two weeks old. He had been gone for four days, and he was still nursing. How had he survived without his mother? As hard as it was to believe, there was really only one possibility. The coyote had nursed our puppy.

That was the only way the little puppy could have survived, but it seemed so unlikely. Dogs and coyotes are mortal enemies. On our ranch, it was not at all uncommon for Lady, our German shepherd, to get into fights and skirmishes, usually with at least a pair of coyotes. The shepherd was bigger and stronger, but the coyotes were quicker and smarter. The coyotes liked to tease Lady when we were out irrigating the fields. One time, we were out on the ditch setting the water. Lady was staying by my side when a couple of coyotes came out. They were about 100 yards away, up a small hill with some scattered oak brush. They started teasing Lady. One of them would run towards us barking, and, when Lady would start towards it, the coyote would turn around and go back towards his buddy.

Lady was too smart and experienced to fall for that trick. So the coyote got bolder and bolder, coming closer and closer before turning back towards his buddy. Lady was getting more and more excited but still resisted the urge to chase one of them. She knew they were trying to get her into a trap. Finally, one of them came down and actually engaged Lady not twenty yards from me. It was a horrific, vicious, deadly battle. Lady was pushing the coyote back, but it was nip and tuck. Then the other coyote joined in. Lady was amazing. She was whipping them both, but could she keep it up? I started running towards them with my shovel to help Lady. Before I could get there, the coyotes quit and took off running towards a pretty steep brushy hill, with Lady right after them. She knew better, but, with the fight started, she couldn't stop. When they were over halfway up the hill, those coyotes stopped, turned around, and attacked Lady. They had her where they wanted her.

Up on that hill, her size and weight were a disadvantage, and their size and quickness were a huge advantage. The battle raged, and Lady was magnificent. It was a fight to the death. She was outnumbered and outmaneuvered, but she wasn't giving up. She was in terrible trouble: when she turned on one, the other attacked her backside. There was no way I could make it up that hill to help. They were tiring her out, and she couldn't last much longer! Lady gathered her strength and made a desperate attack. She went after one with fierce desperation, ignoring the other's attack from the rear. She overwhelmed her first adversary before turning on the second. Making a last-ditch attack, she drove the second coyote back—biting, snarling, and crashing through the brush. Then, before the other one recovered and attacked her again, Lady broke away and came down that hill. I mean, she was leaping and crashing down that brushy hill, leaving a trail of broken branches.

She stopped when she got to me at the bottom. We both looked up the hill for the coyotes, but they didn't want any more of Lady. We watched as they went out of sight over the top of the hill. Lady was bleeding from wounds all over her body, but, thank the Lord, none of them seemed too serious. We went to the ditch, and I petted and stroked her until she calmed down.

Then I washed her in the cold, clear water. Lady would be fine, and those coyotes didn't try to tease her into a trap after that.

Our dogs and coyotes were mortal enemies, but what about the puppy? We all talked about it. What could have caused that coyote to kidnap that little puppy and then bring it back? Our theory on what had happened was that a pair of coyotes had a litter of pups and something had happened to them. We didn't know if it was disease or a bobcat, but something had killed those pups. In their grief, one of them thought our puppy could replace what they had lost. They tried for four days before deciding it wasn't going to work. The puppy was a dog. It would never be a coyote, but it wasn't the puppy's fault. So instead of killing it or letting it die, they brought it back. When it grew up, they would have a worthy adversary.

That was our theory. What do you think?

PEACH THIEF

BY DAN WADE

My dad never talked a lot about his childhood, but I remember a few things. One story he did tell was that, when he was eight or nine years old, his mom and dad were perplexed about the peaches. Something was eating them and leaving the seed pit just hanging there on the tree. This mystery continued for about a week. "What could be eating the peaches?" was the main topic of conversation at the dinner table. Could it be a bird? No, a bird wouldn't eat a whole peach. How about a possum? No, the branches were too small to hold a possum, and they would break or fall off. No one had any idea what could be eating the peaches, but they sure wanted to catch the thief before they lost too many more. It became their mission to catch the thief, and one night they did.

The thief was my dad, young Heber! He had slipped out to the tree after bedtime, pulled a limb down, and was eating one of those sweet peaches without picking it off the tree. His mom and dad heard a porch board squeak and, being suspicious parents, got up and caught him in the act. There he was, pulling down a branch and eating that peach in his underwear, barefoot in the moonlight. I think he got a whipping for doing it, but he still enjoyed telling of the trick he had played on everyone.

Dad enjoyed telling that story, but, if you think about it, there is more to it than a young boy playing a prank. It was against the rules for little Heber to pick a peach in the back yard. Would you have gotten in trouble for that? Probably not. You probably had to sweep them up off the ground before they rotted. But in those days, Dad's parents had a need and a use for each peach. They planned to make jelly out of them, preserve them, or sell or barter them by the bushel. They didn't have a peach to waste on a young boy with a craving.

DRAWING WATER AT GRANDMOTHER WADE'S
BY DAN WADE

Often as children, when we visited Grandmother Wade's, one of us would get the assignment to "draw some water" for supper (the evening meal). This is how we drew water. First, we would take the water bucket from the kitchen out to the well. The bucket was about one-third smaller than a five-gallon paint can, was made out of galvanized metal, and had a handle like a paint can. The handhold was wood. Out at the well, which was just a little ways in front of the house, we set the water bucket down and moved the unhooked well bucket so that it swung freely from a pulley attached to a rafter. I should back up. The well was hand-dug and rock-lined, and I think about thirty feet deep. The rock lining was about four feet in diameter and extended about three feet above the ground. It looked like what you might have heard called a wishing well. There are replicas in people's yards that have a round base and two posts that support a little roof. The ones that are realistic have a pole going from post to post with a crank handle going through the post into the pole. The crank turns the pole which pulls the rope through the pulley, bringing the bucket up and down.

After freeing the well bucket and releasing the hand crank, we would turn it counter-clockwise and lower the well bucket to the water about fifteen or twenty feet down. The bottom of the bucket was hinged so that, when it hit the water, it would open, allow water in, and let the bucket sink. Well buckets look more like pieces of pipe than buckets. They are about eight inches in diameter and almost four feet long. They hold two buckets of water. After our well bucket hit the water, we let it go just far enough to fill up. Then we started turning the crank the other way, raising the bucket. Raising the bucket applied pressure to the hinged bucket bottom, which caused it to close and seal the bottom. Once we got it cranked up near the top, we would reach over and grab the bail or handle of the bucket. After we had a good hold, we could let go of the crank and lift the well bucket high overhead, so we wouldn't spill the water. Setting it on the ground, we'd lean it over to fill the kitchen water bucket, then we would take the water bucket inside and fill a pot to be heated for washing. After filling another pot, we went back and filled the water bucket again, hung the well bucket back in the well, locked the crank, and hauled the water bucket back inside for cleaning up after supper.

Pretty soon one of the ladies would call out from the kitchen, "Supper's ready. Y'all come wash up." Then everyone lined up at the back door where there was a wash pan with warmed water, a soap bar, and a fresh towel on a peg. We each took turns washing up at the wash pan, then took our seat at the supper table. The last one in line washed up in brown water and dried their hands on a less-than-clean towel, but we all washed up. After we were all seated, one of the brothers would say grace. Grace would vary some, but most blessings would be something like this: "Thank you, Heavenly Father, for this day and all of thy blessings. Bless this food for the good of our bodies. Forgive us our sins, as we forgive those who trespass against us. These things we ask in Jesus's name. Amen." A simple, timeless prayer for simple, God-fearing people.

COLD SHEETS

BY DAN WADE

There is one thing I remember that you could experience for yourself if you wanted to: cold sheets. This is a treat that thermostats and central heating have pretty much eliminated, and, in a way, that is too bad. Let me tell you how to have a real pioneer experience just like the old-timers. The first thing you'll need to do is wait for a good cold day. Then make your bed up with about three or four good heavy blankets, open the window, close the heat vent, and shut the door to your bedroom. At bedtime, your room should be ice cold. Slip into your room, and close the window. You'll notice how cold your room is. Go back out, close the door, and get warmed up. Then start thinking about going to bed and how it is going to feel getting into that cold bed.

There really is only one way to do it. This is how it's done. After you get as warm as you can, it is time to go to bed. Go in your room. I know it's freezing, but you have to take off your shoes, socks, shirt, and pants. Put your pajamas on, hurry up and pull the sheets back, jump in bed, and pull those heavy covers up over you. Those sheets feel like ice cubes! Your body's natural reaction is to escape and move away, but you can't move! You have to stay real still so your body heat will slowly start to warm the bed. After shivering for a while in bed, you will begin to feel like you might not freeze, and you will start to relax. This is when you are going to do the natural thing and roll over to get comfortable. HaEeee! That's cold! You can't move, because the only part of the bed that isn't freezing is right where you are. Later (much later), your body will have warmed the bed enough that you can be comfortable under those blankets—safe and secure from the cold. Now let me tell you, that is a good feeling!

LIP BALM

BY DAN WADE

Dad told us of several health care practices from his boyhood that were a little different. I don't remember many. But I do remember that occasionally he had to go to school wearing garlic around his neck—to ward off infection, I think. Also, the kids were sometimes required to take a stool sample to school to get checked for worms, I guess. While they were required to take a sample, there was no container provided, so they had to find their own. Dad told us of a time that one of his brothers used an empty lip balm tin as a container. They were perfect because they sealed up tight and would fit in your pocket. It seemed like a good idea and probably would have been if, after securing the sample late one afternoon, Dad's brother had not put the container back on the fireplace mantle where the lip balm was always kept.

Sure enough, that evening their father came in after a hard day's work, and, before anyone could say a word, he went to the mantle. He took the top off the balm can, got some "balm" on his finger, and wiped it across his lips. The house was in stunned silence for a moment, then their shocked father held the can out away from himself and yelled, "Sh----t!!!" I think all four boys found somewhere else to be.

CHAPTER 6

GOOD TIMES HUNTING

UNCLE NOEL – CAMPING AND COFFEE
BY DAN WADE

Uncle Noel and his family lived in Roswell, New Mexico, for several years when our family was there. My dad Heber and Uncle Noel took their sons Wayne, Jerry, and Wallace hunting in the mountains every year. One year, they all went in Dad's pickup. Dad, Jerry, and Uncle Noel rode up front, and Wayne and Wallace rode in the bed of the truck with all the camping supplies. Once they got up in the Nogal Mountains near Ruidoso, New Mexico, Dad drove his truck up the old logging road as far as he could, so they would be higher than most of the other hunters. After picking a good camping spot high in the mountains, they stopped, and everybody went to work setting up camp. Uncle Noel took charge of organizing the camp kitchen. He was just about finished before he realized he hadn't seen the coffee.

"Heber," Uncle Noel asked his brother in a worried tone, "where did you pack the coffee?"

Dad replied shortly, "I didn't bring any coffee."

"What do you mean? I thought you said you were bringing the coffee," Uncle Noel said tensely.

"Well I didn't, and I never said I was. I guess we'll just have to do without," was Dad's short reply.

Standing up without saying a word, Uncle Noel snorted with disgust, leaned over, picked up a paper grocery sack, and walked off down the mountain. Their conversation had escalated quickly to a sharp aggressive tone, and their sons were afraid that Dad and Uncle Noel were about to lock horns. In later years, both of them said that it had not even been close to that. However, their sons still think it had been too close for comfort. Uncle Noel walked down the mountain until he came to a road with traffic from other hunters coming into the mountains. I can just see this big tall man with arms about a yard long, hands as big as pie plates, uncontrollable hair, and a big infectious grin flagging those hunters down. I can almost hear his voice as he explained the seriousness of the situation. He was in the mountains without coffee!

After his explanation, he was able to get fellow coffee lovers to stop, get out of their trucks, and dig through their gear until they found their coffee. After they had done all that, he would only accept a couple of dippers full, no more than that. He didn't want to be the cause of anybody running short of coffee. I don't know how many hunters he had to flag down, only taking two dippers full at a time, before he had gathered six days' supply of coffee in his grocery sack. When he decided he had enough, he walked all the way back up the mountain to their campsite and, without saying a word to anyone, went about making a pot of coffee. Uncle Noel was serious about his coffee.

DONNA GETS A REST, KINDA
BY DAN WADE

After Donna had asked to go for several years, Dad finally decided that, at nine years old, she was old enough to go with the menfolk on their yearly hunting trip. She really wanted to go with them, and, the first morning when they set out from camp before daylight, she was ready and excited to be part of the group. She was hiking with Dad, Jerry, and Wallace. Going up and down those mountains was tough. Donna tried, but she just couldn't keep up and kept falling farther and farther behind. When Dad and the boys stopped to rest, she was so happy and proud to catch up to them, so she could rest, too. The trouble was that, by the time she had caught up with the others, they had almost gotten their wind back. So it seemed she had barely sat down before they were ready to go again. This pattern repeated itself several times. She would just get caught up, and they were ready to go. Finally she decided that, when they stopped to rest, she would rest, too. She never did get caught up, but she did get some rest. (I've always had this picture in my mind of a little girl huddled by herself on the side of a mountain, watching to see when her dad and brothers Jerry and Wallace got up to go. Then she would get up and go, too.)

Her younger sister Jenny thought it unfair that Donna

got to go hunting and she didn't, even though Donna was two years older. The year she was old enough to go hunting with everybody finally arrived. Now it was Jenny's turn to go hunting—boy, was she excited!—but then almost as soon as they got to the hunting camp, Donna came down with a bad case of the mumps. So they had to take Donna back home; she was really sick. Jenny is still mad that she got sent home with Donna, just in case she came down with the mumps, too. She didn't get to go hunting, and she didn't catch the mumps, and she still thinks it was unfair.

MY FIRST DEER HUNT

BY DAN WADE

In 1967, I was almost twelve years old, and I felt it was high time that I was allowed to hunt deer and help supply meat for the family. So I prepared my arguments supporting my readiness to be trusted with a high-powered rifle off in the woods by myself. After getting my nerve up, I approached Dad and Mom and said that I wanted to take my horse Firecracker, Wallace's .30-30 rifle, and go hunting for a deer. Dad surprised me by saying, "You'll have to be careful, but we could use the meat." I didn't even have to use any of my arguments! Dad said "yes"!

Well, I didn't wait around for him to change his mind. I got Wallace's old .30-30 loaded, saddled Firecracker up, and headed out. I was on an adventure! It was my first time hunting anything besides rabbits, birds, or porcupines. Daniel Boone and Davy Crockett, watch out! There's a new hunter in the woods.

I rode out of the barnyard at noon, armed and dangerous. Being the "experienced" hunter I was from all the reading and listening I had done, my plan was to ride up on top of the hills across the valley from our house and ride the ridgeline. I would ride along the ridge, go to the edge, and then scan the hillside for deer. We were about a mile from the house on the ridge above Chokecherry Canyon when I spotted a spike buck on the hillside about 100 yards below me. Oh, boy! This was it—meat in the freezer! I had heard of even experienced hunters getting excited and missing an easy shot. They have a name for that, "buck fever," and I was determined it wasn't going to get me. I wasn't going to take any chances. That young buck didn't know I was there. I swung down off Firecracker real easy, keeping an eye on that buck all the time. He just had little spikes, but I wasn't hunting horns. There weren't any good rests nearby where I could steady my rifle, and I was afraid to shoot freehand because I was so excited. No trees, no post, just a horse. A horse! Well, why not?

I pulled on the reins, laid the rifle over Firecracker's neck, and took careful aim through those peep sights. Remembering everything that I had been taught, I took a deep breath and slowly squeezed the trigger. Boom! My horse didn't even flinch, and that deer didn't take one step. It dropped dead. Wow! I had done it! I had really done it! I was a great hunter!

What now? No problem. I would just ride down there and field dress that deer. Had I ever done that? No, I really hadn't ever done any more than hold a leg, but I had seen it done. It shouldn't take me too long. I couldn't wait to ride up to the house with that buck across the back of my saddle just like in the movies. Mom and Dad were going to be proud.

I had to go on up the ridge a ways before I found a place to ride down the hill. When I got to the deer, he was in some short brush, and it was pretty steep. I tied Firecracker and climbed down to go to work. All I had was my Barlow pocket knife which I would learn to sharpen in a few more years. I was pretty sure the first thing to do was cut his throat, so that is what I tried to do. Tried is all I did. As hard as I sawed at his neck with that dull old Barlow, I couldn't break the skin. What was I going to do? Well, I had watched my dad sharpen his knife on a whetstone many times. How hard could it be? After I found a flat piece of sandstone, I spit on it and started rubbing the blade on the rock just like I had seen my dad do. I did that for a while, then I tried it on the deer again. No luck. There was more to sharpening a knife than I thought. I knew I couldn't lift the buck to get him on the horse, so I was out of options. Going back to the house and asking for help was all I could do. Firecracker and I made good time down through Chokecherry Canyon and the mile or so back to the house.

I had only been gone a couple of hours, and Mom and Dad were surprised to see me. But they were really surprised when I told them I had killed a deer. "You did what?" Dad asked. Mom and Dad looked at each other. I could tell they hadn't expected this. After a few more questions, Dad said he would take the truck up the road and park there. Then he planned to walk through the hayfield and up the canyon to help me with the deer.

Dad parked the truck by a gap in the fence going into our

hayfield. He had brought a couple of sheets and his knife. I didn't ask what the sheets were for, and he didn't say. We went across the hayfield and up through Chokecherry Canyon—Dad walking and me riding Firecracker. Dad looked surprised when we got up to my deer. He shook his head and looked at me. "That is not a deer." I couldn't believe my ears. "What do you mean?" I stammered. Dad chuckled. "That is not a deer. That is an elk." He pointed to the obvious differences that I had been too excited to notice. The difference in color, shape of the feet, and plenty of other differences. I had expected a deer, so that is what I saw, but it turned out to be a yearling elk. I couldn't believe it. My first deer was an elk!

Dad didn't waste any time. It was getting on in the afternoon, and we had a lot of work to do. We pulled the elk to a spot that wasn't quite as brushy and a little flatter. Then my dad went to work with his knife. Dad had grown up trapping, hunting, and slaughtering cattle and hogs for meat. They didn't have a grocery store around the corner. Then, after Mom and he got married, he was a professional butcher for a while. What he did with that young elk was amazing. While telling me to hold this and pull that, he skinned it there on the ground without letting any meat touch the ground. Then I learned what the sheets were for. Dad had me spread the first sheet out as best I could, then he started handing me pieces of meat. First the hams, flanks, tenderloins, shoulder, neck, and brisket. Then we turned him over and filled the other sheet. When Dad got finished, all that was left was bones.

The meat was sacked up in the sheets, and we tied those sacks onto my saddle. We were ready to go home. The sun was getting low when we started back to the truck. As we were going across the hayfield, we saw a truck coming from way up the road. There wasn't much traffic on that road, and it would probably be a neighbor. If it was, they would probably stop to visit. We had tied one sack on each side of Firecracker's saddle for balance, but we didn't want to visit a neighbor with a sheet full of red meat hanging in plain sight. So, I untied the one on the left side real quick and swung it over to my right side and just held onto it. When the truck came by or stopped, I would turn Firecracker sideways to hide our meat. As we neared the road, the truck was getting close and sure enough it started slowing down. But it wasn't a neighbor. It was the game warden!

Gene Bassett was a good man, and I don't think he really tried to catch us hunting out of season. But he was as tough as they come, and he would not ignore two bloody sacks of meat. While the truck was coming to a stop, we were still a little ways in the field. Dad said, "Just stay here and keep that horse sideways." Then he hurried up to the road. Sure enough, the game warden stopped his truck and got out to visit. Dad leaned up against the hood of the truck and took out his Beech-Nut chewing tobacco, and he offered some to Gene. After getting his chew, they started to visit like they had all the time in the world. I was sweating. The sun had just set so maybe the dripping from the sacks wasn't visible from thirty feet. But trying to keep my horse still with my left hand and holding the sack of meat with my right were really tricky. Plus, Firecracker was a horse that liked to go! Holding him still was not easy. I constantly had to hold him back and keep him sideways.

Were they going to talk all night? My trying to control my horse caught the game warden's attention. "That horse sure wants to go, doesn't he?" he said to me. "Yes sir, he sure does." "Well, you had better be careful. That sure looks like a lot of horse." "Yes sir, I will," I said. What next? Is he going to want to pet my horse? Dad jumped in and said, "We don't want to hold you up any longer." He continued, "I know you want to get home to your family." The game warden replied, "Well, I guess I should go. Good to see you, Mr. Wade." While they exchanged pleasantries, I was trying to hold my horse still and not drop those sacks of meat with all I had. I was sweating bullets. Finally, Mr. Bassett left, and I rode up to the truck. Dad said, just as calm as could be, "Well, that was a good visit. Let's go home."

I was ready. I couldn't wait to see Mom's face when she saw all the meat! Not only was I a great hunter, I was a pretty good outlaw, and my dad could do anything.

I did learn how to sharpen my Barlow pocket knife, and, to this day, the knife I have in my pocket will shave the hair on your arms. There is a lesson there: having a dull knife is about the same as not having one at all.

EASIEST HUNT

BY DAN WADE

Our ranch in Colorado had several hundred acres of alfalfa hay and quite a bit of irrigated pasture. If you shined a light on our fields at night, all you could see were rabbits and deer, lots of deer. In the late fall and winter, it was not unusual for us to have anywhere from 200 to 400 head of elk grazing in our alfalfa fields. They came down from the high country looking for food. Dad believed that feeding that much wildlife gave us the right to hunt elk and deer anytime we needed meat for the table. That's what Dad believed, but we knew the game warden wouldn't agree and would throw the book at us if he ever caught us hunting or, as he would call it, poaching. We were friendly with the warden; he was a good man whom we respected. Dad and he simply had different perspectives. The warden considered all hunting out of season and without a license as illegal poaching. Dad considered "harvesting game"—fattened on our fields—as partial payment for the crops they ate. We kept our freezer full of deer and elk that were fattened on our grass and alfalfa. We did try not to be blatant about it, and the warden might not have watched us as closely as he could have. For Dad, I think it was of out of principle that we never bought a hunting license and hunted whenever meat was needed.

One fine fall day after getting caught up on chores and projects, Wallace and I decided to go out and see if we could get an elk. It was a couple of weeks before hunting season started, so we would have the woods all to ourselves. The elk weren't in the hayfields yet, but we had seen some in the hills behind the house. We both carried a .30-30 Winchester lever-action rifle. We were good shots, but we'd soon find that neither one of us were immune to getting excited at the site of a 900-pound elk right in front of us. "Buck fever" could strike at any time, even though this was far from our first hunt. Starting out in the hills behind the house, we were hunting as soon as we left. We kept a sharp eye out while walking quietly through the hills, but we really didn't expect to find elk until we got about a mile out. We weren't surprised when we jumped about eight head in a brushy flat, a mile from the house. They took off fast, crashing through the brush; we didn't have a chance for a shot. Chasing them through the brush wasn't a good idea. Wallace said our best chance for success was for him to get ahead of the herd by circling around and climbing up on the ridge that they were headed for. I would stay about where we were; in case he turned them back, I might get a shot.

That was the plan; it was a good plan. After Wallace left, I leaned up against a tree and waited. I didn't have to wait more than half an hour before Wallace got in the middle that little herd. When he opened up with that lever-action .30-30, it sounded like a young war. I got worried; he didn't know exactly where I was, and I sure didn't know where he was shooting. There was an arroyo behind me about three feet deep. The bottom of that arroyo looked a lot safer than where I was standing, so I got in it. Wallace was still shooting, but he had slowed way down after reloading. I was lying in the bottom of that arroyo peeking over the top when—low and behold!—a nice spike bull ran up and stopped broadside, just twenty yards away. Oh, wow, what a shot! I jumped up, and that spike just stood there looking at me. He was so close I could have hit him with a rock. I whipped up that rifle, worked the lever, and, aiming from the hip, pulled the trigger. Just like they do in the movies. Boom! Then that spike took off in fine health. I was shocked! I was so close. How could I have missed? I was shaking my head in disgust when, on my other side, a nice fat cow ran up and stopped about twenty yards away just posing for me. I couldn't miss again! No more "buck fever." Carefully levering my rifle, I turned and brought it to my shoulder. I aimed carefully with those peep sights straight for the heart and s-q-u-e-e-z-e-d the trigger. That cow took off running, too. Had I missed again? I thought I'd seen some dust pop up on her side after firing, but I wasn't certain. Wallace called down, "Hey, Dan, did you get one?" "I'm not sure. Did you?" I called. "No, I didn't. I'm coming down." It took a little time for Wallace to get down off the ridge. When he joined me, we exchanged stories.

After leaving me, Wallace had practically gotten run over up on that brushy ridge. He'd never gotten a good shot; they were all over him. He said he was mostly shooting in self-defense. I told him I must have missed that big spike, but surely I'd hit the cow. We decided to follow her tracks. She wasn't easy to trail through the brush, but we stuck with it, and, after 100 yards or so without seeing a drop of blood, we were discouraged. It sure looked like I'd missed, and we would go home without any meat. We stuck with her trail, though, and, at about 150 yards, there she was—lying on the ground, dead. It amazed us; after being shot through the heart, she was still able to run that far. We'd got our elk and over 300 pounds of good meat! Wallace and I were laughing and talking while we did the field dressing. We knew Mom and Dad would be glad to get the meat.

After Wallace and I finished with the dressing, we walked back to the house and reported our success. Dad said he'd come help haul her home. The three of us got in the truck and headed out. Because that cow had run so far downhill, we were able to drive right through the trees and load her in the truck. Back at the house, we decided the weather was cool enough to hang the carcass on our game rack (it was out of sight, behind the house) and let the meat age for a couple of weeks. Then we would cut and wrap the meat and put it in the freezer. From the time we left the house till we got the elk hung and skinned wasn't more than two hours. That was the quickest, easiest, and most enjoyable elk hunt we ever had.

A FAMILY HARVEST

BY DAN WADE

Dad bought the ranch in Colorado in 1963. Growing up, I do not remember ever eating beef. Mom said that elk tasted a lot like beef, but I just had to take her word for it. We ate deer and elk that were fattened in our pastures and alfalfa fields. I guess it could be argued that we didn't hunt, we "harvested." Before Wallace graduated and left home, it was his job to keep our freezer full. After he left home, the job eventually fell to me when I got old enough. Both of us knew every square inch of our place like the back of our hand. We knew where the deer stayed and their habits. If mother told us she was low on meat, we knew where to go to get it.

There were times in the fall, though, that the whole family would get involved in the deer harvest. Our ranch was a long valley with a pretty steep line of hills forming our southern boundary. At the bottom of the hills was a belt of pine forest that was a great habitat for deer. On the western end of our place, those steep hills formed a box canyon. I think it was Dad's idea for the family to work as a team on our deer harvest. His plan was to have our two best shots, himself and one of my brothers (either Jerry or Wallace), posted on the side of that box canyon where they could see the entire canyon. It was all in range of their rifles. Then he would have my sisters, Donna and Jenny, and me get on horses and start riding from the east end of our place in the pines at the base of those steep hills westward towards that box canyon. The three of us would spread out in those pine trees and just ride slowly west, and the deer would move away from us. There was about a mile of forest before we got to the canyon. Some years, there would be over thirty deer in that box canyon before my dad and brother started shooting. The deer could get out of the canyon, but, while they were going up those steep sides, they were in rifle range. My dad and brothers were good shots. Our best year was six deer. They were dressed, skinned, and hung up behind the house before ten o'clock in the morning. Now, *that* was a great harvest!

A GREAT HUNT

BY DAN WADE

One of the first times my cousin Wayne Wade came to our ranch in Corona, New Mexico, to hunt for antelope, he was stressed from work and barely made time for the hunt. On top of being just about worn out from work, he was having a terrible allergy attack. He was determined to have a good hunt even with watery eyes and sneezing all the time. He and I left the house before daylight, but he stopped me in the driveway to go back and get his leather satchel. That satchel must have weighed twenty pounds and was stuffed to the breaking point with files and papers, all relating to his business. I wondered, "What in the world does he want his files for? But, oh well, we're going hunting." I had the headlights on, heading east down the ranch road. Wayne was miserable—wiping his eyes, sneezing, and blowing his nose the whole way. The sun was coming up by the time we got to the hunting grounds. I hoped it would help.

For some reason, I just then remembered to ask Wayne if he had his hunting license. He said, "Yeah. We had better stop and get it out of my satchel." So I pulled over, and we got out. Wayne grabbed his satchel and started trying to find his license. He said, "Gail put it in here somewhere." Even with his reading glasses, Wayne's eyes were watering so badly he could hardly see. Frustration set in pretty quickly. He couldn't see well enough to find it, so I offered to help. This was before I had really admitted to needing glasses, so when Wayne handed me a two-inch stack of papers, I squinted and tried to tell if one of them was a hunting license. We struggled through a couple of handfuls of paper, but it was taking a lot of time, and we were not even close to halfway through. I started getting tickled, thinking how silly we must look. Here we were, standing by a dirt road in the high plains: a couple of middle-aged men who could barely see, trying to find one piece of legal-looking paper in a stack of several thousand legal-looking papers. Soon we were both laughing at ourselves. We decided that, if the game warden stopped us, he could find the dang thing for himself! Of course, Wayne got a nice buck, and we didn't get stopped by the warden before getting back to the house. The first thing Wayne said to his wife Gail was, "Where did you hide my license?" Gail easily picked it out of the mass of papers on her first try. Now, *that* was a great hunt!

THE HUNTING CAMP

BY DAN WADE

I think it was the second or third deer hunt on the Corona ranch that a group of cousins from Mississippi came out, and we all stayed at the "hunting camp" for deer season. It was a new camp. A couple of days before, it had been known as a hay barn. What now made it a hunting camp was a woodstove, newly installed by a real good cowboy, and some military surplus bunks that I had "repurposed" after finding them in the dump. That first night, we didn't build a big fire in the woodstove because we learned that the good cowboy was not a great woodstove installer. The stove smoked really badly, and even a small fire was barely tolerable only because the wind blowing through the cracks in the barn walls cleared the smoke out a little. It was a cold first night in the camp. The temperature dropped way down close to zero, and that barn was so drafty that you practically had to sit on that smoky stove to get any heat. We all spent a long, cold night in our sleeping bags and were glad when it was finally time to get up. I will never forget my cousin Robbie Smith's words when he and I stepped out the barn door. When the cold wind hit him, Robbie said, "Humph! It is a little warmer inside." We had a great hunt, smoky barn and all.

The following summer, I fixed the stove and did a little work on the camp. It was a much better camp for the next hunt.

SIGHTING OL' BIGGIE

by Dan Wade

My nephew Tyler Wade was the first person to go hunting with me on the Corona ranch. It was his first—or almost his first—deer hunt. I tried to help him with what I knew about working through rough country hunting for deer, and he worked hard all day but never got a shot. He kept a good attitude, though, and we left the house even earlier the next day. We bounced around those ranch roads for forty-five minutes before we got to the bottom of Baker Canyon just as it was starting to get light. "Tyler, look!" I said. There in the shadows of a steep hill was the biggest deer I have ever seen. I am talking huge! Tyler scrambled to get a shell in the chamber and climb out of the truck to shoot at the monster. It was almost shooting light, and that beautiful buck was standing broadside at sixty yards. BOOM! Tyler pulled the trigger, and that buck seemed to sprout wings. Up the hill he went. Dang, missed! Then suddenly we heard rocks rolling to our left. There was another buck going up the hill. A big one! He stopped just as he skylined and just looked at us. It was lighter now. Tyler took his time and squeezed the trigger. BOOM! That deer dropped in his tracks. We had him dressed and in the truck before nine o'clock. Another great hunt.

Through the years, that monster who got away came to be called "Ol' Biggie." Tyler was far from the last one to miss a chance to take him home.

OL' BIGGIE WINS AGAIN
BY DAN WADE

One hunting season, cousin Robbie Smith and Jim Peden, a member of the family and a good friend, were out together in a pickup coming back to camp from hunting all day. Robbie had shot a pretty good buck earlier, so he couldn't shoot again. They were driving through some cholla-cactus flats when Robbie spotted Ol' Biggie out about fifty yards in the cactus. Seeing that beautiful monster buck would excite even a casual hunter, and Robbie and Jim are not casual hunters. Robbie jumped out of the truck and, out of habit, took his rifle. Jim was right behind him with his. Robbie was using his scope to look at Ol' Biggie, saying excitedly to Jim, "Shoot him, Jim, shoot him!"

The trouble was that Robbie was standing between Jim and the biggest buck any of us had ever seen with his rifle lined up like he was going to fire. Jim couldn't get around Robbie because of the cactus, and he couldn't shoot because Robbie was between him and the buck of a lifetime. So Jim said, "Move, Robbie!" Robbie couldn't move because of the cactus, so he squatted down, saying again, "Shoot him, Jim, shoot him!" We didn't get to find out if Jim would have shot over Robbie's head because, about that time, Ol' Biggie took off. I don't know what was said between them after Ol' Biggie took off, but, when they got back to camp, neither one of them would say a word. They wouldn't speak to each other or anyone else. When we asked what was wrong, they would just shake their heads. It took days for us to learn what happened. It came out just a little at a time, and it was a year before either one of them could smile about the time they almost got Ol' Biggie. Now, *that* was a great hunt!

BUCKS AND A JEEP

by Dan Wade

My cousins Jesse Smith and James Morgan and a longtime friend of Jesse's father JR, Mr. Pat Pierce, came out from Mississippi to our new ranch near Corona, New Mexico, for a deer hunting trip about ten years ago. I think it was only the second time we had family and friends out to go hunting on the ranch. We sure enjoyed our cousins, and I gained a good friend in Mr. Pierce. The first time we had family out to the ranch to go hunting was a year or two earlier when my nephew Tyler came. He got a real nice ten-point buck and had a good shot at Ol' Biggie. Remember, Ol' Biggie was that monster buck that just took your breath away. In the coming years, several people would see Ol' Biggie. Robbie and Jim probably came the closest to getting him, but nobody ever brought Ol' Biggie down. Ten years is a long time for my memory, but a few things stand out from that hunt. I wonder how those men remember it.

James got there early enough for him and me to take a tour of the hunting grounds the day before the season started. On the way back to headquarters, we saw a pretty good buck on the road. James thought that getting one just like it would do just fine. Jesse and Mr. Pierce were at the house when we got back. We all visited about the hunt, planning to get up early in the morning. James took lead on getting supper put together. I don't remember what it was, probably the Colonel's fried chicken. While doing that, James spilled a little something and needed a broom to clean up. He looked in the obvious places, then he came to me and asked where our broom was. I replied confidently, "The pantry." James said he'd already looked there. A little less confidently, I suggested the hall closet. No, James had looked there, too. "Well, I guess I'm not sure we even have a broom," I was embarrassed to admit. James gave me a look that conveyed incredulity. He decided I was not going to be any help finding the broom and continued the search without me. I soon learned from James that we did own a broom, but I'm still not sure where he found it.

We all enjoyed the evening, then we got a good sleep, woke up early, got a good breakfast, and went hunting. I had an old, open-top, Willys Jeep and a Chevy extended-cab pickup. As I recall, James and I rode in the pickup, and Jesse and Mr. Pierce took the Jeep. For those guys, it was a real cool twelve-mile ride to the hunting grounds. Jesse and Mr. Pierce were cold, but they were having a great time in that old Jeep. I had a plan for the morning's hunt, and we got to the starting point before daylight. I laid out my plan in which Jesse and Mr. Pierce were to drive a big, wide, deep, mile-long canyon. By "drive the canyon," I mean they would start at the top and walk down the canyon, driving the deer in front of them. We should end up with those deer in a sack. Jesse was to stay up on the west slope, and Mr. Pierce was to stay in the bottom and a little on the east side. They would wait to start until James and I got into position. If James or I took a shot, we should turn the deer back towards them. James drove the Jeep down the ridge road to a point I had described to him, parked, then hiked towards the bottom of the canyon, and found a good shooting position near our north fence line. I drove the pickup to the next pasture and went down the fence line, stopped, climbed the fence, hiked to the halfway point of the canyon, and picked a spot where I had a good field of fire clear across the canyon.

We all carried walkie-talkies. When I got in position, I checked in with James. He was in position and ready. It would be shooting light soon. A cold, clear morning with plenty of deer, in the foothills of the Rocky Mountains—it doesn't get better than that. My wife Daina and I had scouted that canyon a couple of times and had seen over twenty nice bucks each time. We'd also spotted Ol' Biggie, a real deal "holy cow" buck. He was so big, we almost thought he was an elk. When you saw him with the binoculars, all you could say was "Holy Cow!" I just may have mentioned him to the guys the night before while we talked about today's hunt. Keying the walkie-talkie, I gave Jesse and Mr. Pierce the go-ahead, and they were ready. The hunt was on!

The sun was coming up and shining on the higher slopes. It would take a while before the canyon bottom saw any sunshine. I could already hear and glimpse deer moving among the trees in the canyon bottom. When Jesse and Mr. Pierce started walking down the canyon, it was going to get exciting! I was seeing more and more activity, and I was sure there would be gunshots at any moment. Being the host, I didn't want to take the first shot and passed on a couple of decent bucks. Then I saw two really good ten-pointers at about 350 yards on the side of the hill across the canyon. I tried, but, on the side of that steep hill, I couldn't get into a good position for a long shot. Didn't someone else see them? James should be less than 100 yards from them. Jesse or James should have had at least as good a shot as I did.

Still, no one had fired a shot. In an excited whisper, Jesse came on the radio and said he was right in the middle of some good bucks! Mr. Pierce keyed his radio, and, in his normal voice, said, "Do you have a shot, Jesse?" Jesse replied firmly, in his best college-vice-president whisper, "Keep your voice down, Pat!" I didn't have to see Mr. Pierce to know that his jaw was clenched and he was gripping his rifle so hard his knuckles were white. Jesse was so excited by the deer, I don't think he even realized what he'd said, but Mr. Pierce did. He knew exactly what he had been told. He had been told to shush. I'll bet his mother had been the last person in the world to tell him to keep his voice down. Certainly not someone young enough to be his son. This situation had the possibilities of getting out of hand if we weren't careful. It could get serious, but, the more I thought about it, the more I couldn't help it. I started laughing! I laughed so hard I almost fell down the hill. Jesse Smith, our future college president, wanted Mr. Pierce to whisper so his loud voice wouldn't scare the deer. But Jesse didn't think to use the little control knob on top of his walkie-talkie marked "Volume."

Jesse and Mr. Pierce were past the halfway point down the canyon. Why hadn't anyone taken a shot? The canyon was full of deer, but why weren't we shooting? I knew that at any moment that canyon was going to explode. All of a sudden it did. James let loose in the bottom of the canyon—one loud boom, then another. Finally, some action! We were probably going to carry at least one deer out of that hole. I was straining my ears, hoping to hear more shots because time was running out. I saw Jesse. He was almost to the north fence, and the drive was over. Somehow our sack had developed a hole. Had we done any good at all? "Do you need help with your deer?" I asked James over the radio. "No," he answered back, "I almost got run over, but I missed." Mr. Pierce and I joined up. He was tense, but we spoke for a while, and he began to see some humor in the situation. He knew Jesse had meant no disrespect; he'd just been excited. Both of us were disappointed that no one had gotten a deer. James and Jesse joined us. We had all seen good deer, but we just hadn't finished the deal, and we all had a story to tell. We were disappointed but not discouraged. There was a lot of time left in the day. All of us walked back up the hill talking about our next plan. We'd get one next time.

When we got to the Jeep where James had parked, the plan was to get in it and go to my truck. Then we would split up and go hunt in different areas. We all jumped in the Jeep, and I turned the key. Nothing! I knew right away why it wouldn't start. If the key wasn't turned off to just the exact spot, the battery would run down. I guess I hadn't explained that to James very well. Luckily there was a downward slope in front of us. A dead battery shouldn't be a problem, because we could push-start the Jeep. With three men pushing and me popping the clutch, we managed to push it all the way down the hill without getting it started. There we were, stuck with a dead Jeep. What should we do? My truck wasn't far away, but I didn't have any jumper cables. It would take almost three hours to go back to the house and get cables. We could all go hunting with my truck, but it would be crowded, and we couldn't cover as much country.

We were all mulling the situation, and the options weren't good. I was kicking myself. I should have explained the Jeep key better to James. I should have had cables in my truck. The Jeep should have started when we pushed it. I got to thinking, what are cables? Wire. We were standing by a fence made of wire! We could get wire. Would that work? I asked Mr. Pierce, "Could we use wire for cables?" His eyes lit up. "Heck yeah, we can use wire." We got my truck up next to the Jeep and borrowed some wire from the fence with the pliers on my Leatherman Multi-Tool. We didn't have clamps, so we held that rusty barbed wire tight to the battery posts on the jeep and my truck, and it worked just fine. The Jeep started up, and we went on with the hunt.

The rest of the hunt is a great story, but it's a story for another time. Or even a story for someone else to tell. Jesse? James?

A TOUGH INITIATION

BY DAN WADE

One year, a big group came out from Mississippi to our Corona Ranch, and, for the first time, my cousin Norman Smith came out to hunt. Mr. Pat Pierce, a longtime family friend, was also there. Before those hunts, I had never really gotten to know Norman. I had met Mr. Pierce once before on a previous hunt. It was because of this hunt that I became good friends with both of them.

After Norman got to the camp, he spent time taking all of his hunting equipment out of Walmart packages. He had just about bought Walmart out: gloves, vest, cap, knife, canteen, binoculars, and plenty of other things. Since he was the new guy that year, Norman got the top bunk, which was sort of tough. I didn't get the ladders built until the following year. After hunting hard all day without success, Norman was discouraged and about worn out. A good supper of burgers and beans helped him feel better. After we all ate, some of us were standing around comparing notes about the day's hunt. At one point, Norman said with disgust, "I am fifty-five years old, and I have never killed a deer!" Having known Norman all his life, Mr. Pierce replied, "Well, Norman, I believe this is the first time you have ever gone hunting." We all laughed and gave

Norman a hard time. It was all in good fun, and we enjoyed the evening. After that, Norman worked hard, hunting every day, but without success.

Norman is not one to discourage easily, though; he came back to try again the next year. That was when Norman killed his first deer. It happened like this. Norman and Robbie are brothers, and, like a lot of brothers, they are alike in a lot of ways and as different as night and day in others. At times, they rubbed each other the wrong way. This hunt was the first time they had spent much time together for a long time. We had all been having a good time, but both of them had hunted hard for three days without any luck. It came to the last day of the hunt, and we were all tired. After lunch, the three of us decided to get in Norman's rental car—a hatchback—and just drive around on the two-track ranch roads to see if we could find a deer. We had bounced around on those rough roads for a couple of hours, not seeing anything, when Robbie and I spotted two deer out about 700 yards in a clearing in the cholla cactus. With binoculars, Robbie and I could tell they were both bucks, but for some reason Norman couldn't see them, and he was irritated about that.

Robbie and I decided that the best plan was for him and Norman to try to sneak up on the deer by walking and dodging through the thick cactus until they got close enough to take a shot. If they were successful, I would follow, picking my way through the cactus in the car. Norman was still irritated because he couldn't spot the deer, but he finally agreed to the plan. They set off through the cactus walking; then, as they got closer, they were bending over going from one clump to the next. I think they crawled the last 100 yards until those bucks were in range, just grazing on the high mesa. To be successful, they knew they had to shoot at almost the same time. They were about thirty yards apart, so they used hand signals to let each other know they were ready, then they fired! From where I was, it sounded like one shot. When I got to them in the car, both of them were grinning from ear to ear. We had two bucks on the ground. It was well after dark by the time we got those deer dressed, loaded, and back to camp. Now, *that* was a great hunt!

ORYX HUNTING

BY TOM WADE

Waylon Wade, my cousin, posted on Facebook recently about being at the Trinity Site, where they tested the first atomic bomb that helped end World War II, and also mentioned he had put in for the Oryx Hunt on the White Sands Missile Range in New Mexico. Waylon, I hope you draw out. It is a great hunt. Your post made me remember the time when, a few years ago, I drew my once in a lifetime permit for that Oryx Hunt.

I was allowed to bring one other person, so of course I asked my dad, Jerry Wade, to go. The day before the hunt, we had to go to a class discussing the differences between oryx and North American game animals. Then we had to go to a class on the hunt areas within the White Sands Missile Range. I was assigned an area in the southern part of the range. It was a two-day hunt. They told everyone to hunt their assigned area the first day, and, if unsuccessful, then we could go to other areas the second day. Dad and I decided we would not shoot anything the first day. This was a once in a lifetime chance to explore the entire missile range.

We spent the first day driving the entire southern half. The southern half of the Tularosa Basin is all desert and a lot of it! Big Country. The second day, we headed north. Totally different country—lots of hills, trees, and many springs. Here we saw many of the old ranches that used to be in the area. We got to see lots of deer, turkey, and several bobcats. One of the things they told us about the north end was to never drive off-road. This was where they did most of their bombing, and there could be unexploded ordinance lying about. This did not keep Dad from exploring some of the old ranch headquarters; the ranchers had been forced to sell out to the government when they decided to develop the missile range. I was quite nervous about getting caught. We had set a deadline of one o'clock to shoot something. We kept pushing deeper into the hills, and around one-thirty we found a large group of oryx up a canyon. I jumped out of the truck and hiked around to a good vantage spot about a half mile from the road. I settled in to select my trophy. I took the shot at 150 yards, and the oryx jumped straight down the canyon and then came running up the other side right at me! I was amazed. Did I miss? No, the huge animal came crashing down to the ground fifteen feet from where I was standing! I stood there for a moment and then went looking for a way to signal Dad. The only problem was, he was not there. Confused, I moved up the canyon to get a better view of the road—still nothing. I could not figure out where Dad had gone. I started walking back to the oryx, and Dad came busting through the brush in my new truck! All I could think of was how they had stressed not to drive off-road, and here Dad had driven a half mile off-road. He burst out of the truck, jumping up and down with excitement. He said that was the coolest thing he had ever seen; he had seen the whole thing through his binoculars. He grabbed his knife and started field dressing the oryx. I asked him if he was worried about getting in trouble for driving off-road, and he just laughed and said, "Naw, we'll be fine."

After field dressing and loading the animal in the truck, Dad and I spent another hour hiking over the hill where we found an old adobe ranch house, a sizeable spring, and pens made out of stone. We ended up pulling into the check station with five minutes to spare. The military police officer had some stern words for us, and Dad had some interesting words for him. It was definitely a once-in-a-lifetime hunt. Dad was always up for an adventure and did so with the energy and excitement of a young person.

MY FIRST ANTELOPE HUNT
BY WAYLON WADE

At this point in my life, I consider myself a fairly competent hunter; however, I began hunting fairly late in life. It was 2000, and I had only recently graduated from college. Dan had a ranch near Claunch, New Mexico (not to be confused with his current ranch near Corona). I had been there one time before and had been impressed by just how flat it was and how many pronghorn antelope he had roaming the place. Since I'd never gone hunting, I was surprised when my dad, Wallace Wade, told me that his brother Dan had a couple of spare hunting tags and wanted to know if we would be interested using them. Of course I jumped at the chance.

Growing up like most boys who were raised in the country, I learned how to shoot. However, it was always with a .22 rifle. The larger guns had more expensive ammo, were louder, kicked harder, and just weren't as much fun to take out and use to make a soda can dance. So I never really felt the desire to shoot anything larger than my dad's single-shot, bolt-action .22, which of course had open sights.

Dad and I got up really early and left Albuquerque on the drive to the ranch, which is about two and a half hours away.

After about two hours, I became curious; I'd never actually seen hunting tags or licenses before. I asked Dad if he could show them to me. "Oh!" was the only word he said to me as he patted his pockets. This is the moment I realized two things: first, that the tags were still sitting in an envelope on the kitchen table some 100 miles away in Albuquerque; and, second, that for the rest of my life I would never trust anyone else to know where my hunting tag was. I asked if we should turn around and go get them, to which Dad replied, "Nah, it'll be fine."

We talked about the upcoming hunt, and Dad mentioned that, when we reached Dan's ranch, we should check to see if the rifles we had brought were sighted in. Now these two firearms were old; the lever-action .30-30 with open sights that I was going to be using was one my dad had bought and used as a teen in the 1960s. Dad would be using Pop's (James Heber Wade) old .30-06, which I knew two things about: first, it had been used to harvest more deer and elk than I would probably ever see; and, second, that the only instances when it had been off the set of elk antlers that had been its makeshift gun rack for the entirety of my life were the multiple times it had been knocked down and landed squarely on the battered scope that it still carried from the late 1950s.

When we reached the ranch, Dan greeted us and asked if we were ready to go hunting. Dad told him we sure were, and we loaded up in his truck. I did ask Dad about sighting in the rifles. "Nah, it'll be fine," he said.

As I mentioned before, the ranch was just thick with antelope, and we drove up on a herd in short order. The three of us immediately hopped out of the truck. I chambered a round in the .30-30 because I thought that was the thing to do. Dan said that we were too far off for me to try with the rifle I had and that Dad should take the first shot. It was at this point that I realized my rifle was cocked and had a bullet in the chamber. I was certain that it wasn't a great idea to have a cocked and loaded rifle if I wasn't intending to shoot. I looked in vain to try and find the safety as Dad was trying to determine which antelope he was going to line up on. I started to panic. Where was the safety? How do I get the bullet out of the chamber? I should at least let the hammer down so the gun wasn't cocked any longer. I placed my thumb on the hammer and pulled the trigger to release it. I didn't feel anything, so without thinking I lifted my thumb which was holding the rifle's hammer. In an instant, that .30-30 went off, the bullet impacting the ground just inches from my toes, and the rifle jumped in my loose grasp while letting out a loud report, which caused Dan, my dad, and me to jump and sent the herd of antelope galloping off at a run. Although his eyes were wide with disbelief that I could be so dangerously incompetent, Dan said simply with a laugh, "Well, Wallace, I guess Waylon didn't want you taking that one after all."

We got back in the truck—my face red and hands shaking with embarrassment—and headed off to find a less spooked group of antelope. Fortunately, we were back on the critters shortly, and it was someone else's turn to look the fool.

Approaching the next group of antelope, we hopped out of the truck, and Dad and Dan started picking out the next target. Once one had been singled out, Dad lined up on him. Now, my father, while not renowned as the best marksman in the family, is a fine shot. He grew up hunting both for sport and for supper, and, in all my years, I'd never seen him look uncomfortable shooting. Well, he looked uncomfortable now. He would line up, then line up again, then line up some more, before having to straighten up and look in the direction of the antelope which were placidly grazing without giving any thought to the three of us. Finally, Dad took the shot; he missed, badly. The critters shuffled around but didn't run off, and Dad lined up again and again missed badly. Dan looked a little perplexed but didn't say anything. Eventually we ran into a lone buck, and Dad managed to make the shot to take him.

We took Dad's antelope back to the ranch house to skin it out. As we were hanging it up and starting to get to work, two things were revealed. First off, that old scope on Dad's rifle was so beat up that it was only slightly more useful than a kaleidoscope. I took it out, and trying to look through it gave me motion sickness in just a few seconds. The other and much more important thing that came to light was that we didn't have our hunting tags with us. Which has to be the biggest noob move in a day that was filled with noob moves. Dan was positively dumbfounded. All he could do was wipe his face and repeat back to Dad, "You forgot your tags?" in astonishment.

Years later, I would find out that, while Dad and I were finishing up putting the antelope in the cooler, Dan sought out a game warden he knew to tell him of the situation involving his foolish family members who had purchased legal tags but didn't think to bring them. From what I gather, the game warden was as astonished as Dan was and told him something along the lines of, "Just tell them not to make things too obvious."

It was now my turn to try and get an antelope, and what followed was just a comedy of missed shots and failed stalks. Remembering it now, I can almost hear *The Benny Hill Show* theme playing as I burn ammo and seriously startle unharmed antelope after unharmed antelope with my ineptitude using that .30-30. To this day, I'm not sure if the gun's sights were off, or I was just that bad of a shot. As daylight was running out, Dan finally insisted that I use his rifle, which was a very nice and accurately sighted-in 6mm. We came up on what was undoubtedly the last antelope of the day. He had no concern for us or the truck and was only fifty yards away as I lined up and proceeded to send a bullet zipping six feet over his head. The creature jogged out to a little over 200 yards and was trotting across the edge of the pasture near the tree line. I chambered another round and lined up again at this shot that was well outside of the range that I had any business shooting. Dan, who by this time had to be exhausted with chauffeuring around his brother and neophyte nephew, was just opening his mouth to tell me not to waste another bullet as I squeezed the trigger. The antelope stumbled and was dropping before the echoes of the rifle report had faded. In what can only be described as a voice that was both breathy with disbelief and giddy at the same time, Dan said, "You hit him.... I can't believe you hit him!" In all my years, I have never seen Dan as surprised as he was in that moment. I am certain you could have knocked him over with a feather.

After we loaded the buck into the bed of his truck, Dan reached into his pocket and handed me a shell casing. He said, "After what I saw earlier today, I would have told you there was no way you were going to make that shot. I want you to keep this, and, whenever you look at it, remember: Never let anyone tell you that you can't do something." I still have that shell casing. I've been on a lot of hunts since that one, but it will always be special; and I am fairly sure both Dan and my dad would tell you the same.

CHAPTER 7

WHATEVER IT TAKES

GROCERY SHOPPING

BY DAN WADE

I had moved with my first wife Debbie, seven-year-old April, and six-year-old Joshua into a mobile home on forty acres on the Red Mesa, a high plateau about eighteen miles southwest of Durango, Colorado. The kids went to a great country school, and we had good neighbors and good friends in the community. We had a couple of horses and a few cattle, the kids had a pony, and there was even a good sledding hill. It doesn't get much better than that. I was also in debt up to my ears.

The year was about 1981; I was seven years out of high school. For some reason, with the economy slowing and interest rates rising, I decided it was a fine time to quit my job and go into business for myself as a contractor. I was wrong; the timing could hardly have been worse. It was a constant struggle to stay busy. I worked hard to develop business by making the rounds each week, talking to insurance adjusters and architects, introducing myself, and offering my services. It took some time, but after a while my efforts paid off, and they began giving me opportunities to bid on work. For a couple of years, work went pretty well—not great—but I was able to support my family and somehow keep up with my payments. As the interest rates continued to rise, it got harder and harder to find work, and getting paid for the work became even more difficult.

That was the situation I had gotten myself into. We were barely getting the bills paid, and every dollar was spent before I got it. I finished a pretty good job where I had had to spend my own money to pay wages and buy materials. After the final inspection on the job was done and I was ready to get paid, my client, who until then had been on the jobsite every day, was suddenly hard to find. I needed the money! I had spent my last nickel on supplies and wages, and not getting paid meant not buying groceries. Not being able to provide for my family was a terrifying prospect. Determined to get the money owed me, I went to town, staked out the client's office, drove by his house, and checked out his favorite watering holes. I didn't find him, and I couldn't get paid. Finally, I gave up and went home. Walking into the house with no groceries and no money and seeing the disappointment in my family's eyes was more than I could take. I had to do something!

It was late summer, and a half mile down the county road from our house was an open field. Almost every evening there was a small bunch of deer grazing there. The gravel road wasn't busy, but it did have some traffic, and it was broad daylight. My family needed meat! I decided to go "grocery shopping." I took my old single-shot .22 rifle and drove down the road. The rifle had been a gift from my parents when I was about ten years old. That old .22 and I had been "shopping" many times before. Sure enough, the deer were there grazing in the pasture about fifty yards from the road. I stopped the truck, pointed my rifle out the window, picked out a nice spike buck, took careful aim, and shot him in the head. He dropped like a sack of rocks. I looked up and down the road; no one was in sight. I drove up the road a little ways. I still didn't see anyone, and the coast looked clear, so I turned around and went back.

I needed to get that buck loaded in the pickup as quickly as possible and head back home. The pasture had a good net-wire fence with two strands of barbed wire on top. That net wire was stretched tight and done right. Dragging the deer under the fence wasn't possible. I would have to lift him over. That wouldn't be easy. He wasn't a big deer, but he still weighed around 250 pounds. I stopped the truck and climbed over the fence as fast as I could, then ran out to grab the buck. When I got to him, I noticed that he only had one antler, but I didn't think anything about it. Grabbing him by his one horn, I dragged him to the fence as fast as I could. After I got to the fence, I let his horn go and started trying to get a grip around his body to lift him over the fence. That's when his missing horn started to make sense. I must have shot his horn off and knocked him unconscious, because he was still alive! That buck came to and started kicking around and got his feet under him. As he scrambled up to escape, I grabbed him by his one horn, jumped on his back, and held on. He might be leaving but not without me! I was riding that buck, determined not to lose him. I grabbed my belt knife with my free hand, pulled back on his horn with the other, reached up, and cut his throat. That buck carried me running another fifty feet from the fence before he finally went down throwing me in the dirt. I jumped up, grabbed that one horn again, and dragged him bleeding back to the fence. Somehow, after that excitement I was stronger. Now I was able to lift him high enough to get his head and shoulders over the fence. After that I just pushed his back end up and over till he fell on the other side. There was blood all over me. I was rushing. I needed to go! Somebody could drive by at any moment. I was not only poaching, I was also trespassing! After jumping over the fence, I dragged the deer through the bar ditch to my pickup. Letting the tailgate down, I managed to get that buck loaded up, shut the tailgate, jumped in the cab, and headed home.

What a relief it was to get back to our driveway! I hadn't been caught or arrested, and there was some good meat in the pickup. I pulled up behind the house, and little nine-year-old April helped me skin and dress the deer there in the back of the truck. After we finished skinning and dressing the deer, I cut us some good, fresh, venison steaks. We had a great supper that night, and I managed to get paid the next day. We bought some *real* groceries, paid our bills, and went on from there. Putting one foot ahead of the other, that's all I have ever known to do.

CRAZY COW AND KIDS IN CHARGE

by Dan Wade

After our family moved to the ranch in Colorado, Dad decided to get a cow herd started. I guess after reading about Charolais cattle that were imported from France, he decided that was the breed he wanted to raise. They are a breed of large white cattle that were just beginning to become popular at that time. Dad found a rancher just across the line in New Mexico who had brought in Charolais bulls to use on his Brahman cows. He had been doing it long enough to have some seven-eighths to nearly purebred cows. Coming off a big ranch and being bred down out of Brahman cattle, those cattle were wild. We started off with ten head of bred cows. They were all wild, but most of them settled down some after we brought them to our ranch. There was one we named Pet, and she was real gentle. Tank wasn't mean, but, when she had a calf, you sure needed to watch her. Several others were protective of their calves, but Ol' Crazy and Spot Eye were just flat-out mean, and, when they had a calf, they were every bit as dangerous as a mama grizzly.

The first couple of years we had the ranch, we fed the cows in a corral by the barn. After a few snows, the corral would become a muddy mess. It would be frozen in the mornings and boggy by the afternoon. The cows would be up to their knees in that mess, and so were we whenever we went in the corral.

Dad started working out of town, and, when I was nine or ten years old, the care and feeding responsibility for the cows fell mainly to me. Donna and Jenny both pitched in and helped feed the cows before school, but their care was my responsibility. My sisters and I were all out in the dark before school on many winter mornings, when the temperature was way below zero, hauling seventy-pound bales out to the cows. When Dad would come home on Friday night, I was the one he looked to for a report on the week. Having to give a bad report was something I dreaded. The biggest concern was keeping the baby calves alive. That was my job. Realizing that I might need some help, Mom and Dad asked our neighbor Mr. Snow to be my backup in case I got in a jam and needed help.

One cold February day, Ol' Crazy, the cow we were most afraid of, had a calf right in the middle of the corral, and it couldn't get up on its feet in that cold, sloppy mess. Donna and I tried to get to the calf, but that cow would put us over the fence whenever we got in the pen. We were scared to death of that cow, so, after talking it over with Mom, she called and asked Mr. Snow to come help. He came right over, and I told him the situation. He listened to me tell how mean that crazy cow was, but I could tell he wasn't impressed. He assured my mom that he would have no problem with just one old cow, and, with a little help from me, we'd have that calf up and going in no time. So Mr. Snow and I headed down to the corrals. He carried a little stockman's whip in his hand. As we walked, I tried again to impress him with how mean that cow was. Mr. Snow just chuckled and told me not to worry.

When we got to the pens, the calf was still there stuck in mud. Ol' Crazy was way off to the side with some other cows. That feed pen was pretty big, about fifty yards across and a hundred yards long. On one side were the feed bunks, and on the other was a good fence and three sheds—each about twenty yards apart, connected by the corral fence. We used one shed for a tack room to store saddles and such, the second was a feed shed for the milking pen, and the third was for storing different things. Despite my warnings, Mr. Snow just walked through the gate and into the pen like he owned the place. I stayed right on his heels. It was, after all, my job to take care of that calf. Ol' Crazy was on the other side of the corral, and she didn't react until Mr. Snow bent over to grab that calf. When he did that, she bellowed and started charging us through the mud. I wanted to run, but Mr. Snow calmly stood his ground, popped that little whip, and yelled "Hey, cow!" in a loud, stern voice. He was sure that cow would stop, but she almost ran over him before he saw that she wasn't stopping, and, at the last second, he leaped to the side.

While Ol' Crazy was sliding to a stop in the muck, I took off running for the side of the corral. Mr. Snow was right behind me running through the deep slop. Before we were halfway to the fence, Ol' Crazy was charging after us again, and Mr. Snow wasn't behind me anymore; he was leading the way. That cow was gaining, and she was almost on top of us when Mr. Snow leaped to the third rail on the fence where it ran into the saddle shed, and from there he pulled himself up onto the roof of that shed. I was right behind him, but I couldn't jump as high, and that cow was charging fast. Mr. Snow reached down and grabbed my arm and pulled me up on the roof, just as that 1,500-pound cow hit the fence. We were safe! Safe, but we were stuck on top of that shed. Ol' Crazy was snorting and bellowing, trying to climb that shed and get us. There we were, trapped on the roof with that cow daring us to climb down. Mr. Snow somehow still had his little whip, but all we could do was sit on the roof and hope that cow would go away. After at least a half hour or so, Ol' Crazy finally lost interest and wandered far enough away that we could climb down to the fence and out of the corral. Mr. Snow decided that as much as he would like to stay and help, he had pressing commitments elsewhere.

That calf was still stuck in the mud, and, if we didn't figure something out quick before dark, it would die. Donna and I put our heads together and decided a different approach was called for. After giving it some thought, we took some bales of hay into the pasture just outside the corral and opened the corral gate, luring the cows out with the hay. It worked! Ol' Crazy came out of the feed pen with the other cows, and we climbed over the fence and closed the gate so she couldn't get back in. We got that baby calf out of the mud, rubbed it with feed sacks to warm it up, and then fed it a little warm milk. Pretty soon it was feeling good enough for us to slip it outside the pen where

Ol' Crazy could mother it. She gave her calf a good licking, and before long it was nursing. That calf was going to be fine. Despite some obstacles, we got the job done. We never bothered Mr. Snow again.

BUILDING FENCE
BY DONNA WADE

Late in the year 1980, I was very lucky to have obtained a brand new small home, just wonderful for my son Tyler and myself. At that time, he was about nine months old, so not having a fenced-in backyard was not a problem. Time went by, and a new house was being built next door. Tyler was about two years old now. I was out with him and the little neighbor girl in the backyard, watching them play. I went inside for just a moment, and, when I came back out, my son was very red in the face and could hardly walk. The little girl said he drank from a can that had been left by the new house. It was paint thinner! Oh, my gosh! He survived, and so did I, but soon thereafter I started putting up a wood picket fence.

Two of my nephews, Tom and Roy—Jerry's sons—who were maybe eleven and ten years old, came and helped build fence all one afternoon. Those pickets they put up weren't as straight as they should have been, but—you know something?—that section they did was very special to me. I loved the fact that they wanted to help me so that nothing like that would happen to Tyler again. A little thing but so very special.

UNCLE NOEL DIVING FOR LOGS
BY DAN WADE

In the heyday of the logging boom in Mississippi, they floated huge rafts of hundreds of logs down the great rivers. Some of these big logs were more dense and heavier than others, and, after some time, they would just sink. Those big rivers had hundreds and hundreds of these sinkers. After the big timber was mostly logged out, people went back for those sinkers. Because of their density, they were premium timber. Since they were completely submerged, they would last forever. All a person had to do to get that valuable timber was locate it, hook a cable to it, and winch it out. Yep, that's all there was to it.

Maybe someone knows how they went about finding the logs. I guess they must have used some sort of a drag, and, whenever they thought they found a log, someone like Uncle Noel would dive down in that murky water, which was probably anywhere from ten to over twenty feet deep. After reaching the bottom, he would have to feel around and find the log, if that is what they felt with the drag. Once a log was identified, a cable had to be secured around it. That log might have been there for years, and silt would be built up all around it. In order to tie a cable to the log, he would have to dig the silt and mud from around and under it, feed the cable under the log, and secure it with a shackle. Only then could he go to the surface and breathe! That's right, he did all that while holding his breath. They didn't have diving equipment, goggles, or lights. What Uncle Noel and others like him had were amazing swimming skills, strength, courage, and a desperate desire to provide for their families.

THE TREASURE IN THE CHICKEN PEN
BY DAN WADE

Our first summer in Colorado was 1964. Dad had worked all winter and spring getting the house livable. Next on the long list of projects was fixing up an old chicken pen. It needed a lot of work. The house part was more like a shed, and the pen was a large enclosure made with chicken wire and some boards. This pen had not been used for years, and brush and weeds had just about overgrown it. I am not real sure what Dad's plan was for the chicken pen, but, as an eight-year-old, I was glad to help. Donna, Jenny, and I were having a lot of fun "helping." Dad and Wallace were really doing the work, but they were enjoying themselves, too. Wallace had the job of digging some post holes, and the rest of us were clearing brush and cleaning up old debris. Dad was straightening up the fence.

Since moving to Colorado and into our new home, several neighbors had told us that, in the old days, our ranch was rumored to have been a rustlers' hangout. Others said it had been a stage stop as well. Whatever it had been, it was our home now, and we loved every bit of it.

Like many kids throughout history, we were completely innocent of any knowledge of our parents' financial situation.

We never heard them say a word about it, but somehow it was still known that Dad was not finding as much work as he had expected, and there was some concern about that. We didn't really understand anything; we were just aware of some concern.

Both of those things started to come to mind when Wallace's posthole digger hit something metal almost two feet deep. What was it? Whatever it was, he couldn't break through with the diggers, so he moved over about a foot and tried again. Same thing! What could it be? Now even Dad was curious, too. He got a shovel and helped Wallace make the hole bigger. They cleaned out a hole almost two feet by two feet, and it was solid steel. We kids figured it out. There was only one thing it could be: a strong box. Had the rustlers buried their treasure? This was it! A whole box of gold! What else could it be? Mama and Daddy wouldn't worry anymore. Dig faster! The hole got bigger, and the strong box lid was still there. Dig faster! They finally found the edge. Dig it out!

The hole got bigger, and they cleaned out around the edge. What is that? Clean it more. Is that...? Oh, no! It is. It's teeth, steel teeth. All of us realized it was no treasure. What we had discovered was a long, buried saw blade. Dad and Wallace went ahead and dug it out. It was a big forty-eight-inch, circular saw blade buried in the dirt—who knows how long ago or why? If we had not believed that steel Wallace had hit with the posthole digger was the lid to a great treasure, we would have been excited to find that great old saw blade. It wasn't a treasure, though. It was just a saw blade. We went on with our work that day, but the sun wasn't nearly as bright. Mom and Dad would still worry, and there wasn't a thing we could do to help. None of us ever had a bit of interest in that giant old saw blade.

CASH MONEY
BY DAN WADE

While Dad was growing up, his family grew or made almost everything they needed. But there were things they needed that required what they called "cash money." They sold their cotton crop for cash, but, too often, most of that money was owed to their creditors. They had to borrow money almost every year to put in the new crop and to use for living expenses. Any cash left over after paying off the loan had to be put away for the next year, only to be used for absolute necessities and emergencies. You never knew what might come up.

For things that weren't absolutely necessary like shoes, shirts, pants, or maybe a new hat, they had to get "cash money." They did many things to earn some "cash money." One thing they did was cut stove wood. For a wood cookstove, the wood has to be cut just right: twelve inches long and split into pieces no bigger than two inches thick. This wood was sold by the cord. A cord of wood measures four feet by four feet by eight feet long. The wood had to be stacked honestly. If a buyer saw a lot of air in the stack, he knew he was being cheated.

They cut the wood with a crosscut saw and an ax. I don't know how you can appreciate just how much work that is unless you have done it. Let me try to describe the process so you can understand how it was done. First, you find a good tall tree, say about sixty to a hundred feet tall and three to four feet in diameter. Score it really well in the direction you want it to fall, then, using your two-man crosscut, cut that big tree down. Now the work starts. First, with ax and saw, cut all the limbs off and set aside the ones big enough to make firewood out of. Get your saw, go to the end of the log, and mark a spot twelve inches from the end of that three-foot-in-diameter log. Cut it all the way through, one long saw stroke at a time. Do that about sixty or more times, and keep that saw moving. Now that you have it blocked up, there are sixty twelve-inch-by-thirty-six-inch blocks to split. Get your ax, your wedges, and your sledge hammer. Start splitting those blocks. Remember those blocks have to be reduced to two-inch stove wood, twelve inches long. Are you tired yet? After you get it all split, start loading it onto a wagon, and haul it with your mule team to your customer's house. It will take two trips. Stack it up into a cord, and stack it right because they will check it out. If it is not stacked tight, they will make you do it again, and they will think you were trying to cheat them. Do you get the idea? Anyone that cuts a cord of stove wood with a crosscut saw and an ax isn't afraid of work—hard physical work. The going rate for a cord of stove wood was about the going rate for a day's work: less than five dollars. Do you want to tell the men who did this about your hard day at work?

SKINNING SKUNKS

BY DAN WADE

Another way they earned "cash money" was trapping game to sell the fur. They usually caught raccoons, possums, foxes, and sometimes skunks. Dad said they made pretty good money on most of the fur, but the skunks didn't pay as well as the others. Their hides only brought about a quarter apiece. My dad and his brothers trapped, skinned, scraped, and stretched skunk hides for twenty-five cents apiece. Think about it. They could have opened the trap and left them to rot, but they needed that quarter. They needed it bad enough to skin a skunk!

Several times in my life, I've found myself in a jam for money. During those times, I've worked very hard for very little pay and been glad to get it. All the while I was working for just enough money to buy some groceries, I always consoled myself with the thought that things might be pretty tough, but "I've never yet had to skin a skunk."

How badly would you need money to get you to skin a skunk?

PROTECTING THE HAY STACK
BY DAN WADE

Growing up on a ranch in Colorado, alfalfa hay was a big part of our lives. All of us were involved with hay in some capacity. Donna and Jenny spent many hours on a John Deere tractor, mowing and raking. They helped haul it, too. The first year or two of hauling hay was a real family affair—Dad, Jerry, Wallace, Donna, Jenny, and me. The girls and I all learned to drive a pickup with a standard transmission in the hayfields. We all had fun. It was an adventure the first few years; after that, it turned into my work. Donna and Jenny decided they didn't like their arm muscles developing like a man's. Jerry and Wallace got busy with life and came home less often. Dad started to work out of town, so I slowly became the hay-hauling specialist. It seemed to me sometimes that my life was consumed by alfalfa hay. Haul it all summer; feed it all winter. In the winter, we'd put the cows in a fifty-acre trap, right next to the haystack. Every morning, we'd load about forty bales of hay on the trailer and drive the tractor into the trap, often through two or three feet of snow. When Dad was home, he'd drive the tractor, and I'd throw the hay from the trailer as he drove. When he was out of town, I would be by myself. So, after I got the trailer loaded and drove the tractor into the field, I'd throw a few bales from the trailer; then I'd get back on the tractor, pull up, and do it again.

One winter, when we had more snow and colder weather than usual, a herd of maybe fifteen or twenty elk decided to stay on our property. They found our haystack and would push the fence down just about every other night. Elk can jump fences just fine, but they often seemed to enjoy tearing them down. Dad didn't like fixing the fence or feeding those elk alfalfa, but what really made him mad was that those elk wouldn't just eat the hay; they climbed all over the stack. They'd tear up the bales, making a big mess.

Dad decided he'd had enough. It was time to do something, and he decided to kill two birds with one stone. We could always use meat, and the elk needed to be scared off from our haystack. So he developed a plan. First, he would wait for a bright, moonlit night. Second, he would dress real warm—long johns, coveralls, coat, and gloves. Next, he would load his .30-06 and walk the quarter mile from the house to the haystack. He didn't want to take the truck and have the neighbors wonder why it was on the road by the haystack at night. We didn't like to draw attention and considered that what we did on our land was nobody's business. Now that he had a plan, all he had to do was wait for a moonlit night. It soon came. On a cold clear night with a full moon, Dad got prepared, and, after walking up to the haystack, he climbed to the top and moved some bales around, building a snug windbreak. Now all he had to do was wait for the elk. They should be coming soon.

That night was cold (fifteen degrees below zero!), clear, and moonlit. Dad would be able to see well enough to shoot. He had gotten into position and settled in by six o'clock. The elk finally came out of the trees across the valley about a half mile away at eleven o'clock. He had been waiting for five hours; the long johns, coveralls, and coat weren't enough. Dad was cold—shivering, bone-chilling, can't-feel-your-feet, freezing cold. Coming home and trying another night would have been reasonable, but the elk were right there! Surely they would come across to the haystack soon.

He watched them coming; they weren't in any hurry, just fooling around crossing the valley. Dad was freezing. It was after midnight when they finally came through the fence to the haystack. Dad was a very good shot normally, but he was shaking so badly that aiming the rifle was tough. After lining it up as well as he could, he took a shot. It was a hit, but not a kill shot; the elk was hit in the shoulder and ran with the others, back across the valley. Half the job was done. Those elk wouldn't be back, but he couldn't let that wounded elk go if he could help it. Somehow, he steadied himself and fired, knocking that elk down about 200 yards into the pasture.

It was about one thirty when Dad woke me up to go help. He hugged the coal stove, warming up while I got dressed, and he filled me in on the situation. Our plan now was to head back to the haystack, drive the tractor out to the elk, field dress it, and then drag it back to the stack. We made quick work of the field dressing. While Dad drove the tractor, dragging the carcass, my job was to kick snow over the blood trail. Sounds easy, doesn't it? It was almost impossible to do.

The snow crust was strong enough to hold me up for just a second before breaking, and then down I'd go. Three feet of snow up to my hips. Then, I would do it again. The crust was about six inches thick and would break into large pieces. The snow underneath was like powder, and, when I kicked it over the blood, it was like kicking dust. I covered the intestines with crust as well as I could and kicked the powdery snow at the blood trail.

Dad and I were both freezing by the time we got back to the haystack. We threw a tarp over the carcass after we dragged it to the haystack and headed back to the house—and the stove. It was only about one hour until dawn. The game warden often drove past our place just a little after daybreak while patrolling for poachers, and we wanted to make sure that we hadn't left any evidence in sight. After warming at the stove, we headed back up to the haystack before sunrise. It was light enough to see that we were in trouble; the blood trail was pretty clear. I hadn't done a very good job kicking that powdery snow over it.

Dad and I loaded that hay wagon in record time. Dad drove the tractor right on his tracks from the night before and I threw the hay on the blood trail. The cows lined up, eating the hay. As we pulled back to the stack, the only evidence left was the carcass beneath the tarp.

We saw the warden's truck coming, and then he stopped

his truck up on the road. He would often stop and come down to the haystack to visit. On most days that was fine; however, on this day, we had a fresh-killed elk under a tarp. Dad rushed up to the road, greeting the warden like a long-lost friend. They had a good visit there on the road. I stayed down by the stack, acting busy; my clothes had quite a bit of elk blood on them. After the game warden finally left, we had work to do. Dad had been up all night, but we still had that elk to deal with. We hauled it back to the house and went to work. Mom, Dad, and I managed to get that elk cut, wrapped, and in the freezer by early afternoon.

It was a good feeling when we finished. We had meat in the freezer, and those elk wouldn't be tearing our fence down and eating our hay or destroying our haystack. Dad almost froze, and we almost got caught. But he didn't, and we didn't. He got his two birds with one stone.

JERRY AND UNCLE HASKELL

BY DAN WADE

Jerry and I flew to Jackson, Mississippi, and Jerry rented a car as soon as we heard that Aunt Willie Mae, Uncle Haskell's dear wife, had passed. We were there to support Uncle Hack and to represent the Western Wades. We got there late in the afternoon and spent the evening trying to be a comfort to our uncle. Uncle Hack was a strong man but brokenhearted, and we could see his pain. I think we all finally got a little sleep that night.

The next morning Uncle Hack had some errands he needed to do. We all got in the rental car, Jerry drove, Uncle Hack took shotgun, and I sat in the back. I would soon find out I had the best seat in the house. Our first stop was going to be the pharmacy. Jerry, of course, depended on Uncle Hack for directions. As Jerry pulled away from the house, Uncle Hack pointed him in a general direction, towards a busy street. We were at the stop sign for a minute before Jerry got the word to turn left. Off we went; there was no conversation, grief was heavy in the car. "Turn here," Uncle Hack said loudly and impatiently, as if Jerry should have known where to turn. We were right at the turn when Jerry got the direction, and he almost had to lock the tires to make the turn. That's how it was at every turn. Jerry did really well, getting yelled at, for the entire trip. I know he was glad when we finally got to the pharmacy, but the trip wasn't over yet. As we pulled into the parking lot, Uncle Hack ordered Jerry to "Stop here!" Jerry did, and Uncle Hack got out of the car and walked over to a plainly marked empty parking space. He then turned and whistled to get Jerry's attention and, with both hands held high, directed Jerry into the parking spot, making sure Jerry knew how to turn the wheels and when to straighten them all the way to the curb. I was trying really hard not to laugh, but Jerry wasn't finding anything funny at the time.

Of course, we were there to pick up some medicine, but Uncle Hack was in no hurry. He took us up to a clerk working in the aisle and introduced us. "Adam," he said, "I want you to meet my nephews." Then he made sure he had Adam's full attention before he continued. "This is my youngest brother Heber's oldest son. They moved west when he was fifteen, but he was born over in the Myrick community. He now lives out in Farmington, New Mexico. That's up near the Colorado border." He continued, "Jerry's a homebuilder with his father." He waited while Jerry and Adam shook hands and exchanged pleasantries. "Now this is Dan. He's Heber's youngest son. He was born out in New Mexico, but he was mostly raised on a ranch in Colorado. Dan is the youngest son of a youngest son. He still lives in Colorado. Dan was named after me. My first name is Daniel, too." Adam and I shook hands. I could see he was confused; he just wanted to get back to work. He had seen

Uncle Hack enough to say "hi" to, but he sure had no interest in his nephews. We were introduced several more times all around the store. Everyone stopped what they were doing for Uncle Hack. He had a presence about him that held people's attention.

Jerry and I stayed with him through the funeral, then we had to get back home. Uncle Hack sure missed his dear Willie Mae. It was sad to leave him all by himself. We could only hope he'd be okay. He was ok, but terribly lonely. David Wilson is Uncle Haskell's brother Noel's grandson. At that time, he was struggling to find his place in the world. I believe the good Lord was watching over both of them. David moved in with Uncle Haskell soon after the funeral; they were an unlikely pair, but helping and being helped was a true blessing for both of them. One was in his final days, and one was getting a fresh start. They were good for each other; they were family.

DIGGING STUMPS
BY DAN WADE

I remember Uncle Noel telling us about digging up stumps for "cash money" during World War II. The United States Department of War used the sap or resin in the making of munitions. That Mississippi country was full of old stumps from all the logging of those old giant long-leaf pines. Those stumps sold by the pound. They might be three to four feet in diameter. The job was to dig down all around the stump and chop the roots with an ax until you could pull it free with a team of mules, then load that stump on a wagon. They would try to get as many stumps on the wagon as they could haul, then take the load to the railroad station to get them weighed and loaded on the train. They got paid by the ton. Think about it. The next time you feel like you're overworked, think again.

CHAPTER 8

LESSONS FROM LIFE

COTTON PICKING

BY JENNY WADE CHILSON

Why does no one see me?

Why does no one hear me?

Hello! I am here!

Really, just give me a chance! I want a life, too!

For most of my life, those were my inner cries.

I was six years old at that time. But not just ordinary six years old. I was the fourth child and the second daughter. And, I had a baby brother. The perfect birth order for being the forgotten kid, the invisible kid.

My parents were busy doing whatever parents do. And, that included watching after Jerry, Wallace and Donna and helping them go to school, do sports, go to work, play with friends, and do all kinds of fun things outside of the house. That also included watching after the baby, my little brother, Dan. And, then, there was me. Instead of grouping me with the verbal kids and letting me have independence and responsibility, I stayed "grouped" with the baby! No matter how hard I tried to show I was more like the real kids than the baby, I just had to wait.

That's what they always told me. Just wait. Day after day I waited. Finally things started to change after turning six years old! That magical age meant I got to go to school! Finally, I left the baby behind. No more being in the baby group for me!

Life was finally getting to be something I could enjoy! One beautiful Saturday morning, Daddy was going to go to a job site to do some work and he was taking Jerry and Wallace along with him to work, too. Daddy was very big on building character in his kids through work. He decided that Donna and I should do some character building work while they were gone. So, he took us aside and told us that the first thing we should do that day was take some cotton-picking bags out to our cotton field and pick some cotton. He wanted us to each pick fifteen pounds of cotton.

Well, that was great. This was the first time we had ever had this job. And, I was sure it was going to be an easy one! I loved being a real kid, a big kid, at long last!

We were just headed out the door to go to the cotton field when our neighbor friend Kay Mahan rode up on her bicycle. We were so happy to see her, but I was especially glad to see her, since I had only recently been allowed to start being a part of the big kid group. Donna was eight years old, and Kay was even older, she was eleven. I loved Kay because I thought she knew everything, and she treated me with respect; not like I was someone that just got released from the baby group.

Kay wanted us to go for a bike ride with her. We told her that we couldn't do that until we completed our cotton-picking job. That didn't bother her at all. In fact, she said the cotton-picking sounded fun, and she could join with us and pick fifteen pounds, too; then we could all play! Well, that's what you call a good friend. Someone that wants to have fun with you, no matter if it is working or playing! So, the three of us each got our big long cotton bags, and we headed out to the field of cotton. We were full of chatter and laughs. The sun was bright and hot. We started picking cotton, and it seemed easy. The cotton was soft and pulled out from the boll easily. We pulled out the cotton, then opened our bags and dropped it in. Then, we reached back, got scratched a little, and picked some more. We picked and picked, and it got hotter and hotter. Donna said we should weigh our bags to see if we had enough. We dragged our long bags over to the scale over at the side of the field, and the scale barely moved! We didn't have enough cotton. How could that be?

Well, we were disheartened, but we knew we had more work to do; so the three of us went back to our cotton rows and picked and picked some more. Our laughing had mostly stopped as we became more serious at our work. Our hands kept getting scratched by the cotton plants, and we kept looking up at the sun beating down on us and getting hotter and hotter. I looked at my bag and was sure it must have enough cotton in it, so I said it was time to test the scale again. So, over to the scale we went, dragging our cotton bags behind us. Again, the scale disappointed us. We were barely at five pounds!

So, back to the cotton row we dragged our bags. Our steps were slower, and our shoulders were drooping. This was hard work! We knew we had hours to go to finally pick our quota of cotton! We had just started picking cotton again when Kay suddenly said she had an idea!! She bent over and picked up a nice big clod of dirt! She held it up, and she said if we put clods of dirt like that in our bags, our bags would weigh more! I looked at her in amazement. There she stood, holding up a dirt clod with the most genius idea I had ever heard. I really thought beams of light were radiating down on her from heaven. She was such a genius. It made perfect sense. The three of us suddenly had our happiness back! We each started grabbing dirt clods and putting them in our bags!! There were thousands of dirt clods!! We didn't have to stop at fifteen pounds!

We drug our bags back to the scales, and we had bags to be proud of! Our bags weighed over thirty pounds! Oh, Daddy was going to be so happy with us. I vividly remember wondering if he was as smart as Kay, and, that if he didn't know this trick, I should tell him so that he could make more money.

We left our cotton bags at the scales, and then we headed out for good times on our bikes! The day just got better and better. Soon Daddy and the boys returned, and Kay left for her house. I knew dinner would be a happy time after Daddy saw our great success for the day.

Donna and I were on the sidewalk playing jacks when I looked up and saw Daddy coming toward us. Something was wrong. I was sure he had been to the cotton scales, but he looked mad, not happy. He got near us, and he told us to come inside with him. We knew something was very wrong. He took us into his bedroom and had us stand side-by-side. He stood in front of us and told us that he found dirt clods in our cotton bags. He asked us if we put the dirt clods in the bags. We looked up and shook our heads up and down.

I knew by the sternness of his face and the anger in his voice that what I had thought was pure awesome genius was something very bad, instead. He confirmed that with his next words. He told us that putting dirt clods in our bags was a form of lying and cheating. He said he was very ashamed that we would try to lie and cheat instead of doing honorable work. He said that we had to be punished for what we had done. But he said that we could choose our punishment. We could have a verbal scolding, or we could have a spanking.

Donna looked straight at him and said, "Spanking." I quickly looked at up at her. I was shocked that she would make the wrong choice, and I answered, "No, scolding!" But, Daddy said it was too late, Donna had spoken first, and I wouldn't get a choice. So, he grabbed Donna and started spanking away. He was holding her by the arm and spanking away at her bottom. She stood as still as a post, looking straight ahead without giving any reaction. I was standing there watching the punishment I was about to get, and I was paralyzed with fear and wishing I could disappear. Then, Daddy let Donna go and grabbed my arm and started spanking away. I was running away in a circle around him and crying out every time he hit me. It hurt so much! Finally, it stopped, and Daddy told us to go to our bedroom. We ran down the hall to our room and shut the door. I was still crying when we got into the room, and I yelled at Donna, "That was stupid to choose a spanking!" She just shrugged. Then, she spoke the words that hurt more than the spanking.

"You're a baby," she said.

HOW TO SHAKE A MAN'S HAND
by Terry Wade

My Uncle Dan's stories are great, and, since he mentioned at the get-together last night that others should write some of their recollections, I thought I would add an early life lesson from Pop, my grandfather (Heber Wade). I was still pretty young—likely around eight years old or so. Jerry Wade, my dad, and Pop had taken me to a work site where they introduced me to another man who shook my hand. After the man left, Pop sternly (at least it seemed sternly to my young mind) informed me that, when you shook a man's hand, you did it firmly and looked him straight in the eye. It was what men did, and you could tell a lot about a man by his handshake.

That lesson has stayed with me, and I notice it at every Wade get-together—certainly with my dad, Jerry Wade, and his brothers, Dan and Wallace. It has also been great to shake hands with my nephews Bryce, Matt, and Garrett Wade and to see that it has been successfully passed to following generations. My daughter Tara knows the importance of a good handshake, too, to the extent that she once was telling me about a boy at school and said, "You would like him; he has a good handshake." Just one of many good life lessons that Pop passed down.

STRENGTH IN FAMILY
BY APRIL WADE TURK

It's been a rough week for our family. Uncle Jerry passed away. We as a family spent a lot of time together. It is time that I will always treasure.

Friday was a day that none of us could have ever been prepared for. For me, it was one of the hardest days and one to always remember. When I look back on Friday, I will remember the loss, but I will also remember family holding on to each other as we said goodbye to someone we all loved so much.

We cried together, we loved each other, we comforted each other, and we were together. When we gathered after the services, stories were told. We talked politics, we talked about the big fight that was happening over the weekend, we updated each other on what was going on in our own lives, we played games, and we teased one another and laughed.

The laughter filled the house. The laughter was contagious. For me, the longer we laughed, the more a sense of comfort came over me. Uncle Jerry's laugh was absent Friday, and it will be forever missed. However, I know he was laughing with us and smiling down at us.

I know things will be different with his loss, and, in the coming years, we may not talk much about Friday; but that time together was needed by all of us to draw strength from each other.

As we told stories, we discussed the idea that we need to write these memories down. I wanted to write this because, as I watched our family together, I realized why we are so truly blessed. We share a common bond; we are "family."

POTATO CROP
BY DAN WADE

In 1943, Mom and Dad had been married a few years. Dad was working at the Masonite plant in Laurel, Mississippi. After some time, they saved enough money to make a down payment on a farm. Jerry was only two or three years old. Dad built their first house on that farm in the community of Myrick, working nights and weekends. I don't know if our brother Tommy Felix was born before or after they moved onto the farm.

Like a lot of young couples, Mom and Dad had gone into debt getting started in life. Meeting those obligations was about all they could do, and there wasn't a penny to spare. Also, like a lot of young couples, they had hopes and dreams for better days. One year, the market for potatoes looked really good, and their farm had good loose soil that was just right for growing potatoes. During the winter and early spring, they made plans and preparations to put in a big crop. Like all business ventures, they calculated the expected returns on their labors. It looked good, the banker agreed, and they got a small loan to put in the crop. If they just raised an average crop and the market held, they figured to make pretty good money. Of course, if they worked real hard and the rains came just right, their crop might just about set a record, and the market price for potatoes just might get better. If that happened, they planned to pay off some bills and have money left over. Like all young couples, they had plenty of plans for what they might do with the extra money.

Spring came, and they worked hard plowing, disking, and harrowing the field with a mule, then planting potatoes carefully in long straight rows. The rains came, and they worked and kept the weeds chopped. They had never seen such a beautiful field of potatoes. It sure looked like their crop was going to be a record-buster, and the market was rising a bit. They couldn't help but look at the Sears, Roebuck and Company catalogue in the evening, dreaming and making plans for what they would do with the money. Finally, the day came to start the harvest. The plan was to dig and pile the potatoes, then come by with the mule and wagon, load them up, and take that load of potatoes to market. It was going to be a great reward for all their hard work, and they could hardly wait.

Dad started turning the soil, digging those potatoes before daylight one fall morning, and, man! They looked good! Each plant had a bunch of great big potatoes. Man, oh man, it was going to be great! Then daylight came, and Mom came out with little Jerry to help. It was while making that first pile that they noticed something was wrong. "Blight." Those big beautiful potatoes were infected with blight! They were worthless! Dad and Mom stared at those blighted potatoes with sinking hearts; then, with faint hope, they went to the other end of the field and dug up another bunch. They were blighted, too—the whole crop! Not worth a dime. Oh, they would be okay to eat. You could just cut the blighted part out, but they weren't worth a dime to sell on the market. Nobody would buy a blighted potato.

All their dreams were out the window. Instead of having some extra money, they had more debt than they had started with. Things would be tighter than ever, but, looking on the bright side, they would have plenty to eat. Potatoes and more potatoes. (Can you imagine how hard it was to dig, haul, clean, and store that crop of potatoes? It's backbreaking work. They had borrowed money to put that crop in, and they had invested all their hopes and dreams.) Mom said she tried every way of cooking potatoes she could think of, and then she invented a few more. They had potatoes for breakfast, potatoes for lunch, and potatoes for dinner. Mashed, scalloped, fried, boiled, and baked. Potato soup, potato pancakes, and potato chips. They ate potatoes until they were sick and tired of potatoes, then they ate some more. They didn't spend much more time looking at catalogues.

WORKING FOR JERRY
BY RYAN CHILSON

When I was eleven years old, Jerry offered to let me do some work for him. This was around the time that Artistic Homes, Inc. had just moved into its new office on the west side of Albuquerque. He picked me up in his truck, and I remember being quite nervous to work for him. Jerry made me feel really small—not in the negatively charged way that we usually use that term, but in the fact that Jerry was the most gigantic force I had ever known. The way I felt around Jerry was similar to how one might feel sitting at the edge of the Grand Canyon: fear, awe, and inspiration.

We arrived at Artistic Homes, and Jerry showed me what I would be doing for the day. I would be stacking heavy containers (containers of what, I do not remember) onto some new shelving that had just been installed in the garage bays of the Artistic Homes office.

It was a pretty simple job. I needed little instruction, even for an eleven-year-old. Pick the containers up off the floor, and put them on the shelves—simple as that. Jerry instructed me to come get him when I got a certain number of containers on the shelves.

The task was daunting to my eleven-year-old brain and body. But it was just what I needed. As a young man, you begin to yearn for validation of your utility. Jerry was the embodiment of utility and, as such, would be a near-perfect source of validation for me. I believed I could impress Jerry and wanted to do so badly.

So I worked and worked and worked until I completed the task. After a short rest, it dawned on me that I could continue loading containers onto the shelves; doing more than I had been asked would surely bring the admiration and confirmation that I sought.

So I kept on. I stacked and stacked and stacked. I put containers on those shelves until I had exhausted every fiber in my body and, even more so, my willpower. The only thing I had left in me was my desire for Jerry's approval.

I went into the office to go find Jerry and show him my work, as he had instructed. Predictably, Jerry was very busy, and I ended up waiting for him to come look at my work for a fair amount of time. Jerry finally freed himself from the pressing matter of the moment and started walking with me toward the garage to inspect my work.

We stepped into the garage, and my world turned upside down. What I saw I couldn't believe. I started to panic. While I had been in the office waiting for Jerry, the shelves had buckled and folded right down the middle—collapsing from the pressure of entirely too much weight. Not just one or two shelves, but every single shelf; and there were rows and rows of shelves. I had uniformly distributed the containers that Jerry has asked me to put on the shelves, and, when I decided to do all of the extra work, I had just dispersed the extra containers across the shelves so that each shelf would receive the exact same number of containers. Had I actually loaded up a single shelf with all of the containers they would eventually receive, I would have seen the first shelf collapse very early on. However, I distributed all of the containers across the shelves evenly as I went. In doing so, I delayed the collapsing of any single shelf until I had gone into the office to get Jerry.

Jerry's eyes went wide. He said two or three curse words. He didn't direct the curse words at me, but rather at some invisible point six inches away from his face. The moments during which I watched Jerry absorb the failure of my work were the longest seconds in my short life. Seconds turned into eons as I watched Jerry's look of shock fade away from his face. I braced myself, anticipating an incredibly volatile reaction.

And then...

Nothing.

Jerry just accepted it and let it go right there. What was done was done. He literally just rolled his sleeves up and suggested that we start unloading the shelves. I felt incredibly ashamed as we worked side-by-side, but it was just one of the many feelings going on inside of me. I felt guilty that he had not only forgiven me but was now having to help me unload the shelves. I also felt frustrated. I had sought an experience of validation and had instead only given myself empirical evidence of my complete lack of utility. Would I ever become a man? Container by container, these feelings softened, and, by the time we were done unloading the buckled shelves, my feeling of shame had almost completely subsided.

Jerry and I did a few more odds and ends around Artistic Homes before it was time to go home. We hopped in the cab of his truck, and the AM radio came blaring back on. The last five seconds of the current radio program played out and then went right into a commercial break.

The commercial was for Artistic Homes. I remember looking at Jerry's face as the commercial blared over the radio, waiting to see him show the expression of egocentric pride that anyone would display while hearing their own radio commercial.

Nothing. The commercial was nothing to him. It was just as boring to him as drinking water or waiting in line at the bank. He didn't care at all.

Jerry's complete lack of reaction to his own commercial was a transformative moment for me. This moment would be the basis of nearly everything I ever thought or felt about Jerry afterward. I had sought an experience of validation and didn't get it—which was tough—but something entirely different was going on inside of me at that moment. A great realization was taking place.

At that very moment, there was only one person in the entire world riding around with the man they were talking about on the radio and that person was me. Words really can't describe what that feeling is like for an eleven-year-old. Not only was I friends and family with the great man, but this man loved me and so much so that I could accidentally destroy his property and he would forgive me for it—and without hesitation. Whatever I had thought our relationship was worth to him, I could now be certain that it was worth more than the thousands of dollars of shelving I had just destroyed. I felt larger than life. I had one of the great forces in the universe on my side, and, even if I messed up, he'd still be on my team.

I had yearned to impress Jerry and receive an experience of validation. However, in this very moment, I was experiencing something that was far beyond the reach of anything I had hoped to gain by "impressing" Jerry. My paradigms about manhood were permanently shifted that afternoon and have remained in a near similar condition ever since.

As I imagine, my experiences on that day were not unlike what others have experienced in Jerry's presence. Jerry was so big, it could make you feel small—yet, in the end, the net effect was that you yourself became a permanently bigger person. Jerry showed us that we should never, ever sweat the small stuff. Even more importantly, however, he showed us that life is entirely made up of small stuff—small stuff like shelving. Jerry expanded my consciousness and introduced me to new possibilities of what I could become. There will always be a great force inside of me that wants to receive Jerry's approval through my work. And I see nothing wrong with that.

APT TO DO

BY DAN WADE

I was about nine years old when our neighbors, Slim and Ruby Campbell, gave me a Shetland pony. Mr. Campbell was a tall, distinguished-looking man and thin as a whip. The Campbells were known to have been in the racehorse business. They were new to the neighborhood, so Mom, Dad, and I had stopped by their house for a visit. Mr. Campbell asked me if I would like to own their Shetland pony. "She's not broke, but she's real gentle," he said.

Sure, I would like to have that pony. I rode horses all the time, but to get on a regular-sized horse at my age, I had to get the horse to stand by a fence so that I could crawl up the fence and jump on. Sometimes it took a while to get Jubilee, our gentle old horse, to stand still long enough for me to climb up the fence and jump on bareback. Just as I got up on the fence and was ready to jump on, she would move just far enough away that I would have to crawl down, pull her back to the fence, and try again.

If I had that pony, I could jump up on her back without climbing on a rock or a fence, and she would be all mine! You had better believe I wanted her, but I tried not to show how much. So I asked, "How much money do you want for her?" I only had about ten dollars of birthday and coke-bottle deposit money saved up, so I had my fingers crossed. But Mr. Campbell didn't want to sell her. He said, "I don't want your money, son. Here's the deal. If you can ride her, you can have her."

Well, that wasn't the first time I'd heard that proposition, and I was a little gun-shy. In Roswell, before we moved to Colorado, Dad, Wallace, Jerry, and I had stopped at some man's house for them to talk about some business thing. The man had noticed me, gap-toothed and burr-headed. I was hard to miss. He could tell that I was fascinated with some goats in his pen and offered to give me his billy goat if I could ride him. Have you ever noticed that some adults have a twisted sense of humor? I couldn't believe it! Did he really say that all I had to do was ride that billy goat, and he would be mine? How hard could it be? We had a deal! That goat wasn't even wild. He let me walk right up and get on his back. This was going to be easy, I thought.

Then, suddenly, that billy goat went crazy—running, leaping, dipping, and rearing. I fell off before we were halfway around the pen. I'd ride him next time, I said. Getting on him again, I was determined to do better with my arms around his neck and my legs around his middle. I got over half way around the pen that time. That goat threw me over the front, off the back, and sideways. No matter how hard I tried, that billy goat threw me every time. The goat wasn't going to go home with me. After about six or seven tries, I figured out what everyone else had known to start with: I wasn't going to ride that billy goat. All I had accomplished was getting beat up, stepped on, head-butted, and dragged. I was covered with goat hair and corral dirt. Providing entertainment for everybody didn't make me feel better, and it sure hadn't been my goal. I had to ride all the way home in the back of our pickup because Jerry and Wallace said I was dirty and smelled like a goat. When we got home, my good brothers had fun washing me off with the garden hose before they let me go in the house.

I really think the only reason Dad let me get into that deal was so that I could learn a lesson. Well, it worked. I did learn a lesson. I learned that I didn't like providing entertainment by getting the heck beaten out of me and eating corral dirt.

So when Mr. Campbell said that I could have the pony if I could ride her, I gave it some serious thought. I remembered that billy goat, and I wasn't going to make the same mistake again. Providing entertainment for the adults was the last thing I wanted to do. So I asked Mr. Campbell, "Do I have to ride the pony right now?" "No," Mr. Campbell said, "you don't have to ride her right now." He continued, "What did you have in mind?" "Well, how about giving me until tomorrow and letting me take her home until then?" I asked. "What time tomorrow?" Mr. Campbell asked. "If I rode her back by five o'clock, would that be okay?" I was hoping against hope that I hadn't blown the deal. Mr. Campbell smiled and said, "Let's shake on it." We had a deal now. All I had to do was ride that pony.

I felt a little silly leading that pony down the road all the way home. It was about a mile and a half, but I wasn't going to get on that pony until I was out of everybody's sight. After we got home, Dad let me take the pony into the hills behind the house by myself. I was determined to ride that little horse. So while walking home, I had given it plenty of thought. We wouldn't be in a corral, and, if I fell off and lost the reins, that pony would probably be long gone. My solution was to tie one of the reins to my wrist. That way if I fell off, that pony might drag me for a ways but it was staying with me. Boy, did I ever fall off! That pony threw me off all afternoon. She would take off running, then stop suddenly, and I'd fall over her head. She would be running, then turn on a dime. She reared, and she bucked. Off I'd go, hitting the dirt time after time. I kept getting back on her, though, and I slowly got better at staying on. That little pony was getting tired. By late afternoon when I could stay on her most of the time, we went back home. I put her up, put some hay out, and went to the house—tired, sore, and proud. I had done it. That pony was going to be mine!

The next day, while I was riding back to Mr. Campbell's, I only got thrown off twice. I think he was a little surprised when I rode that little pony into his yard. He smiled when he saw the rein tied to my wrist. After watching me ride the pony back and forth for a minute, Mr. Campbell invited me to get down. He told me, "Dan, you've held up your end of the deal. The pony is yours, so take good care of her." I thanked him and promised I would. We shook hands to seal the deal. Mrs.

Campbell brought us each a glass of iced tea. After drinking the tea and having a short visit, I rode back home as happy and proud as I could be. I had made the deal; I had ridden that pony, and nobody was laughing at me.

That little pony was all mine. I named her Apt because she was "apt" to do anything. She would throw me off many more times, and I would continue to keep one rein tied to my wrist for quite a while. That little pony and I had some great times and made many "treasured memories." Perhaps more importantly, I learned to think about any deal that I am offered and to negotiate the terms to my best advantage.

ALL WORK AND NO PLAY...
BY DAN WADE

It was 1992 when I decided that I needed to develop a hobby; I was thirty-seven years old. For most of my life, if I wasn't working, I was looking for work. Oh, we had always gone camping and exploring and generally found ways to have a good time, but I had never had a hobby. Golf, fishing, biking, racing, stamp collecting—nothing like that appealed to me. I do read a lot, but that's not much of a hobby. I wanted something that my wife Daina, my children April and Joshua, and I could all enjoy doing together.

One day, Joshua and I stopped at a yard sale. There on the side of the house was a homemade plywood sailing canoe. It was barn red and about fourteen feet long with a great, beautiful sail. For seventy-five dollars, I couldn't resist. The first time we took it on Lake Cochiti, Daina said she would stay on the bank, so she could tell rescuers where we went down. Joshua and I had a good time trying to sail, but it was clear that we had a lot to learn. The canoe was fun, but it had its limitations. I started looking for something that we could all enjoy. A seventeen-foot MacGregor sailboat with a swing keel was what I found. Daina and I both completed a sailing course with the United States Coast Guard, and we were ready to go.

We all had some fun adventures sailing on Lake Cochiti, a small lake near Albuquerque. The seventeen-footer was so much fun that we all thought that a little bigger boat would be better. So it wasn't long before we found a 1973 twenty-six-foot MacGregor and started going to a larger lake in northern New Mexico called Heron Lake. It is a beautiful mountain lake surrounded by tall pines and mountains. On one of our first trips there, we found a great camping spot by accident. Daina and I had just been on the water a little while, and there was a good gentle wind filling the sails. We were on the north side of the lake, cruising along, and it was a beautiful day. All of a sudden, from out of nowhere, we got hit with a gust of wind that knocked us completely over. The top of our mast hit the water on the starboard side. Daina and I were both hanging on to whatever we could grab for dear life!

The boat righted itself, but then the wind picked up to a high gale. What had been calm water was now three-foot swells, and it was time to start the motor. We both fought to strike the jib and the mainsail; with the boat being tossed around, taking the sails down was no easy job. It was our first time in a heavy blow. Getting the sails down and tied off and the motor started felt like a success, but we still needed to get off the water because—even without the sails—the wind and waves were tossing us around pretty good. I really didn't know what to do, so I just headed south, away from the wind. But it is not a very large lake, and soon we were approaching the rocky shore. Turning left into the waves or running into the shore were the only options. When I turned, we saw an opening through the rocks and found a hidden cove completely protected from the wind and just as calm as it could be. It was a great cove. Since then, we have camped there many times. Those are special memories of starry nights, swims, and cook-outs. Then the National Park Service put in a new road and developed camping spots nearby. It was no longer just our special cove.

There were many special times sailing with the kids and family. One time, a bunch of the family rented a big cabin at El Vado Lake. Jerry brought his boat for water skiing, and we had our sailboat. We all had a great time. A treasured memory for me is that, on one moonlit evening, I took all the young people for a boat ride; they ranged in age from about nine to fifteen. I sat at the back with the motor running just above idle. They all scattered around the front of the boat. Waylon, Weston, Alaena, Ryan, Max, Joshua, and April were all there, I think. They all got to talking between themselves about life and hopes and dreams, seeming to forget I was there. The youthful innocence was wonderful to hear. Another time, on the drive back to town, we all got treated to the most beautiful rainbow display. Vibrant colors of the entire spectrum and double rainbows that went on and on. Daina and I were in the truck, and April was driving Daina's Celica with a car full of cousins. There are a lot of great memories with the boats and the lakes.

Daina and I enjoyed sailing, and we were a good team, but there were times of tension between us. When the wind got up to where we could really start cutting through the water,

Daina wanted to take down the sail and use the motor just when it started getting fun. If the water was a little rough when we were loading the boat onto the trailer, the tensions could get high. Daina's job loading the boat was usually to stand on the dock and help direct me onto the trailer, which was backed into the lake. I would be at the back of the boat with the outboard, trying to hit the trailer, and not let the wind and waves push me off course. On a rough day it might take three tries to get it right. There were never any cross words, but it sure came close. We would sometimes drive for an hour on the road before our jaws unclenched. I finally asked her while we were eating a hamburger on the trip back home after a good weekend of sailing and a hard time loading the boat. "Why do we get mad over such a small thing as getting the boat on the trailer?" Daina and I talked for a while, and I felt pretty stupid. I should have figured it out years before. Daina told me that she had always had a fear of water. All that time that she was trying to enjoy sailing with me, she was fighting her natural fear. That was our last time on the boat. Camping was great; we had both enjoyed being outdoors, but sailing was out. After parking the boat, we never sailed again. We were going to have to find another hobby.

That, Grandchildren, is how we came to own a ranch. Business had continued to improve, and I was surprised when I realized that my dream of owning a ranch—that I had long ago put aside—was now possible. After looking at half the state, we bought a nice ranch south of Mountainair, New Mexico. Daina had grown up on a farm and was unsure about ranching. I told her not to worry about it because all there was to ranching was watching the grass grow. She is still a little mad about that, but I think she suspected I might be stretching the truth a little.

Ranching has been good for us, and we have all had some good times. Daina and I have worked the ranch over the years, driving down to the ranch from Albuquerque almost every weekend. We found her a big palomino Missouri Fox Trotter named Peak to ride and, for me, a great cow horse called Clover. We had some great antelope hunts and good times on that first ranch. We found that we both enjoyed ranching, and business continued to improve, so we decided to sell our first ranch and buy a bigger one that could be a more serious business. After closing on the new place, April, Daina, and I went exploring Lavadee, which was our southernmost pasture. We were driving around looking at things, having a good time, when the fog came rolling in pretty quickly. We couldn't see fifty yards in front of us. After driving around lost in that five-section pasture for about two hours, we finally found the gate. It sure was a relief.

Daina and I are both still in awe of our high desert ranch. It looks like we'll stick with this "hobby" because it hasn't turned into work yet. I learned that for the two of us to have a "hobby" or in this case a second business, it works best if it is something we both love.

HAY IN THE FIELD

BY DAN WADE

One summer when I was a teen on our ranch in Colorado, I had fallen behind hauling hay. My dad was working in New Mexico during the week building houses with Jerry. On the weekend, he would come home and cut and bale hay, check my work, and lay out any projects he had in mind for me to do. My job was to take care of the ranch—irrigating, fencing, checking and caring for the cattle, and hauling hay out of the fields to the barn or the haystack. I had decided that 150 bales a day, or 750 bales a week was about all I could haul and do my other duties as well. Dad was baling about 850 bales every weekend, this meant that the hay was staying longer and longer in the field. I did still find time to ride my horse and read a little Zane Grey in the shade. Dad never said a word about the hay staying longer and longer in the field, but there came a time when he came home Friday night, and the field he wanted to cut on Saturday still had most of the bales from the last cutting—500 bales that were next on my list to haul.

That Saturday, I had something to do off the ranch; it seems like it was school or sports related and took most of the day. When I came home late in the afternoon I was surprised to see my dad on the tractor cutting hay where those 500 bales had been. I went in the house and asked my mom, "Who hauled all the hay?" "Your dad did," she said, a little tersely. "Who helped?" I asked. "No one," she replied. "he hauled it all and stacked it in the barn by himself." I felt about two feet tall. My dad—at sixty years old—had done my work and his too. He never said a word about it to me; I guess he knew he didn't have to, after showing me the difference between a man and a boy. I wanted to be a man, and that day I made a vow to myself that he would never have to haul hay again. He never did.

KEEPING UP WITH YOUR ELDERS
BY RUTH BEARD SMITH

The hay story reminds me of when Steve and I bought our home in Nashville, Tennessee. The yard was a complete overgrown mess. Harold and Juanita Smith, Steve's parents, along with Juanita's sister Virdee, came up from Mississippi to spend a few days helping us clean up our property. We had all worked hard the first day, cleaning the overgrown brush from our backyard. All of us had been tired and went to bed early. Steve and I were still asleep early the second morning when we heard voices and shovels outside our window; they were already working again. Steve and I could barely move—we were so sore from the day before—but we vowed to not let three seventy-somethings outwork us. It was very humbling to know that they were sacrificing to help us, but they were also out-working us!

UNCLE HASKELL AND A GLASS OF WATER
BY DAN WADE

I don't have any idea where we were going, but, as a young boy, I was traveling with Uncle Hack. We stopped at a little, one-pump gas station at a place called Ramon, half way between Roswell and Vaughn, New Mexico. It was about forty-five miles to town either way. Uncle Hack asked the gas-station attendant to fill it up. When he finished pumping the gas, we went inside to pay; that's what we did in those days. In my entire life, I never saw Uncle Hack in a hurry, and he wasn't then. After paying for the gas, he asked for a glass of water, thinking he might visit awhile. The man running the place went to the back and came back with a glass of water, set it on the counter, and said, "That will be twenty-five cents." I could feel Uncle Hack tense up as he reached in his pocket for a quarter. As he carefully laid it on the counter, he said, slowly and clearly, "I hope I'm never so poor that I have to sell water." The man gave Uncle Hack a hard look and then said, "Well, I hope you never have to drive ninety miles for every drop of water you get."

Uncle Haskell drank his water, wished the man a good day, and we left. We both learned about making judgments without all the information.

LESSONS WE LEARNED
BY DAN WADE

While growing up, we were all taught lessons. Many of them were taught without my ever realizing that I was learning:

- Don't quit, and don't complain.
- Do your best.
- Don't lie, and don't cheat.
- Take great pleasure in simple things.
- Stand up for what you believe.
- Be grateful to a loving God.

We knew that this was how honorable people behaved. The list could go on and on.

And there are the lessons that I knew they were teaching:

- Sit up.
- Keep your elbows off the table.
- Don't speak with your mouth full.
- Don't chew with your mouth open.
- Respect your elders.
- Don't talk back.
- Ladies first.
- Yes ma'am, yes sir.

This list could go on and on, too.

Somehow my parents, who had not finished high school, knew how to teach and instill values. They not only knew how but seemed to do so without really trying. They were believers in the biblical adage of "spare the rod and spoil the child," but they raised us in such a way that the rod wasn't necessary very often. I can remember my mother teaching me lessons a few times with a switch off a tree when I was a boy. It was my sisters' job to go get her the switch. They still claim that they thought it would hurt me less if all the leaves were stripped off, and I believe them. Not! The times my mother used a switch on me are just a faint memory, and what I may have done to deserve a whipping is long forgotten. However, there is no doubt in my mind that I was deserving. Having my mouth washed out with soap for saying "damn" at ten years old has stuck with me.

Mother's reaction to a statement that I made when I was thirteen made a lasting impression. I had been reading a little book of quotes; it was called Leaves of Gold, if I remember right. It was a book that had unattributed quotes on different subjects. At that time, I had plans to get rich when I grew up, and I read the quote, "It is easier for a camel to pass through the eye of a needle than for a rich man to enter the kingdom of heaven." I wanted to get rich and go to heaven, so that got me to thinking. After giving it some consideration, I decided that whoever had said that was plain wrong. Later that day, Mother and I were sitting at the table talking. I guess I wanted to impress her with my opinions on what I had read. I told her about the quote I had just read and opined that whoever said such a thing about rich people was a "fool." The next thing I knew, Mother slapped me hard across the face. She was angrier than I had ever seen her as she told me that "Jesus Christ is the one who said that! And he is no fool. You will not blaspheme in this house!" That had a huge impact on me. Being slapped by my mother shocked me more than it hurt—and it did hurt—but seeing her anger and passion rocked me to my roots. This was important to her! That is a lesson I have never forgotten.

Dad's word was law. He didn't say a lot but what he did say, we all took to heart. Not doing what Dad said to do just never occurred to me. When I was ten, I got a bolt-action, single-shot .22 rifle for Christmas. Dad gave me strict safety and care instructions: never point a gun at anyone; never bring a loaded gun into a house; set the rifle down before crossing a fence; don't shoot anything just for the sport of it; and keep your rifle clean. Those rules about guns are ones I live by to this day.

When we moved to the ranch in Colorado, our house was on the county road at the south side of eighty acres of rocky hills and woods. It was fenced all around but not well enough to pasture cows. It was winter when we got to Colorado, and the snow was hip-deep, so there were no worries about my wandering off like I had always been prone to do.

In the spring after the mud dried some, Dad knew that his

young boy would soon be off exploring. He took me out one day, and we walked to the fence line of that eighty acres. He told me that I could explore it all I wanted, but I was not ever to cross that fence. Eighty acres is a big place to explore for an eight-year-old, but, by the time I was eleven it was getting small. I had explored it top to bottom and front to back. The back fence was a long way from the house, and no one would know if I crossed it; but my daddy had told me not to cross, and I didn't, but I sure wanted to. Sometimes, I would stand at the fence just wondering what hidden wonders were on the other side. I was twelve years old the day I worked up the courage to ask Dad if I could cross the fence and explore further. He seemed confused for a moment. I think he had forgotten about having set that boundary years before for an eight-year-old, but then he said, "Yes, you can; just be careful." The lesson was that, once he had set limits, I was trusted to stay within those limits. I wanted to deserve that trust.

My parents had one rule that I really don't remember being enforced very often, but it did send a clear message. The rule was: "If you get in trouble at school, you are in bigger trouble at home." The result of that rule was that they never had to listen to complaints about my teachers. When I got paddled in grade school for talking in class, my parents didn't hear about it from me. When I spent almost an entire semester of recesses at my desk because my teacher wanted me to write cursive better, I never said a word. Usually, whatever trouble I got in was well-deserved, but once or twice my punishment was unjust.

The lesson I learned was that my teachers may not always have been right, but they were always my teachers. In later years, I learned that my mother somehow knew almost every time I got in trouble and had spoken quietly behind the scenes in my defense when she thought it was needed.

Once, when I was a freshman, an upperclassman named James C. was picking on me every morning in the hallway right before school. He would poke me, push me, do anything to bother me, then laugh and act like it was funny. It wasn't funny to me. Finally, one morning I'd had enough, and, when he flicked my ear that day, I turned around and punched him in the face. Then the fight was on! We were going at it like cats and dogs, one on top then the other, when our English teacher got between us. She grabbed each of us by our arm and marched us to the principal's office. This was serious. We were in big trouble. Fighting at school was not tolerated! My shirt was torn, I had a black eye, and there was no way that Mother wasn't going to know. This time I knew I was going to be in trouble at home. I knew it was going to be bad. Dad would probably get involved. Thank goodness that my sister Jenny was a senior that year, and she came to my defense. She told Mother that I was right to stand up for myself and said the whole school was glad that the bully had finally gotten what he deserved. Because of that and my explanation, Mom let me off the hook, but she made it clear that she didn't want it to happen again.

The principal was a wise man who had once been a young

man himself. After assessing the situation, he punished the two of us by giving us the job of cleaning up the mess after the homecoming bonfire. We had both thought we were going to be suspended from school, so we were glad to clean up after the fire. Sometimes it is funny the way things work out; before we got the ashes from the bonfire cleaned up, James and I had become friends. I learned that there are times you do need to take a stand, and rules are meant to be enforced by wise people.

I once heard my mother say that she had learned to never say that "No child of mine would ever do _____." My parents had come to understand while raising the five of us that even good kids could make bad decisions. I was no exception. I made more than my share, and the lesson I learned was that, no matter how badly I disappointed my parents, they still believed in me. That was the lesson, and, when I have failed, their belief in me has given me something to live up to. I am still trying to live up to their belief in me. I always will.

When Mom passed away, I was struggling to make a living and keep my family together. I couldn't afford to buy a suit for the funeral. She worried about me. I was almost on my feet financially when Dad died, but things were still a bit shaky. Their belief in me, to some extent anyway, has finally paid off. I hope—I believe—that they know that I am good now.

SAYINGS FOR THE GRANDCHILDREN
COMPILED BY DAN WADE

Dear Grandchildren,

You have been inundated with information, and knowledge, almost anything you want to know about is at your fingertips. With just a few keystrokes on a computer or the press of a button on your phone, you can access information that might have taken hours, days, or longer to gather not too long ago. What you haven't been inundated with is wisdom. In the grand scheme of things, wisdom is more important. You can become wise by living long and learning from all your mistakes (which will be painful), or you can gain wisdom by learning from the mistakes of others. Sayings and adages are a way of passing hard-earned wisdom down from one generation to another. This list of sayings put together by your family members contains some old and time-tested sayings along with contemporary ones. Other things these sayings are called are truisms and axioms. Most of us have learned at least some of them the hard way, and you probably will, too. You may think that some of these are old-fashioned or out of date, but they are not. "A penny saved is a penny earned" is as true today as it was when Ben Franklin wrote it in the 1760s.

Sayings are guidelines for living, and this selection of family sayings is led by our Lord's rules for living, the Ten Commandments:

1. Thou shalt have no other gods before me.
2. Thou shalt not make unto thee any graven images.
3. Thou shalt not take the name of the Lord thy God in vain.
4. Remember the Sabbath day, and keep it holy.
5. Honor thy Father and thy Mother.
6. Thou shalt not kill.
7. Thou shalt not commit adultery.
8. Thou shalt not steal.
9. Thou shalt not bear false witness.
10. Thou shalt not covet.

Those are the good Lord's rules of life. They are the RULES. If they weren't rules, they would have been called the Ten Suggestions.

The following family sayings are in no particular order, but you should know that an older family member thought they were important enough to share with you. They represent knowledge that has been gained by life experiences. That, Grandchildren, is WISDOM.

The Big Sixty

1. Righty tighty, lefty loosey. - Dan Wade
2. Buy a plunger before you need a plunger. - Waylon Wade
3. Listen at least as much as you talk, preferably more than you talk. - Michael Turk
4. When you can't say something good, say nothing at all. - Doris Smith Peden
5. If you pray for rain, be prepared for mud. - Donna Wade
6. If you're gonna be dumb, you had better be tough. –JR Smith (Anthony Nix)
7. Always choose to love rather than hate. - Beth Touchet Morgan
8. Do the best you can with what you have. - Grandmother Minnie Ozella Wade (Nancy Wade)
9. Pay yourself first. - James Heber Wade
10. Pretty is as pretty does. - Dan Wade
11. When it is too tough for the rest of them, that is just the way we like it. - James Heber Wade
12. Choose your spouse as the person who will raise your children. - Janis Terauds (Daina Wade)
13. When life gives you lemons, make lemonade. - Elizabeth Shoats
14. The harder I works, the luckier I gets. - April Wade Turk
15. *Carpe diem.* - April Wade Turk
16. It is better to be silent and thought a fool than to speak and remove all doubt. – Abraham Lincoln (Jim Peden)
17. Measure twice, cut once. - Dan Wade

18. Learn to create and stick to a budget. The less money you have the more important this is. - Waylon Wade

19. If something is worth doing, it is worth doing right. - Jenny Wade Chilson

20. The hand that rocks the cradle rules the world. - LaGuewn Wade Wilson

21. If you can't hide it, decorate it. – LaGuewn Wade Wilson

22. NEVER date someone you would not want to marry. – LaGuewn Wade Wilson

23. "Yes Ma'am, No Ma'am, Yes Sir, No Sir" may be Southern and old-fashioned, but it will open many doors for you in life. – LaGuewn Wade Wilson

24. The truth will set you free. – John 8:32 (Robbie Smith)

25. Sometimes it is better to keep your mouth shut! Ask yourself, "Is this fuss and bother gonna matter in a year?" - Amanda Smith Robertson

26. When seeking direction from God, remember he doesn't make suggestions. - Daina Wade

27. Blessed are the meek for they shall inherit the earth. - Matthew 5:5 (Amanda Smith Robertson)

28. Write it down! A short pencil is better than a long memory. - Tom Wade

29. If it's not broke, don't fix it. – Barbara Zell Wade Moore

30. "Can't" never could do anything. - Jenny Wade Chilson

31. Do unto others as you would have them do unto you. - Jesus Christ (Dan Wade)

32. Compliment a woman's choice in shoes and

accessories. They appreciate it when you notice these details. - Waylon Wade

33. Never lend anything you aren't prepared to lose or can't repair. - Waylon and Gail Wade
34. Common sense does not grow in everyone's garden! – LaGuewn Wade Wilson
35. Never speak quickly from a place of hate, jealousy, anger, or insecurity. Evaluate your words before you let them leave your lips. - Kaye Smith
36. Sometimes it is best to say nothing at all. - Kaye Smith
37. Don't lie, cheat, steal, or tolerate those who do. - West Point Cadet Honor Code (Dan Wade)
38. Prayers need legs. - Minnie Lee Wade (Gail Wade)
39. When you get thrown from a horse, get up, and get right back on the horse. Of course, this is literal for horseback riding; figurative for the rest of life. - Jenny Wade Chilson
40. This too will pass. - Kowana Moore
41. There is a lid for every pot. - Thomas Wilson
42. There is honor in all work. - James Heber Wade
43. Always treat others with respect, from the president to the guy that dumps the trash. - Ruth Beard Smith
44. "That's OK, Mom. Your job is to raise me until I reach maximum sustainability." - Jackson Smith (Jackson's advice at eight years old to his frustrated mother.)
45. Make friends from different nationalities, socio-economic levels, and ages. You will always have a rich tapestry of people to draw wisdom, encouragement, and strength from throughout your life. - Ruth Beard Smith

46. Easy come, easy go. - Dan Wade

47. Let your Yes be Yes and your No be No. - Jenny Wade Chilson

48. If you don't know where you're going, how do you get there? - Donna Wade

49. Is that a want or a need? (Understand the difference.) - April Wade Turk

50. Today is a new day. - Gail Cromer Morgan

51. "If you haven't eaten by now, you're too stupid to feed." - Dan Wade (This is what I told my kids, after coming home from a long work day when they told me that they were hungry. They were about nine and eleven years old. Not my best moment.)

52. A penny saved is a penny earned. - Ben Franklin (Robbie Smith)

53. A sane six beats a crazy nine. - Waylon Wade

54. A house divided cannot stand. - Robbie Smith

55. Never quit on a bad day. - Alaena Chilson Hyatt

56. Someone wrapped up in themselves makes a mighty small package. - Minnie Lee Wade

57. There is no elevator to success. You must always climb the stairs. - Doris Smith Peden

58. You get what you get, and don't throw a fit. - Kindergarten saying (Gail Wade)

59. Keep your words short and sweet, for you never know from day to day which ones you'll have to eat. - Dan Wade

60. When you get to the end of your rope, tie a knot in it and hang on. - Ann Morgan

61. Diplomacy: thinking twice before saying nothing. - James Morgan

62. We do not stop playing because we get old; we get old because we stop playing. - James Morgan
63. There is a Right and a Wrong. (What you think or feel does not change that.) - Dan Wade
64. Be particular. – Daniel Haskell Wade
65. If you want a better wife, be a better husband, and vice versa – Dan Wade
66. Remember that before you became old and wise you had to first be young and stupid – LaGuewn Wade Wilson
67. If it sounds too good to be true, it probably is. – Dan Wade
68. Choices have consequences. – Daina Wade
69. Before you speak, ask yourself: Is it true? And is it necessary? – Dan Wade
70. Don't worry about the mule, just load the wagon. – James Heber Wade

I am sure you noticed that there are a few more than sixty sayings. There is a lesson in that, too. It is best to under-promise and over-deliver.

Some of these sayings have stories behind them. For instance, my dad taught me many things in many different ways. His advice to "pay yourself first" was about the only financial advice I can ever remember him giving me. As simple as it seems, I was probably thirty years old before I really understood what he was telling me.

I bet others have stories behind their sayings as well.

FAMILY COMMENTS

FURTHER INSIGHTS ON THE STORIES

CHAPTER 1 – FAMILY NOT FORGOTTEN

MOM AND DAD
BY DAN WADE

<u>LaGuewn Wade Wilson</u>   This is a wonderful insight to your parents. What a wonderful tribute to two loving people!!! I could see them both, just as you describe. Aunt Sue surrounded by her favorite colors, in her car, this was probably one of her happiest times. And the scenes at the cemetery must have cost you some tears to remember. What strength did that take for him to make those steps, and even more for you guys to watch! It is easy to see how all of you guys share the same strength.

<u>Michelle Ferguson Wade</u>   Oh Dan, that was so beautiful. Thank you for sharing the amazing people I was never lucky enough to know. I think I'll read this to my children today, so they'll get a small sense of who their great-grandparents were.

<u>Weston Wade</u>   Pop set the benchmark for all of us Wade men on how to be a man and how to always do the right thing. Never taking short cuts or cheating others in life. Even at a young age I saw how I should act and treat others. When things get tough, you grit your teeth and bear it. We have a long history of very tough men and women in the Wade family, and I want to teach my kids all the same things that I have learned in life. Thanks, Dan.

Donna Wade   Selling the ranch in Colorado and moving to Roswell was also fulfilling a promise Dad made to Mom. Mom never took to living in the country the way the rest of us did, she was raised a city girl, and Dad promised her that when all the kids were grown he would move her back to a town with nice things, and he did.

Carla Huish Wade   He was an amazing man! So blessed to have known him and to take him milkshakes when he wanted a smile.

Linda Smith   This was wonderful, Dan. RV said he can remember your mother being so glad to see his family when they visited. He can just see and hear the four Wade brothers telling their funny growing up stories.

Alaena Chilson Hyatt   Wow, this is so powerful and touching. I really enjoyed reading this story, Uncle Dan! I love learning more about my grandparents/family through these stories. I was so young when they passed away, so I appreciate getting to know them through your stories. Thank you!

WINTER FUN IN THE SNOW
BY DONNA WADE

Dan Wade   Saving Jenny's life when the ice broke wasn't easy; that pond was pretty deep with steep sides. You and Jody were both in danger but didn't hesitate.

<u>Jenny Wade Chilson</u>   Dan was there the day I fell through the ice, too! He was kind of trapped on the ice when I went under! That was really a close call. I sure appreciate how you guys saved me that day!

THEY ARE ALL MY CHILDREN
BY DONNA WADE

<u>April Wade Turk</u>   Thank you, Aunt Donna. This is so special. All of us are lucky to have you. You helped raise us. I tell people that I was lucky because I had my aunts, and they were always there for me. I so miss those camping trips we had, and, yes, I remember that ice cold water. I treasure all of our adventures. We need to plan another camping trip.

<u>Nancy Wade</u>   Sweet memories, Donna. You were such a special aunt to all of these children. My boys have fond memories and wild stories about Aunt Donna.

<u>Alaena Chilson Hyatt</u>   This is such an awesome collection of memories, Aunt Donna! Thanks for always being there for us. Thanks for petting me when I was born! haha! Ryan and I always LOVED our trips to Bloomfield to visit and would be overwhelmed with excitement the moment we went over the hill into Bloomfield—anxious for unending adventures with our cousins and your amazing sweet tea! Love you so much.

TORMENTED BY MY OLDER SISTERS
BY DAN WADE

<u>Tom Wade</u> Bryce Wade can relate to the hazard of being the focus of two sisters and the frustration of having all activities being based on their wishes.

<u>Alaena Chilson Hyatt</u> Hahaha! Love the story! Ryan, can you relate?

<u>Ryan Chilson</u> Just watching you and Mom mix all your food is a special kind of torture.

CHAPTER 2 – YOU CAN NEVER HAVE TOO MUCH FUN

SCARED, SO SCARED, BUT TRYING TO ACT BRAVE
BY DONNA WADE

<u>Dan Wade</u> I had more fun in those dark woods than ought to be legal. You guys not only armed yourselves, but that little cooking fire practically became a bonfire!

<u>Jenny Wade Chilson</u> I don't think we ever paid Dan back for that! I guess it is not too late!

BULL IN THE HOLE
by Wallace Wade

LaGuewn Wade Wilson   That bull probably saved your life. With that kind of determination you probably would have completed the quest!! Several things could have happened to you, none of them good.

Jenny Wade Chilson   It is fun to have this story to read, Wallace! Well told. I love recalling so many of these classic moments from our growing up years. I do not remember ever, ever being bored!!

MAGIC MOMENTS
by Melita Wade Thorpe

Dan Wade   Melita's story took me back to warm summer nights long ago. After a fun day of playing and swimming in the creek, it would be time for ghost stories. There were harrowing tales of creatures called goof-a-nanners and woof-a-nannies. After the stories, we would go to bed, knowing our parents would keep us safe from harm.

ROCKET LAUNCHES AND GRANDMOTHER
BY WALLACE WADE

<u>Jenny Wade Chilson</u>   What a special connection with Grandmother! I do remember her as being such a smart woman and so interested and curious about things. That is fantastic that you and Dad actually saw the rocket launch at White Sands!! It is probably good that Google Earth didn't exist back when you were making and launching all of your rockets!! Satellites would probably have zoomed in on you for sure! Haha! That is interesting about Grandmother being able to make herself wake up at whatever time she wanted. Jerry and Donna have always had that ability! I wonder if that is where they learned it.

<u>Donna Wade</u>   I knew Jerry and I both had the wake-up ability thing but did not know it was inherited from Grandmother Wade. How the world has changed in Grandmother's lifetime from horse and buggy to rocket ships, WOW!

<u>LaGuewn Wade Wilson</u>   Didn't she also make you a shirt, using newspapers for a pattern?

<u>Barbara Zell Smith Moore</u>   I seem to have that wake-up ability, too.

<u>Kearney Hall Morgan</u>   I have the ability to get up, sometimes, at the time I want to, but I don't trust myself. I remember so well where I was when John Glenn went up. I was a tank platoon leader in West Germany and happened to

be in our big tank park. I listened to the whole thing on Armed Forces Radio Europe on my miniature radio.

Burney Wade Morgan   I remember when I visited after Uncle Noel and family had moved to Roswell. Wayne and I were looking at the launching ramps you had built, and Wayne warned, "We better stay clear of Wallace and his launching ramps. He might blow us all up!" Ha!

CHAPTER 3 – CHARACTER(S) REVEALED

NOT JUST A HORSE STORY
BY DONNA WADE

Dan Wade   I remember you were riding Gander in the county queen contest. You were beautiful, with your fancy outfit on.

MOM AND MAYNA
BY DAN WADE

Nancy Wade   Wallace agrees he could always find your mother. She had a lot of friends. She was very good at explaining things, especially to children and young people. I still remember some of her words of wisdom. She was a very special lady.

TRAVELING WITH POP
BY APRIL WADE

<u>Dan Wade</u>   You just wouldn't get on the plane, so Dad took you across town to the bus station. The bus was a five-hour trip; the plane would have been forty-five minutes. Dad never gave it a second thought.

THE LEGACY OF THE EIGHT-DOLLAR SHOES
BY WAYLON WADE

<u>Weston Wade</u>   Great story; ironically enough I'm reading this right after my run. My feet just ache thinking about running in eight-dollar shoes!

<u>Robbie Smith</u>   Wow, I really enjoyed that! I had a time in my life when I did the same thing, not to impress anyone. So glad you shared that.

<u>Jenny Wade Chilson</u>   What a difference in many lives Wallace's fitness decision and those eight-dollar shoes made!! It is always the little things that are the big things!! Wallace did get in great shape. Jerry started running when Wallace was running! One of my favorite memories with Wallace and Jerry was the three of us got together and did a four-mile run there in Bloomfield! I was a runner at that time, too. None of us knew what pace to set, though, because we had never run together. We just kept going faster and faster, because none of us wanted

to be the weak link! Haha. It was so much fun, though. I have a photo of us when we started out on the run. I am so glad you got me back into running, Waylon!! Your support has been awesome. I enjoy our races so much!! Guess what? Riley and Madison told me that they may join us for the Thanksgiving Day run!!

<u>Nancy Wade</u> Wallace liked this story. He says the shoes were a good investment.

CONFAR HILL
BY DAN WADE

<u>Jenny Wade Chilson</u> It was a rough beginning of a rough first winter on our ranch!

<u>Nancy Wade</u> I've heard this story, and, having been born in Colorado, I never really thought what it was like for your parents. Your mother was a very brave southern lady, and your dad resourceful and hard working. Colorado winters take a lot of preparation, and, if you are not crazy when it starts, you will be by the time it is over.

THE UNCLES
BY DAN WADE

<u>April Wade Turk</u> I remember that visit and the dinner. They brought a lot of laughter with them.

<u>Robbie Smith</u>   Thank you for sharing this time you had with your father and uncles, even though they were during very hard times. I agree, they were great gentlemen. We miss them very much.

CHAPTER 4 – PASSING DOWN

RETIREMENT
BY WAYLON WADE

<u>Dan Wade</u>   Jerry never worked a day in his life. He said a good test to see if you loved what you do is, "Would you do it for free?" Jerry loved building, and it certainly was put to the test.

UNCLE VARDAMAN AND HARMONICA SALES
BY DAN WADE

<u>Waylon Wade</u>   I remember the trip Uncle Vardaman and Aunt Beatrice made out to New Mexico. It's one of the clearest memories I have from childhood. They had flown into the Durango airport. Weston and I went with Dad to pick them up. On the way home, we hit a deer. I remember Aunt Beatrice commenting, "We knocked the poor thing's tail off," and thinking how strange Uncle Vardaman seemed because he

was a very tall and dignified man that I couldn't understand at all because of his shakes and possibly a southern accent on top of it.

Jenny Wade Chilson   Uncle Vardaman and Aunt Beatrice were both special people. As a young girl, I was in awe of beautiful Melita (daughter of Vardaman and Beatrice Wade)! Once, when she was a teenager, she had me spend the night with her. I felt like the luckiest girl in the world. She made me feel so special.

CHAPTER 5 – A DIFFERENT TIME

COTTON HOER
BY WALLACE WADE

LaGuewn Wade Wilson   There are a lot us of who picked cotton. I think it would be very hard to find this kind of help now. I know that my dad and your dad were very proud of you both. Chopping cotton is one thing, but chopping cotton smart is all together something else!!   "Bless your cotton-picking heart" is an endearment to us cotton hoers.

Gail Wade   Wayne said, "From one hoer to another, that's a very accurate description. Good job!"

SNAKE HUNTERS
by Wayne Wade

<u>LaGuwen Wade Wilson</u> He didn't tell that they sometimes brought them in alive—inside a mason jar—when called in for lunch. When placed on the dinner table, his tail was in trouble!!

HORSE BREAKING
by Dan Wade

<u>Donna Wade</u> When I read this, it is like yesterday. We were the wildest kids on horseback. For sure we would all faint if we saw any of the kids riding this wild today! I am sure the many times I fell off and was thrown off is why I have pain in my backside today. This was all part of a very wonderful childhood

JERRY AND TOMATOES
by Tom Wade

<u>April Wade Turk</u> When I was little, I refused to eat tomatoes. One summer we were at your house in Bloomfield, and we helped Max pick some tomatoes. He talked me into eating one. We washed it off and cut it in half. Max loaded on the salt. It was really yummy. I still cut my tomatoes in half and add some salt.

<u>Donna Wade</u>   Dan called for another sibling get-together in September (2016) to play dominoes. It was one year from our last get-together, the last time all the siblings were together. It was full of sad and happy emotions. The last thing my brother Jerry ever said to me, as we passed around a bowl of small tomatoes I had brought, was "Are these from your garden?" and we made eye contact and smiled. Jenny and Jerry had dancing. Jerry and I had tomatoes; we loved them. We loved trying to grow them. He would have loved to see—and eat—my garden tomatoes this year. This has been the first year I have achieved success in growing big, beautiful tomatoes. It has only taken forty-five years, but I have enough to have sharing be fun. Jerry was not able to say much the day of our sibling gathering, but, when he said those words, they made my day. "Are these from your garden?"

CHAPTER 6 – GOOD TIMES HUNTING

UNCLE NOEL – CAMPING AND COFFEE
BY DAN WADE

<u>LaGuewn Wade Wilson</u>   Thanks, Dan, for that story, so wonderfully told. Heard it many times. The emotions were very real; you didn't separate the man from his coffee. We even placed a Folgers coffee can on his grave with a Styrofoam cup. You just never know! Dad loved his coffee.

MY FIRST ANTELOPE HUNT
BY WAYLON WADE

<u>Nancy Wade</u>   Wallace says he was there and still doesn't believe it. I'm just glad I didn't have to be there. Ten years later is a good time to hear this story. Great story, Waylon.

<u>Dan Wade</u>   I've been on quite a few hunts in my life, they've all been fun, and I've never had a bad one, but a few stand out. This hunt with my brother Wallace and nephew Waylon is in a class all by itself. Daina and I laughed till we hurt.

CHAPTER 7 – WHATEVER IT TAKES

BUILDING FENCE
BY DONNA WADE

<u>Dan Wade</u>   What a special section of fence, I don't remember Tyler drinking paint thinner, but I remember the cedar fence—six feet tall and at least 160 feet long. I've always felt bad that I didn't help. I'm not sure, but it seems that you were determined to do it yourself. That yard may have been played in more than any yard in history. Tyler and his friend Freddy wore it out.

<u>Nancy Wade</u>   I remember how badly you needed a fence

and what a big job it was for you, but you got it done with some help from Tom and Roy. You must have gotten your money's worth out of it, because a lot of fun happened in that yard. I know my boys played out there a lot.

CHAPTER 8 – LESSONS FROM LIFE

STRENGTH IN FAMILY
BY APRIL WADE TURK

LaGuewn Wade Wilson   Beautiful April!! I think one of our common threads in the family is the ability to laugh through good times and bad. I remember Dad and his brothers doing the same thing. I bought a little plaque many years ago that says, "Lord, please teach me to laugh again, but never let me forget that I cried." I have repeated that many times in my life, and that prayer has always been answered. Thanks for sharing this with us. It is important for those of us who could not be there.

Jenny Wade Chilson   That is a sweet and poignant recognition, April. Thank you for taking the time to write it. How wonderful it was for Dan and Daina to plan and provide so much family support time for us all at their beautiful and welcoming home on both Thursday and Friday. Many of us stayed there until midnight both nights. It meant so much to all of us. It just helped so much to be among family and in a place that Jerry had often been for our previous gatherings of laughter and good times. Had it been any of the rest of us, Jerry would have wanted us to do the same thing.

WORKING FOR JERRY
BY RYAN CHILSON

<u>Dan Wade</u>   Ryan, what a great wealth of lessons. I'll bet Jerry had a similar experience as a young man. Our father was one you just naturally wanted approval from, and it wasn't easy to get.

<u>Ryan Chilson</u>   Remember the time I destroyed your fence with the front-end loader? This story repeated itself completely from end to end, but with you as the main character.

Jesse Felix and Minnie Ozella with Family

WADE FAMILY TREE

GENEALOGY

Isaac Wade [born 1776 in North Carolina: died 1858] married to Phebe and Charlotte

↓

Sebron J. Wade [born 1802 in Georgia: died 1876] married to Sarah J Shows

↓

Daniel Webster Wade [born 1830 in Mississippi: died 1908] married to Cornelia Ann Knight

↓

Jesse Felix Wade [1868-1931] & Minnie Ozella (Stringer) Wade [1878-1973]

Talmadge Vardaman Wade* & Beatrice (Shows) Wade
Malita (Wade) Thorpe
    Daniel
    Zita Beatrice Star (1)

Robert Sylvester Smith & Beulah Olivia (Wade) Smith*
Harold Smith & Juanita (Leggett) Smith
    Richard Harold (1)
    Steven Lloyd (2)

Harlin Dean Smith Sr. & Sara (Myrick) Smith
  Harlin Dean Jr. (3)
  Norman Lee (2)
  Robert William (2)
  Mary Sue (2)
  Wanda Christine
Barbara Zell (Smith) Moore & Joseph W. Moore
  June Janeice (5)
  Joel Wesley (2)
Myra June (Smith) Montgomery &
Richard Hugh Montgomery
  Dianne Lynn
Beulah Vonniece (Smith) Butler & Paul Brooks Butler
  Paul Lavaughn
  Larry Brooks (2)
  Phillip Todd (2)
Reginal Veston Smith & Linda (Stringer) Smith
  Gregory Boyd (5)
  Reginald Vance (1)
  Dennis Ray (2)
Jesse Roland Smith Sr. & Doris (Sumrall) Smith
  Jesse Roland Jr. (2)
  Stacey Robin (3)

Kearney H. Morgan Sr. & Lola May (Wade) Morgan*
Kearney H. Morgan Jr. & Gail (Cromer) Morgan
  John Prentiss (2)

David Wade

Chris Cromer Gardner (2)

Scott Gardner

James D. Morgan & Myrtle Ann (Smith) Morgan

Burney Wade Morgan &

Martha Kate (Thompson) Morgan

Todd Thompson (1)

Stephanie Lynn (4)

Jesse Byron Morgan & Debbie (Sauer) Morgan

Joshua Byron (3)

Caleb

Cherith

Noel McFaniel Wade* & Minnie Lee (Taylor) Wade

Rebecca (Wade) Holliman & Charles Edward Holliman

Lori Denise (3)

Clayton Lyle (4)

Fay LeGuewn (Wade) Wilson & Mike Wilson

David Michael (1)

Thomas Noel (1)

Nolan Wayne Wade & Gail (Beauchamp) Wade

Marcus Wayne (1)

Aimee LeGuewn (5)

Roma Lee (Wade) Kidd & Bob Kidd

Daniel Haskell Wade* & Willie Mae (Rainey) Wade

James Heber Wade* & Betty Sue (Bryant) Wade

   Jerry Lane Wade & Stephanie Kay (Brown) Wade

      Alicia Ann (3)

      Terry Lane (3)

      Thomas James (3)

      Roy Lane (2)

      Max Aaron (4)

      Jordan Virginia (1)

      Justin Richard Brown

   Wallace Heber Wade & Nancy (Peterson) Wade

      Waylon James

      Weston Mark (2)

   Donna Sue Wade

      Tyler Magnus

   Jenny Darlene (Wade) Chilson

      Alaena Leigh

      Victor Ryan

   Daniel Lee Wade & Daina (Terauds) Wade

      April Marie (2)

      Joshua Lee

*The six children of Jesse Felix and Minnie Ozella Wade

Jesse Felix and Minnie Ozella Wade raised 6 children, and those children produced 21 grandchildren. Roughly there are 49 great-grandchildren, and 84 great-great-grandchildren and counting.

THOSE WHO CAME BEFORE US

LETTERS FROM DANIEL HASKELL AND
WILLIE MAE WADE'S GENEALOGY BOOK

INTRODUCTION
BY DAN WADE

The following letters were written in the 1980s at the request of Uncle Haskell and Aunt Willie Mae. The two of them spent countless hours researching and compiling our Wade family history. They put together a book of all their research, which is a wonderful resource. Uncle Haskell regretted not getting more family information from older family members when he was a young man. These letters are his way of introducing us to some special people who came before us. Through their work, we have a glimpse of our forefathers going back to the 1700s. We all owe those two good people a debt of gratitude for the years of work they did.

MY GRANDFATHER

BY DANIEL HASKELL WADE

My grandfather, Daniel Webster Wade, was born in Jasper County, Mississippi, on June 26, 1830. His parents were Seborn James Wade and Sarah Shows Wade; his grandparents were Isaac and Phebe Wade. Daniel Webster Wade married my grandmother, Cornelia Ann Knight, in 1853. They made Jones County their lifelong home.

Grandfather was a cotton farmer and owned his own farm; he was also a hunter. At that time, deer and turkey were plentiful in that country. Neighbors got together to have big deer drives with their best marksman placed in a blind to get a good shot. Daniel was usually the man in the blind; he rarely missed. There was no retirement plan for farmers, and he continued to farm and plow with a mule or a horse well into old age. In his later years, he would sit and rest at the end of each row until he gained the strength to do it again. Old age slowed him down, but he didn't quit. That tells you something about the measure of the man.

Grandfather, several brothers, and three brothers-in-law enlisted in the Confederate States Army and fought in the Battle of Vicksburg. His sister Phebe's husband—Narvel

Robert Duckworth—was killed there during a lull in the battle. Grandfather was beside him when he was shot. Grandfather told of walking over dead mules and horses to get to a stream of water where he would see Yankee soldiers getting water as well. They would visit with each other before going back to their trenches and shooting at each other again. He once put his folded blanket over a tree branch, and a sniper put eight holes in it.

After Vicksburg, Sergeant Wade's next major battle was the Battle of Nashville in December 1864. He was captured during that battle and sent to Camp Chase, near Columbus, Ohio. When they got to the prison camp, there was no shelter ready for them. It was a cold December night in Ohio. The first night they marched and jogged in a circle all night to keep from freezing, and by morning the place looked like a cow lot.

The war ended, and Grandfather was released from prison camp in June 1865 and had to make his own way almost 800 miles home to Mississippi without a dime in his pocket. He and a few others from Mississippi managed to hitch boat rides and work their way part of the way down the Mississippi river to Vicksburg. From Vicksburg, they hiked 130 miles to their homes in Jones County. Grandfather told of living on berries, small game they snared, and a few eggs from generous people along the way. He said that they would listen for a rooster crowing in the mornings, then go towards the sound, hoping for a bite to eat. The people they saw had very little to eat themselves. The Yankee cavalry had taken most of their livestock and much of their seed corn. He said that during this trip he prayed, asking the Lord to help him make it home and promising to never complain about anything again if he did. According to those that knew him, he kept that promise.

Finally arriving home, he was met by a mean guard dog. It was his dog! Grandfather had been gone so long he had been given up for dead, and even his own dog didn't know him. He had to hit the dog with a gourd to get in the yard. He found his family in a bad situation; about all they had to eat was a little corn. Some of that needed to be saved for seed. There was none to spare for the pony that they would have to use as a plow horse. There were no draft animals left in that area. They had all been taken by the Yankees or eaten by starving people. Before setting to work to feed his family, he took them to visit the cemetery; his three-year-old son Isaac had died while he was away. After that, he took that underfed pony and managed to put in a small crop. It was a start.

Years later the president of Mississippi State College was honored with a "Dr. Ben Hilbun Day" at the Big Creek Baptist Church where Grandfather was an ordained deacon. During President Hilbun's speech, he mentioned several local men, saying, "Daniel Wade is a modern-day Moses and a peacemaker in the community."

OUR FATHER, JESSE FELIX WADE

BY VARDAMAN WADE

Our father, Jesse Felix Wade was born 1868, three years after the Civil War ended. He enjoyed competitive games. He also was studious and hard working.

He received his formal education at Pinnelville in the Centerville community. His subjects were: Blue Back Speller and McGuffie 3rd Reader, which he mastered.

It was at this time at twelve years of age that he was stricken with ill health. By following the doctor's advice and instructions, he cured himself in a few years. He enjoyed hunting and was an expert marksman, and at the same time he worked on the farm.

He believed in principles of living right and treating everyone right. He was a total abstainer of strong drinks. When enticed to drink, his answer was an emphatic, "NO!"

As a farmer he established new improved farming methods, such as green manure crops, using litter and contour plowing and planting.

He was a good salesman, selling his farm produce which gave him an opportunity to talk on eternal things. He was a devout Christian and member of the Providence Primitive Baptist Church of Jasper County. He believed in the spiritual philosophy of predestination and fore-ordination. He practiced that and lived that all his life.

He loved and believed in his family. In 1912 Glover Lee was born and only lived one month. Mother took blood poison and was dying. Dad gathered the children around the bedside and looked up in tears and said, "William, if you can pray, pray." (William was our Dad's brother who was a minister.) The next morning mother was better and lived sixty years longer. This act of providence was a spiritual lesson to the entire family

My father loved his family and gave advice and counsel to us children, "All we are and all we ever hope to be that is worthwhile we owe to our parents."

REMEMBERING OUR FATHER
by Daniel Haskell Wade

My father, Jesse Felix Wade, was born February 3, 1868, at what later was known as the McAndrews farm, located in the Hebron community of Jones County, Mississippi. He died November 8, 1931, in the Big Creek community. He married Minnie Ozella Stringer March 2, 1902 in Jones County, Mississippi. Her parents were James McFaniel and Louania Angelian Wade Stringer.

My father lived on the farm in the Hebron community until he was about ten years old. Today there is a park, lake, and campground there. About this time, 1877, Grandfather Wade traded that land to John P. Rainwater for a place on Big Creek. My brothers and I still own a portion of this land.

My father would tell about going with Uncle Henry to Pennelville to school, about a half mile northwest of their house. It was near what is now called the Jack Hilbun branch. In one part of it was a great big pool of water which was very cold. People called it the Blue Hole as the water was so blue and cold.

Dad said his mother would cook a pone of cornbread and fill a quart jar with milk. The jar would have a string tied to it to hold it in the pool, where it would be put to keep it cool. Thus they would have cornbread and cold milk for school lunch. So, it looks as though they were the first to have refrigeration and that without an electric bill.

My Dad was a small farmer, growing corn, cotton, and other crops for the home supply and to sell. He was one of the first men in his generation in the community who plowed under all the litter that was left on the land from the previous crop year. He would not burn it unless it was impossible to plow through it. He said it would injure the land; besides, the litter would keep the ground more fertile.

He read the Bible every day and many times aloud and asked us to listen. He lived by it as much as anyone could. He and mother have taught us that there was no substitute for honesty, and all of us have tried our best to live by that.

MY MOTHER, MINNIE OZELLA STRINGER WADE
BY DANIEL HASKELL WADE

My mother, Minnie Ozella Wade; I never saw her but a very few times that she was idle. When she wasn't doing the housework, she was busy with needle work, crocheting, sewing, or mending clothes. She was a very good seamstress. She also saw to it that we had a good vegetable garden, so we could have flowers in the yard and garden, winning several prizes on them at the fairs. She also was a good cook and remained so until her last few months of life, even then doing some of her own cooking. She was almost ninety-five years old when she passed away.

Many times I think back when we kids were sick, she would stay up and wait on us, and afraid we'd get pneumonia. I can't help thinking back and wonder when she ever got much sleep during those times.

She made the girls' dresses, sometimes remodeling them so they'd feel as if they had new dresses. When we were quite young, she made us boys' shirts and pants, which was done by mothers in those days...not much opportunity to buy ready-made clothing.

When it came to memory, Mother was a walking "card

catalog." I used to sit up with her when she would be doing some needlework, making clothes or other things, and get her to tell me about when she was a young girl.

She was born near Morton, Mississippi, in Scott County. They lived there until she was fourteen, then they moved to Jasper County, near Stringer, Mississippi, and later moved to Jones County.

She told about when they moved; on the day they started, it began snowing and continued most of the day. There were several men with their wagons and their teams. They stopped at an elderly colored couple's house; just the two of them lived in a real large house with the kitchen made off to the back. The man told them they could use the main big house, and he and his wife would use the kitchen. They were a modern-day Samaritan! So that's where they spent the first night on the road.

My mother was a strong Christian. She was not the type to give up. She worked right up to the very last. She was ninety-three when she passed away. Just a few minutes before she passed away, she was pleating the sheet, as though sewing or preparing something to be worked on.

For the period in which she lived, she was considered as having a reasonably good education and would have been qualified to teach school. She wrote a beautiful hand (writing).

The Run Away: When Heber, my brother, and I were

real young—I was about five or six, and he about three or four years of age—Dad and Mother took us to Soso, about nine miles northeast of our home. I think Mother wanted to see the doctor, even though it was Sunday…They did in those days.

Dad had put a tongue into a single buggy (it was change-able from shafts). Dad was driving a pair of Mustang Mules. When we started back out of Soso, one of the breast straps broke. These straps go up to the collar and harness and to the breast yoke.

My father said, "Whoa," and he still had hold of the lines in his hands as he got out, going to fix the straps. When the mules stopped, the straps, being broken, ran against the mules; it frightened them. They jerked loose from Dad, throwing him against the fence, where he cut his forehead. The team took off "like a hired hand."

The buggy had a rumble seat. I remember I was in it; my brother was in Mother's lap. I remember Mother reaching back and holding me and hollering. The lines were flying in the air! About one and a half miles down the road, some men stopped them. My father still had the scar, two or three inches on his forehead, for the rest of his life.

Just a few months before Mother passed away, she visited with us several days, in Jackson, Mississippi. She especially enjoyed it as Willie Mae let her wash dishes. Can one imagine anyone really enjoying washing dishes? She did! Then she also enjoyed doing needlework by the picture window, as she could use the sunlight and floor lamp to help her to see. Her son, Heber and family from New Mexico, came through going to spend a few days with her at her house, near Laurel. She was delighted to see them and went to her home with them, but when they got ready to return home, she packed her things and came back to our home to finish her visit. It was a really good time for all of us and is such a pleasant memory!

She did beautiful sewing. After Beulah's, her daughter's, death, Mother did the sewing for the children. She enjoyed it. Very, very seldom did she sit down without a piece of needle-work of some sort.

IN LOVING MEMORY OF OUR PARENTS,
BEULAH OLIVIA WADE AND ROBERT SYLVESTER SMITH
BY HAROLD, HARLIN DEAN, BARBARA ZELL,
JUNE, VONNIECE, RV AND JR

Our mother died when we were all quite young, but the memories that we have during her life reflect a loving and caring mother. At her early death, our dad was left with seven children to raise, and that he did, with God's help, for nearly three years. Then he married Gwendolyn Craft.

Daddy's love for God and family made life a joy at our house. Even in times of troubles, he could see the sunshine after the rain.

GWENDOLYN CRAFT
BY WILLIE MAE AND DANIEL HASKELL WADE

All of the Wade families had a deep love and respect for Gwendolyn for coming into a large family and showing such love and devotion to all the Smith family. She had not been married before, and one can only imagine the tact and love it took to win over the children. On the other hand, it was really "great" for them to have someone to do the cooking for them and looking after their needs; they welcomed her with "open arms," but still with strong remembrances of their mother.

A TRIBUTE TO MY MOTHER, LOLA MAYE WADE MORGAN

BY KEARNEY H. MORGAN, JR.

The eyes of an eleven-year-old boy are not able to observe people and things in an adult manner. However, I believe my experiences and perceptions of my mother have been processed and interpreted in a more mature way in the thirty-eight years since my mother's death. The kind of mother and wife she was, was clouded by the great loss my father, brothers, and I felt at the time. Only the years and thoughts I've had since that time about our wonderful mother have given me opportunity to reflect on what an ideal mother she truly was.

My mother, if she were alive today, would fit the mold of a Super Mom—but in an old-fashioned and much more valued way. She loved her family deeply. She was a homemaker in the truest sense of the word. The most appropriate way I can relate how effective she was would be to describe the daily routine she had during my preschool days. While she worked in the morning to clean house, put everything in order, and prepare for the evening meal, she allowed us to play in the fenced-in backyard. At lunch time, we came in for our baths, lunch, and a nap. After resting, we would be dressed in clean clothes and allowed to ride our tricycles on the front sidewalk. She would have also bathed and fixed herself up for my dad when he returned from work. She watched us as we played, waiting for him; it was a daily routine. It must have made my dad happy to be greeted by a wife who was neatly attired and looking pretty for him. Her house was always immaculate and each thing in its place. It was so important to her. She was genuinely happy in her role because I recall her singing as she went about her day's work.

She was a joyful, fun-loving person. Someone described her laugh to me as infectious. Time has obscured my memory as to how her laugh really sounded. I can recollect she and I playing with one of my birthday presents when I was quite young. She would put it back in the hiding place each day before Dad came home until my birthday. Her nieces loved to visit Aunt Lola, and I think that it was because she was such a pleasure to be around.

She was a God-fearing woman. On each Sunday, the entire family went to Sunday school and worship service. She encouraged us to study and know more about Christ. I remember so well the night I accepted Jesus Christ as my saviour as a small boy. She and Dad were elated, as you might imagine.

I thank God for giving me the kind of parents he gave me, as many are not as fortunate. I recently ran across a get-well card to her which was sent to her by Miss Ferris's first-grade room mother. Our mother was loved by many people, and I cannot keep myself from speculating about what life would have been like had we all been blessed with her presence for a while longer. Mothers are special to us all. However, this wife and mother was an exemplary ideal. The biblical writer of Proverbs gives a description of a worthy woman:

An excellent wife, who can find? For her work is far above jewels. The heart of her husband trusts in her, and he will have not lack of gain. Strength and dignity are her clothing, and she smiles at the future. She opens her mouth in wisdom, and the teaching of kindness is on her tongue.

She looks well in the ways of her household, and does not eat the bread of idleness. Her children rise up and bless her; her husband also, and he praises her, saying, "Many daughters have done nobly, but you excel them all.

KEARNEY HALL MORGAN, SR.
(HUSBAND OF LOLA MAYE WADE)
BY JAMES MORGAN

As most children do, my brothers and I thought a lot of our dad—the person he was and what he stood for. Some children have to reach adulthood before they really grow to appreciate their parents. I can say with all honesty, for myself and I'm sure for all my brothers, that we have always had a love and appreciation for Dad, even through our teen years (sometimes known as the rebellious years).

Dad was small of stature but had a big heart. Working as a milkman for almost thirty years, he was also a "people person." He cared about people and seemed to get great satisfaction from performing a service for them. Many of his customers left keys to their houses so he could put the milk in the refrigerator. He always received many presents from his customers at Christmas. He was appreciative of his customers, and they of him. Opportunities were presented for promotion to a supervisory position, but he preferred to remain a delivery-man. During his rough years, he generally worked from 3:00 a.m. until 3:00 or 4:00 p.m.

Before Mother died, Dad promised her that he wouldn't put us boys in an orphanage. I'm sure he would not have done this, promise or not. He arranged for his sister, Ester Tisdale (with her daughter, Nina) to come and live with us and help raise us, thus keeping his promise to Mother.

I think Dad longed to move back to the farm. One day, after Mother died, we were at Grandpa Morgan's. He took the three oldest boys to the cornfield for a talk. He let the three of us decide whether we wanted to stay in Jackson or move to the country. Not realizing what Dad probably wanted to do, we chose to stay in Jackson.

Dad was a determined man, yet compassionate and softhearted. Tears could often be seen in his eyes during a sad TV program. He was a Christian and a deacon in the Baptist church. The IRS did not believe he gave ten percent of his salary to the church until he proved it one year. I remember of him loaning small amounts of money to some people seemingly down on their luck, knowing it would probably never be repaid.

It can probably all be summed up in a few words. Dad was a man of high moral character and integrity and cared about people. His nickname around the plant was 'Pappy.' Everyone that knew him seemed to hold him in high esteem, and, in retrospect, I am sure this is the reason I feel that, by example, he taught these values to his sons.

ESTER MORGAN TISDALE
BY WILLIE MAE AND DANIEL HASKELL WADE

Kearney Hall Morgan, Sr. was a man that, although short in stature, was tall in the eyes of the people he worked with. He was a friend to everyone. He never said a harsh word about anyone. He was a friend whom others went to with their joys, worries and sorrows. He served as a milkman for a great many years, until his retirement. He worked for Pet Milk Company. He started out driving a wagon pulled by a team of horses, then eventually the company changed to trucks. He was a friend to his customers and would go out of his way to do nice things for them. He was a really honest person; he would walk a distance to pay someone a few cents or to make correct change for his customers. Many left house keys where he could find them so he could put milk in their refrigerator.

After his wife, Lola Maye Wade Morgan, passed away when their son Byron was born, he persuaded his sister, Ester Morgan Tisdale—wife of Clinton Tisdale—and her daughter to live with him and his boys and to help raise them for him. She took over the housekeeping and looking after the needs of the family. In order to earn a little extra money, she kept children for neighbors who were working. She and Kearney together raised a good family of honorable men, who are doing quite well in their fields of work. Her daughter, Nina Tisdale Bratt, is an outstanding person her field of work. In fact, Nina and her husband, Charles Bratt, are doing the index for this book— *Issac Wade and Wives Phebe and Charlotte and Descendants 1776-1988* by Daniel Haskell and Willie Mae Wade—on their computer.

Ester also worked for the nursery or kindergarten section of their church on Sunday and Wednesday nights. After Kearney's death, Ester worked as housemother at the Baptist Children's Home until her retirement. Ester is a strong Christian and loves her daughter and the Morgan boys as much as her own

A TRIBUTE TO NOEL AND MINNIE LEE WADE
BY ROMA WADE KIDD

It was a typical autumn day when Noel and Minnie Lee were married. Hardly youngsters, the bride and groom, age twenty-four and twenty-eight years respectively, had "slipped" into the Laurel Courthouse on November 5, 1935, for a private wedding.

Minnie Lee was the daughter of Charlie Andrew and Martha Anzaline Beeson Taylor, and the third of eight children. Her paternal grandfather, John Henry Taylor, had immigrated from Dublin, Ireland, as a young boy. Her maternal grand-parents were from the "Carolinas," her grandmother being a Reynolds who raised tobacco. Minnie Lee's father, Charlie Taylor, was a mixture of Irish and American Indian; and it was that quickness he passed onto his daughter.

Noel, on the other hand, was a man given to patience and determination. With the strength physically and spiritually of "Lil Abner," his quiet reserve was generally broken by a joke which he especially enjoyed it if was at the expense of a brother.

In 1936, a little less than a year after they were married, they moved to the eighty-acre farm where they reside today. From the onset, ownership of the land came as hard as the farm life would continue to be. But the two were armed with persistence, love, a willingness to work hard, and a strong abiding faith that allowed them to endure many hardships. Throughout the marriage, the priority has been consistent: family comes first. This was and is clearly understood by the children in their lives which include, but not exclusively, their four—"Becky" (Nola Rebecca), "Gwen" (Faye LeGuewn), Wayne (Nolan Wayne), Roma (Roma Lee), Vester's (Smith) "kids," and Bernie Morgan during summers they were lucky enough to have him visit. Later the "family" grew to include the children's spouses (Edward Hollimon, Mike Wilson, Gail Beauchamp Wade, and Bob Kidd), the grandchildren (Denise Hollimon Bradley, Clayton Hollimon, David Wilson, Thomas Wilson, Marcus Wade, Aimee Wade), and five great-grandchildren at this writing.

While they never achieved any great futures, their life is one of great wealth. For they believe that the measure of a person is in those values claimed; and when applied, those values become the essence of who the person is. Therefore, the measure of Noel and Minnie Lee can be quantified by the following exemplifications:

LOVE: Making sacrifices and being strong enough to look straight forward and not only that sacrificing was a privilege, but to believe it.

COMMITMENT: Choosing to count blessings when hardships are more obvious.

INTEGRITY: Getting ahead by breaking only one back,

your own, from hard work and not someone else's you stood on, held down, and used like a step ladder to get to the top.

HONESTY: Believing that what you say and who you are, are synonymous, and further believing above all else, "to thine own self be true."

TENACITY: Continuing when life would rather you quit.

JOY: Making a conscious decision to be happy and then realizing that your spirit was already convinced.

GENEROSITY: Doing for someone else...instead.

PATIENCE: Smiling and saying, "that's okay," when you haven't the foggiest idea where the money, time, or energy will come to fix whatever is broken and being able to pass it off when it can't be.

ASSURANCE: Knowing that if enough love is poured on during the growing period, the kids will come out "in the wash."

FAITH: Holding firm to the God who made us, resting on the knowledge that just as we are here for Him, He is here for us. For like the mightiest eagle who befriends the tiniest sparrow, He leads us to soar by His side to new heights and then lets us glide on His wing when we are weary.

By these gifts and more, the four children, family, and friends have been benefited by Noel and Minnie Lee Wade. Just as the richness of the soil in which they placed the seeds of their crops, so is the richness which nurtures all those who are touched by their lives.

DANIEL HASKELL WADE
BY WILLIE MAE WADE

Daniel Haskell Wade is a person who believes in having fun, especially joking with people. He is quite a historian; the books he has read just since living in Jackson would probably fill an ordinary-sized room.

His greatest love is horses; it would be hard to find one who loves them more. At present time, he has about a dozen ponies and horses and a large number cattle. Many people recognize that "yellow" truck as he makes his round each day.

In his earlier years, at the death of his older sister Beulah, quite a number of summers her children, who were quite young then, were spent with Haskell and their grandmother Wade. Haskell spent much time with them, as he knew they were so lonesome and longing for their mother as well as their father, who was at home.

Haskell's father died when he was a young man. He and his brother, Heber, remained at home longer than Vardaman and Noel to make a living for their mother and themselves.

Haskell is known for growing beautiful gladiolus. He handpicks and selects his bulbs for their colors. People put in requests for them months ahead, and he grows them to give away to his friends.

He remembers birthdays, seldom letting any of his friends slip without a greeting of some sort.

He does amateur rope tricks and is quite good at it. The younger children always want him to 'do rope tricks' for them and to teach them how to do them.

He and his brothers enjoy 'pulling a good one' on each other and then telling about it, if it was at the others' expense.

He has a deep love and respect for his relatives and forebears and wishes he had asked the older family members more questions. He suggests: Ask questions and record answers!

He recalls many happy times when he took his nieces and nephews to the swimming hole in the Big Creek nearby where they lived. The water was quite cold, regardless of the time of year. When they were spending time visiting him and their grandmother Wade, it was a "must" to go swimming every day. He recalls one time when his mother had shampooed Barbarazelle's hair and asked that she not get her hair wet. Barbarazelle was picking at Haskell, and he temporarily forgot about her hair and ducked her. He was not "very popular" for a while that day. Barbarazelle still remembers that.

He has been the "guiding hand" in researching and compiling this book—*Issac Wade and Wives Phebe and Charlotte and Descendants 1778 – 1988*. He has helped with the research, remembered events, and saw to it that the book contains the right research and information. He has also been patient when his meals were not ready and the information was scattered in different areas of the room, perhaps having to carefully step over some.

REMEMBERING WILLIE MAE RAINEY WADE

BY ROSALIE ODOM NELSON

Willie Mae Rainey Wade is a cousin of mine. She lived above us out in the Rainey community. The Rainey community was founded by our great-grandfather, Thomas R. Rainey, and wife Rebecca Tisdale Rainey.

Willie Mae was born to William Thomas Rainey and Clara Mae Patrick Rainey, June 26, 1916, in Winnsboro, Louisiana.

Willie Mae finished high school at Ellisville, attended Junior College there, and finished at University of Southern Mississippi at Hattiesburg, Mississippi, earning a Master's Degree. She became a teacher, taught in Mississippi public schools, Draughon's Business College. During WWII she taught the electrical system of the B24 bomber airplane at Keesler Field. She had the privilege of cranking one of the airplanes and doing all the operations, except the last one, to take off. She even cross-fed the engines from the one wing to the other.

Her last twenty-three years were at Pear Junior High School, where she served as Chairman of the Social Studies Department. She was one of six district winners for Mississippi Teacher of the Year. In 1977 she was one of forty-two individuals selected from throughout the United States to receive a State

Merit Teacher Award from the National Council for Geographic Education in recognition for her work on the state and national level to promote and upgrade the teaching of geography.

Willie Mae married Haskell Wade August 23, 1947, in Hattiesburg, Mississippi.

Willie Mae helped my sister and myself to write the book *Thomas R. Rainey and Rebecca L. Tisdale and Descendants* in Mississippi by Rosalie Odom Nelson, Jessie Odom Tisdale, and Willie Mae Rainey Wade, 1983. We spent many hours in courthouses, cemeteries, archives, and talking with relatives. I do know she hunted for Wade, Rainey, Knight, Stringer, and Odom families. We had a marvelous time, had many a good laugh. We went out in the cold, rain, and heat to find any available information.

I love Willie Mae very much.

TRIBUTE TO BETTY SUE WADE
BY JENNY WADE CHILSON

(ADAPTED FROM AN ANONYMOUS SOURCE)

Our Mother… there's no other word that says so much… It brings to our minds Her sunny smile and sunny laugh, Her understanding, gentle heart, Her warm and thoughtful way… Her forgiveness and quiet strength, unfailing, come what may… Her caring and putting others first, concern and patience, too. We have always loved dearly, Our Mother, Betty Sue.

ABOUT THE AUTHOR

Dan Wade is the youngest of five siblings raised on a Colorado ranch by parents with roots in Mississippi. Close family ties, clear rules of behavior, and strong Christian values defined his parents, his siblings, and Dan.

Following a path started by their father in the construction industry, Dan and his oldest brother, Jerry, founded their own companies and pursued successful careers as General Contractors. Dan chose carpentry as his path, developing his skills and passing them onto his employees, thus giving each of them a skillset to carry through their lives.

As a child, Dan was a voracious reader, exhausting the local library and testing his parents' patience at bedtime by reading under the covers by the light of a flashlight. Dan's skill for writing emerged gradually, reflecting a blend of his family values and his abiding love for his extended family, for the South, and for the freedom of the "Wild West."

Dan and his wife Daina currently live in Albuquerque, New Mexico, where Dan is busy overseeing his construction business—Aesop's Gables—and spending weekends on their ranch in Lincoln County, New Mexico.